VISUAL EXPERIENCES IN CINQUECENTO THEATRICAL SPACES

Visual Experiences in Cinquecento Theatrical Spaces

JAVIER BERZAL DE DIOS

UNIVERSITY OF TORONTO PRESS
Toronto Buffalo London

Toronto Buffalo London
utorontopress.com

ISBN 978-1-4875-0388-8

Toronto Italian Studies

Library and Archives Canada Cataloguing in Publication

Berzal de Dios, Javier, 1977–, author

Visual experiences in Cinquecento theatrical spaces / Javier Berzal de Dios.

Includes bibliographical references and index.
ISBN 978-1-4875-0388-8 (hardcover)

1. Theater – Italy – History – 16th century. 2. Theaters – Stage-setting and scenery – Italy – History – 16th century. 3. Theater audiences. 4. Italian drama – to 1700 – History and criticism. I. Title.

PN2091.S8B479 2019 792.02′5 C2018-904969-3

University of Toronto Press acknowledges the financial assistance to its publishing program of the Canada Council for the Arts and the Ontario Arts Council, an agency of the Government of Ontario.

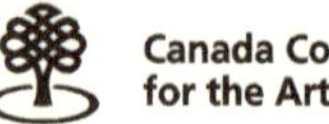

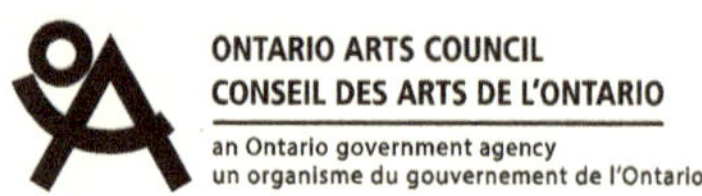

Funded by the Government of Canada
Financé par le gouvernement du Canada
Canada

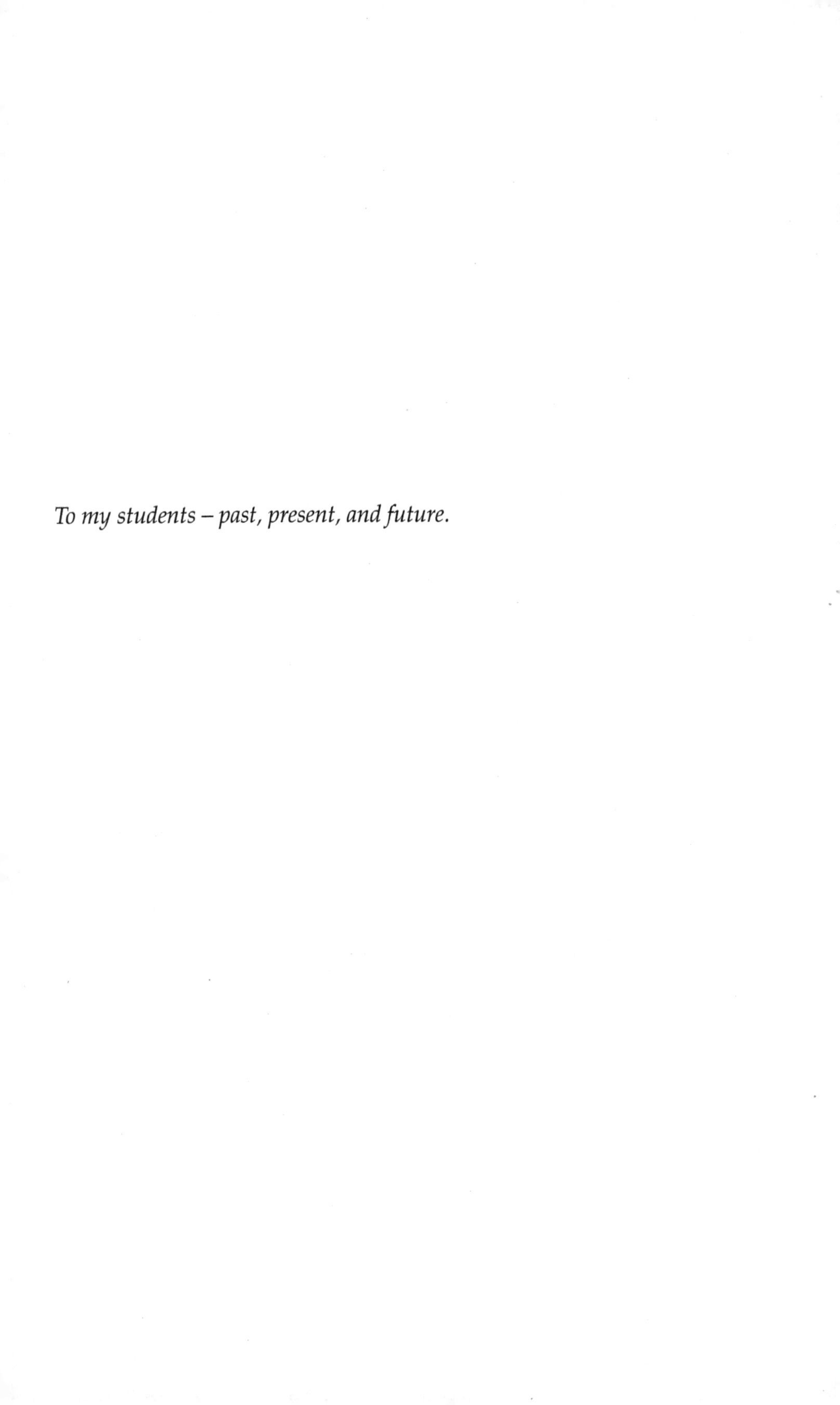

To my students – past, present, and future.

Contents

Illustrations

Acknowledgments

The germ of this manuscript was an undergraduate research paper supervised by James Saslow at City University of New York (CUNY), Queens College. This project owes much to his scholarship and initial guidance. For the support during my years at Queens College, I am also grateful to John Nici, Christopher Atkins, Harvey Burstein, and Hilail Gildin. I am indebted to the encouragement provided by the faculty at the Ohio State University's Department of Art History, especially Christian Kleinbub – I truly could not have wished for a better doctoral adviser. I am also in debt to Lisa Florman's attentive notes and Byron Hamman's interventions as well as to the advice and illuminating courses offered by Barbara Haeger, Andrew Shelton, Myroslava Mudrak, Karl Whittington, and Aron Vinegar. I never was a complaisant student, and I am, therefore, twice as grateful for their assistance and encouragement. Dissertation research was made possible by various funds at the Ohio State University: the Sara Pyne Memorial Scholarship Fund in the Visual Arts, the Aida Cannarsa Snow Endowment Fund, the Cathleen M. Murnane Travel Scholarship Fund, the Nicholas Howe Research Grant, and the Dr P.K. Chu Memorial Award.

I thank the two manuscript readers for their comments, which have decisively strengthened my manuscript, and the staff at the University of Toronto Press, especially Suzanne Rancourt. Financial backing to finalize the book manuscript was made possible through generous grants provided by Western Washington University's College of Fine and Performance Arts and a Publication Support Grant provided by the Office of Research and Sponsored Programs. I am grateful to my colleagues and staff at Western's Department of Art and Art History and throughout the university for creating such a special place to work.

A special thanks goes to James Hansen, a brother-in-arms through the years, and to all my friends throughout the academic journey, especially Becca Howard, Bob Calhoun, Tommy Kivatinos, and Mike Bocchino. This book would not exist without Sarah Schnadelbach, whose care and encouragement pushed me to the finish line. Finally, my most heartfelt gratitude goes to my mother, Felisa de Dios, for her many sacrifices.

VISUAL EXPERIENCES IN CINQUECENTO THEATRICAL SPACES

Introduction: Striking the Stage

> HISTRION I: Okay, okay, so I made a mistake. No need to crucify me! It's only a play!
>
> HISTRION II: Yeah, you're right. It wouldn't be fair or proper to crucify a person over something as trivial as that.[1]
>
> Pietro Aretino, *La Cortigiana*

This book presents a critical engagement with the heterogeneous practices of sixteenth-century theatre architecture and design. Theatrical spaces are here studied as neither ideal nor geometric locations but, first and foremost, as constructed artworks in relation to viewers. An attentiveness to this material pull encourages us to explore the performative aspects of visual paradoxes and the complexities of spectatorship. In this sense, Cinquecento theatrical spaces reveal themselves as sites of exceptional dynamism that provoked viewer response at an individual and social level. Accounts of theatrical experiences, I argue, cannot be reduced to visual unity and illusionism – two prevalent notions in the scholarship that neglect the experimental concerns of the period. It is my intent, borrowing from Walter Benjamin's concept, to *engage with* the resonating pulse of sixteenth-century Italian theatres and stages.[2]

Despite (or perhaps because of) the richness of its interdisciplinarity, theatre design finds itself stranded in an academic no-man's land. Developments in one field are frequently neglected in others, and actual practices, tensions, and complexities are bypassed to enhance the teleological narratives of particular fields. Theatre studies has privileged a close reading of the textual over the visual elements of performances.[3]

In the art historical literature, theatrical spaces are often superficially noted but seldom reconnoitered. Art history has often distilled scenography into a practice of merely pictorial values, focusing on visual correlations between theatre designs and paintings.[4] Books dealing with linear perspective regularly incorporate a brief section on scenography, though these accounts are often cursory and marginal, in turn emphasizing a routine understanding of the material that reduces stage art, with all its complex functions, to the position of illusionistic painting.[5]

While fifteenth- and sixteenth-century stage design can be a pigeonholed subject, the word "theatrical" outspreads in contemporary art history as a generalizing epithet equally applicable to spectacles, architecture, and sculpture. Though John Shearman's more nuanced "transitive art" could often better articulate the relationship between viewers and artworks, perhaps its technical overtones are less intuitive than "theatricality," a term equally used by experts and laypeople.[6] Hence, the word "theatrical" has come to define a visual engagement in its most general sense in art: as used by Michael Fried, for example, to reveal the anticipated presence of spectators.[7] My interest in the theatrical is literal: I am concerned with staged drama in order to stress not only the presence of the spectator, but also to emphasize the fictive and dramaturgical character of the spaces at hand. The main concern here is thus narrower than "performative," which would also encompass discourses on executions, parades, political displays, architectural programs, and other events and visual modes that are not dramatic in nature (though these topics will occasionally appear).

A rhetorical use of "theatrical" as an element in descriptions of artworks not made for theatrical events may be useful and even fitting, but it creates interpretive difficulties. When a cityscape is called theatrical, it is immediately understood to have a "picturesque" quality, as having been constructed with a point of view in mind, and as being framed. There is something economical about the word "theatrical." Its rhetorical use is graceful and evocative. Its popularity is understandable. But metaphors and analogies merge, and the transference of meaning in the word "theatrical" becomes bidirectional: the city becomes a stage; the stage, in turn, a city.[8] What is a theatre when a town square becomes a public stage? What is scenography when cityscapes are backdrops to the actions of citizens? A stage becomes a copy, a repetition, a reiteration. At the same time, the tectonic solidity of the city is lent to the stage. The stage can be understood by the same theoretical means as a city. The tensions that emerge from the primacy of these usages permeate this study, and I seek to disentangle the metaphoric from the material. The purpose is not to banish the metaphorical, important as it certainly was in early modern consciousness, but to amplify and explore the experiences of theatrical spaces *qua* theatrical spaces.

While the "theatrical," broadly conceived, has invaded discourses on early modern architecture, stage design of the period continues to be studied as a pictorial two-dimensional medium associated with perspectival drawing and the rationalization of space. As a consequence, scholars of stage design have characterized early modernity as a rudimentary foil for the modern stage, a dynamic space for the shared kinesthetic experiences of performers and spectators.[9] Pamela Howard asked contemporary stage designers to devise their own definition of scenography. The answers were exceedingly diverse: "the visualization of the dramatic text"; "the visual intersection of the ordinary and the imaginative"; "graphics to be seen by theatre spectators"; "the visual direction of the stage"; "the art of space in action"; "the suggestion of space which transforms in the head of the spectator to anything possible."[10] This sampling of the dozens of answers Howard transcribed shows the profuse artistic conceptualizations that pervade stage design today – a fertile world of signification that is seldom applied to early modern theatres. The aim of this study is to show the rich visual articulations that permeated the stage designs of early modern Italy. In this sense, my focus is the *apparato* rather than the *prospettiva*. The latter detaches the stage set and its perspectival scenography from the spatial context of the theatre as a whole.[11] The *apparato*, in contrast, is a comprehensive term that signifies the stage and scenographic set, the auditorium and its decorations, and the spectators' act of viewing as made possible and conditioned by the space.[12] In this sense, I explore the protean experiences made possible by theatrical spaces, embracing the ephemerality of the objects at hand and their fundamental plurality – from conception to construction and performance – rather than reconstructing the spaces or lingering over questions of authorial intent or attribution.

The chronological scope of this book focuses on scenographic experimentation in the Cinquecento, broadly understood, a framework that remains connected to medieval theatrical experiences and the visual arts of the Italian Renaissance (a term here denoting a pliant temporal boundary). By bracketing mid- and late-seventeenth-century developments, I call into question the assumption that linear perspective in sixteenth-century practices prefigured Baroque cultural, political, and philosophical developments.[13] Indeed, the presence of two late-sixteenth-century theatres in this study, the Teatro all'antica in Sabbioneta and the Teatro Olimpico in Vicenza, will show that even at the threshold of the seventeenth century, theatres actively challenged the putative primacy of unity. Historicist methodologies and deterministic chronologies have elucidated many a significant connection, but they have also generated a series of obstructions that enforce linear discourses. My goal is to explore resonances and dissonances. In this process, I take up Manfredo Tafuri's stance: to respect the problems, contradictions, and paradoxes of the past, allowing them to remain living and unresolved.[14]

Arnold Aronson's essay on scenography, "Postmodern Design," contains a concise, albeit poignant, description of the Renaissance: "a period in which the scientific desire for unity clashed with an appetite for diversity and delight in incongruity."[15] Aronson presented this definition as somewhat indisputable, though in truth only the first part of that definition (the desire for unity) has been properly explored. Unity itself has traditionally been a pictorial indicator of the Italian Renaissance ideal. In the influential work of Erwin Panofsky, perspective guarantees "a fully rational – that is, infinite, unchanging and homogeneous – space."[16] The Kantian overtones of Panofsky's space have been addressed by James Elkins, who revealed the problems inherent in thinking about perspective as producing pictorial unity.[17] A systematic artistic approach to a given problem does not imply a unified, singular result, much less a codified epistemological framework. Michael Baxandall and John White advocated the necessity of taking precautions when engaging with perspective, a subject determined by and through inclusive artistic practices rather than mathematical proofs.[18] Despite these reconsiderations of perspective, the lineage of theatre scholars remains traceable to the pioneering, mid-twentieth-century work of George Kernodle, who stressed that perspective allowed for the presentation on stage of "a complete illusionistic picture of an actual place" as "all the space of the stage picture was unified by the concept of one picture place and one frame."[19] Kernodle's position would find an influential supporter in Allardyce Nicoll, who stated that the Renaissance stage was "looked upon as a kind of single 'picture.'"[20] Kernodle's and Nicoll's positions regarding the pictoriality of the stage linger in the scholarship.[21] In David Rosand's words, "the unified spatial setting of Early Renaissance painting became an important ingredient in the evolution of the new humanist theater."[22]

My approach begins with an interest in spatial practices informed by recent developments in art history to incorporate a nuanced approach to visuality and viewership as well as theoretical awareness regarding perspective and representation. The latter will remind us that theatrical spaces, despite their seemingly naturalistic qualities, articulate irreducible questions in regard to figuration and representation – the legible and the visible. "Legible" and "visible" may be modern terms, but, as has been noted, they have been present in artistic discourses since antiquity and are integral to understanding the artistic and historiographic goals born out of early modern practices.[23] This theoretical attentiveness challenges the epistemic gravity of the so-called perspectival realism, which, it has been argued, engages the "gaze of the spectator, who is the true accomplice in the deception that ambiguously intertwines reality with theatre."[24] The problem of images and their relationship with reality becomes intensified in the theatrical spaces. Alexander Nagel comments on Savonarola's criticisms of painters' use of people as models in the depictions of religious figures, which exposes a sense of doubleness that invokes a theatrical effect: "Images that trouble identity, revealing an 'actor' behind the figural mask, pervert the representational functions images are meant to serve ... But theatre itself responded to the concerns by exposing its own duplicity"[25]

By stepping away from the customary fixation with linear perspective and illusionism, we can disentangle the scholarly association of scenography with mathematics, visual coherence, and unity. Invoking the power of perspectival illusionism, W.J.T. Mitchell stated, "One thing that cannot be seen in an illusionistic picture, or which tends to conceal itself, is precisely its own artificiality."[26] A corollary follows from such a postulate: images that do not attempt to conceal their artificiality cannot be illusionistic – those images, whatever their medium, are not meant to play the role of invisible thresholds or windows. Adopting this position, I move away from the habitual overemphasis on the power of illusionism to explicate the presence and aesthetic function of pictorial displacements, visual anomalies, and architectural paradoxes. Instead of *a priori* mathematics and purely pictorial practices, I focus on how theatrical spaces operate in an open system where tactics of expression are in dialogue with tactics of viewership.

In chapter 1, "Magic and Mimesis: *La Calandria* and the Idea of Rome," I set forth a nuanced interpretation of Baldassare Peruzzi's seminal 1514 stage design for *La Calandria* by addressing the spatial dissociations found in the drawing. Eschewing traditional and overarching generalizations about scenography, which envisioned the sixteenth century as a homogeneous phenomenon whose goal was unity and illusionism, this chapter shows that Peruzzi consciously produced a fantastical space. Between fact and fiction, famous monuments are displaced, resized, and conjoined. The impossibility of Peruzzi's Rome brings forth the city not as an individual instantiation but as a conceptual entity.

In the wake of this analysis, chapter 2, "The Artificial City on Stage," shows that Peruzzi's deviation from illusionism was not an isolated case. Rather, it was an established practice in which displacements were emphasized to great effect. Textual and visual evidence demonstrates that period stages were understood as dramaturgical spaces rather than open windows to independent and autonomous worlds. I argue for an understanding of scenographic projects as fictional yet tangible sets operating in the liminal space between the two- and the three-dimensional, and as bringing forth, while distancing, the identity of urban spaces.

Chapter 3, "Palladio, Scamozzi, and the Built Theatre as Enclosure," explores the performative aspects of theatrical spaces. Although throughout the fifteenth and sixteenth centuries we encounter abundant cases in which the prince was granted a privileged position, artists and theorists remained interested in the audience's plurality of experiences. Focusing on the *apparato,* I propose that theatrical spaces were predicated not on seeing-through, but on seeing-within – in other words, that enclosure, and not the detachment of the stage, defines period theatrical spaces.

The political implications of linear perspective are studied in chapter 4, "The Medici Theatres, Political Aspirations, and Cognitive Autonomy." Discord and interpretation are fundamental to the performative. The presence of linear perspective, I argue, does not limit responses; vision is not a passive procedure of image reception, but a social process incorporating dissent, jesting, and insincerity. Indeed, if theatrical performances had symbolic capital, it was not because only the prince or duke enjoyed the stage alone or because the stage rhetorically anticipated utopian visions, but because the patron made possible a sumptuous event that everybody in the audience collectively enjoyed.

Italian sixteenth-century theatre is ubiquitously interpreted as a world of political rhetoric, a codified mode of spatial domination through linear perspective, and a space of verisimilar replication. But wandering away from these paths, one encounters a heterogeneous and experimental impetus. To be clear, my proposal is not that the Italian Renaissance theatre rejected the import of pictorial naturalism or the Aristotelian notions of mimesis and dramatic unity, but rather that those were malleable values at the service of the spectacular and the marvellous. My aim is to excavate what the scholarship has kept covered, consciously or unconsciously: to sate that appetite for diversity and delight in incongruity. The period's architect-artist-designer did not operate in a purely abstract mode. Theatres manifested a pragmatic interest in collectivity and an awareness of the stage's materiality. Before we capitulate to the power of illusionism, ideal emplacements, and spatial order, let us recall Michel de Certeau's words: "the surface of this order is everywhere punched and torn open by ellipses, drifts, and leaks of meaning: it is a sieve-order."[27]

Chapter One

Magic and Mimesis: *La Calandria* and the Idea of Rome

> [T]hey are both in Rome today, and you will see both of them appear here. Do not imagine, though, that they were suddenly transported here from Rome by necromancy. The city you see here is Rome, which used to be so ample, so spacious, so large that, triumphing, it could contain many cities, and towns and rivers. Now it has become so small that, as you can see, it can easily fit into your own town.[1]
>
> Bernardo Dovizi da Bibbiena, *La Calandria*

Aristotle famously systematized dramatic structure in his *Poetics*: "a whole is what has a beginning and middle and end."[2] This tripartite structure was later reorganized into five sections by Horace and Seneca, although Aristotle's overall theory persisted: a plot is introduced, tribulations arise, and tensions heighten into the climax of the story, which is finally resolved.[3] A highly effective and ingrained concept in Western consciousness, it is a narrative structure that has permeated historiographic thought. Here, it is particularly relevant not only because of the dramatic nature of our topic, but also because the discourse on sixteenth-century theatre design and architecture itself embodies such a conventional plotline. This narrative begins in the late Quattrocento with a vigorous and resolute departure from the aesthetic values of the medieval stage, implementing linear perspective to synthesize two- and three-dimensional elements into a coherent and believable locale (an artistic problem that remained at first untamed). Early protagonists in this sequence include Pellegrino da Udine and Girolamo Genga with their respective designs for *La Cassaria* in 1508 and *La Calandria* in 1513. The challenges and solutions of these developments herald the mid-sixteenth-century climactic codification of artistic canons and practices by Sebastiano Serlio and Giorgio Vasari. The narrative of the unified Italian Renaissance stage culminates in the architecture of Palladio's Teatro Olimpico and the set designs of Bernardo Buontalenti, which, resolving the visual problems previously introduced, portend Baroque theatre and scenography.[4]

A historiographic, theoretical thread plaits these achievements. From Pellegrino to Buontalenti, Renaissance scenography is consistently interpreted as consolidating a sense of visual and spatial unity that, aided by linear perspective, denotes the humanistic absorption of Aristotle. Within this art historiographic narrative, Baldassare Peruzzi (1481–1536) occupies a preeminent space. His scenographic projects epitomize the moment of transition that will make the developments of Vasari and Serlio possible.[5] An artistic coup, the design for *La Calandria* (figure 1.1) is understood to decisively produce a unified stage in which a perspectival, painted backdrop was fully integrated with a three-dimensional set and the space of the stage itself. What is more, this scenographic design is seen to manifest Aristotle's theory on unity of action, which mid- and late-sixteenth-century commentators like Ludovico Castelvetro conjoined with the unity of time and the unity of space, to craft the famous doctrine of the Three Unities.[6] The drawing for *La Calandria* has become the keystone that upholds the narrative arch through which modern scenography was born. Given its significance, it seems justified to begin this study with this drawing, *in media res*, in order to understand the design's tensions, resonances, and paradoxes that historiographic narratives have commonly overlooked.

The drawing for *La Calandria*, today housed in the Galleria degli Uffizi, quite probably corresponds to what ultimately appeared on the stage, and it is widely attributed to Peruzzi.[7] The "learned comedy" (*commedia erudita*) was written by Cardinal Bernardo Dovizi da Bibbiena, produced by Leo X in honour of Isabella d'Este, and staged by Duke Francesco Maria Rovere.[8] The drawing is the most finished and complete of the few surviving examples of Peruzzi's theatrical works.[9] Despite the limited number of these drawings, their historical significance is by no means small. As we have mentioned, Peruzzi's scenographic designs signal a crucial step in the developments originated by artists like Genga, who had designed the stage for the inaugural 1513 production of *La Calandria* in the city of Urbino under the direction of Baldessar Castiglione, and whose set featured a view of a city, likely in perspective.[10] Additionally, Peruzzi's designs may have been intended

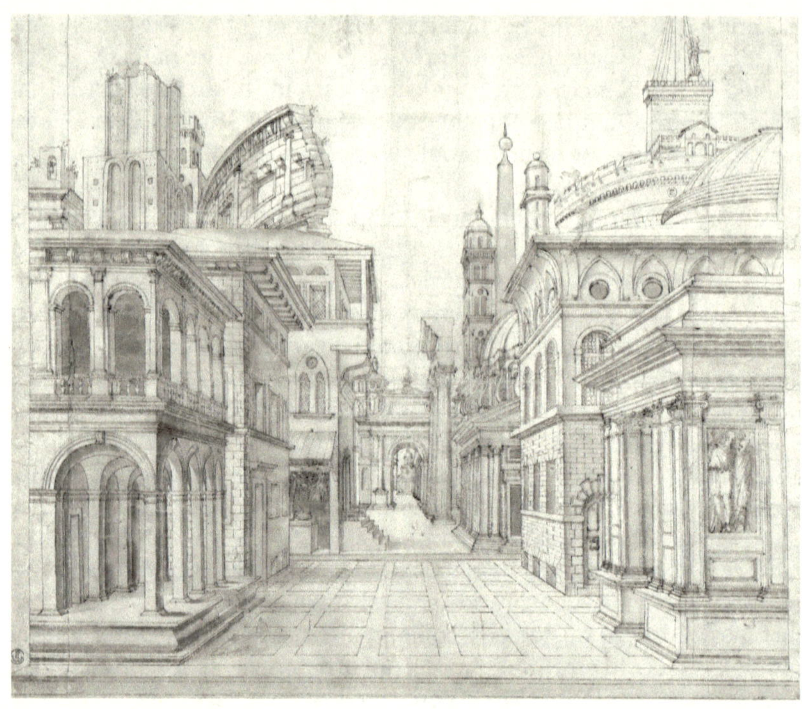

1.1 Baldassare Peruzzi, stage design for *La Calandria*. Pen and ink drawing. Florence, Uffizi, Gabinetto Disegni e Stampe. Image from Artres.

as a compilation of drawings of Rome made to illustrate a never-published commentary on Vitruvius. These drawings certainly fertilized the scenographic tradition. It has been frequently argued that Serlio may have retained them after Peruzzi's death, later using them as models for his influential tragic and comic scenes.[11] Within the larger sixteenth-century cultural context, the scenographic works of Peruzzi and Serlio have been seen as directly informing highly regarded works of art and demonstrating the early modern fascination with theatricality.[12]

Vasari expresses an unequivocal admiration for Peruzzi's theatrical skill, highlighting that his designs were a turning point in Italian scenography.[13] In his *Lives*, Vasari explicitly mentions two plays for which Peruzzi produced stage designs. One of them is *La Calandria*, which was performed in the late months of 1514 and probably repeated in January 1515.[14] The other play is not named, and its identity has become the subject of scholarly speculation.[15] Vasari praises both the text of *La Calandria* for its use of the vernacular and Peruzzi's scenography for having laid the foundations for contemporary sets. This is something especially remarkable, in the Tuscan writer's opinion, given that comedies, and consequently scenery for comedies, had fallen into disuse in the Middle Ages, replaced by festivals and mystery plays.

In the scholarship, Vasari's triumphal rhetoric has traditionally been taken up in order to see Peruzzi's scenography as heralding a new age of scenographic unity and illusionism. The design for *La Calandria* has been characterized as a *tour de force* in which the advances of Renaissance painting are finally deployed in theatrical performances. Leaving behind medieval practices, where geographically disparate locations where simultaneously visible on stage, Peruzzi's groundbreaking drawing is understood to stipulate the new values of the Italian set design: the importance of verisimilitude, the scientific use of linear perspective, and the revitalization of Vitruvius's theatrical architecture.[16]

In developing Jacob Burckhardt's neglected prioritization of aesthetics over illusionism in the period's scenography,[17] my intent is to explore the anomalous elements in Peruzzi's drawing that reinforce a pragmatic, aesthetic concern with active modes of visual engagement. The spatial disassociations in Peruzzi's design, far from being idiosyncratic, exemplify the heterogeneity, plurality, and experimentation of sixteenth-century Italian theatrical art. Peruzzi's drawing juxtaposes a legible, perspectival ground and an impossibly flattened and condensed Rome, unbound from restrictive mathematical, perceptual, and cognitive expectations. In his design, Peruzzi presents a marvellous artistic apparition in which the spectators encounter Rome as a monumental, overflowing concept. Congested and teeming with monuments, Peruzzi's presentation displaces the viewer's phenomenological expectations to conjure an overwhelming presence of the city that is truer to Rome than any factual, single view of the city can be.

Unity, Verisimilitude, and Truth

The scholarly emphasis on Peruzzi's creation of a verisimilar stage is not ungrounded. A glimpse of Peruzzi's design evidences a well-constructed perspectival stage, with the receding orthogonal lines of the floor leading our eyes to a central point on the horizon in the way famously proposed by Leon Battista Alberti's *On Painting*. Although sixteenth-century artists of Peruzzi's calibre would have had little difficulty in drawing a projected, three-dimensional space, it is notable how effortlessly we accept the monochromatic and unfinished lines of the design as a credible space – an open, urban space that we can easily navigate.[18]

Despite its putative illusionism and visual uniformity, Peruzzi's urban scene depicts two spatial entities. The drawing ostensibly differentiates those elements that are three-dimensional from the flat backdrop with a double horizontal line that separates the checkerboard-patterned pavement from the area beyond it, which belongs to the backdrop.[19] The checkerboard pattern marks a rectangular piazza, the physical place that would be occupied by the living bodies of the actors. This space of action is framed by two edifices on both the left and the right, that are noticeably more volumetric, homogeneous, and proportional than the structures behind them. Beyond those four buildings, a city thronged with monuments emerges: this is the backdrop – a flattened space that would have remained purely pictorial on the stage.

The ersatz and paradoxical amalgam of monuments appears initially less peculiar than perhaps it should. Peruzzi demonstrates his pictorial skill and his capacity to divert the gaze of the viewer, who intuitively apprehends depth. However, the contrast between the two spaces is subversive. Lacking a factual topographic arrangement, the planate monuments crop up as mutilated, stacked segments. And there is the predicament of scale. The buildings' sizes have been modified without reference to a fixed perspective ratio, and thus lack the appearance of continuous proportionality. The Colosseum is a conspicuous example. It is fancifully shrunk, and a carved-out section of the monument protrudes into the space of the third house, hovering over its roof. Opposite, the dome of the Pantheon awkwardly appears in front of the Castel Sant'Angelo, occupying an impossible space.

Peruzzi's design for *La Calandria* is, therefore, not a mimetic representation of a specific location. On the contrary, it brings forth an impossible and imaginary point of view from which a wide array of famous Roman architecture becomes visible. In addition to the above-mentioned monuments, we encounter the Tower of the Milizie, the three columns of the Temple of Castor and Pollux, an impossibly tall rendition of the obelisk from Piazza del Popolo, Trajan's Column, the Palazzo Senatorio, the bell tower of San Lorenzo in Miranda, and an arch inspired by that of the Argentari in the Forum Boarium.[20] The perspective of the central avenue, an anchoring rachis, is nonetheless disjoined from the city's monuments, which, bereft of grounds, linger in a nimble dissonance at the margins of mathematical reason.

The image of a lackadaisical or inept Peruzzi who was technically unable to correct the picture into a geometrically coherent whole appears altogether incongruous. His knowledge of perspective was praised by early authors, and works like his Sala delle Prospettive in the Villa Farnesina speak to his capacities.[21] Peruzzi's proficiency forces us to view the less coherent aspects of his stage design through a different prism, one in which the artist and architect was engrossed not in the recreation of an antiquarian (and arguably narcissistic) dream based on spatial surveillance, but in devising a formulation purposefully inattentive to the categorical dictates of technical norms, in this case optical and mathematical ones.[22]

The proposal that Peruzzi disregarded spatial unity may seem at odds with the pervasive body of scholarship on early modern Italian set design, which is anchored in Kernodle's thesis: "The purpose of perspective scenery – to create the illusion of an actual place – required the complete unity of the stage setting."[23] Nevertheless, multiple voices have raised issues regarding the significance of pictorial mathematical unity based on perspective. In other period contexts, scholars like Elkins have challenged the assumption that the goal of perspective was the creation of a unified picture plane, as it may have been a tool designed to depict individual objects and not space as such.[24] Moreover, there is a tradition in the scholarship, exemplified by John White and Michael Baxandall, that has argued that pragmatics and artistic realities took precedence over mathematical demonstrations.[25] Indeed, even arithmetic historians have argued that early modern mathematics need not be seen as articulating principles detached from experiences; fifteenth- and sixteenth-century mathematics were reflections of everyday life still dependent on the abacists' tradition of reasoning by example.[26] Hence, it seems probable that mathematical correctness was not the priority of artists; rather, linear perspective was one of many tools, all of which were at the service of the artistic process. Therefore, potential understandings of theatrical productions in which the intrinsic virtues of correct spatial constructions are seen as conjuring a unified visual field need to be contextualized within art historiographic developments and the realities of the period itself. In cases of accomplished artists like Peruzzi, we must maximize the rationality of the artists' choices and be receptive to the positive potential aspects of seemingly incoherent spaces, as such spaces can elicit active cognitive engagement. In the words of John White, "Multiple viewpoints greatly increase the organizational range and effectiveness of perspective."[27]

The fragmentation of pictorial space is not incompatible with the humanist preoccupation with Aristotle's dramatic unity, which stipulated a main action without subplots. "One," in this sense, means "whole" or "complete."[28] After all, the scene, as the semantic centre of a play, can operate as a conceptual unity through the embodied engagement of viewers and actors in the visually designed space of the stage.[29] Unity, in this sense, would be not a static, monolithic apparatus, but a malleable set of relations that is established through the engagement between each viewer, the space of that viewer, the performers, and the space of the performance. Besides, we may question the extent to which Aristotle's *Poetics* would have been interpreted in 1514 as stipulating a unity of space, as the application of the doctrine of the Three Unities would only become pervasive in the second half of the sixteenth century, having its notorious early exponent in Castelvetro's famous 1570 exegesis *Poetica d'Aristotele vulgarizzata e sposita*. Although it is possible that Peruzzi either directly or indirectly knew Aristotle's treatise through Giorgio Valla's 1498 Latin translation, through the 1508 Venetian printing of the Greek original, or even from one of the many copies of the texts that existed in the fifteenth century, the *Poetics* as a whole, beyond specific doctrines, was not generally well known until the middle of the sixteenth century.[30] As has been pointed out, neither Gian Giorgio Trissino's *Sofonisba* (written between 1514 and 1515, published in 1524) nor Giovanni Rucellai's *Rosmunda* (performed in 1525) adhered to the rule of unity of place.[31] While unity of action was a concern for late critics like Gregorio Comanini, who argued in his 1591 *Il Figino* that painting and drama should both enact a single action, it may be more difficult than is often assumed to ascribe to Peruzzi a definite interpretation of Aristotle's text.[32]

Displacement and Memory

Let us, then, engage with space, as Alberti proposes in the opening paragraphs of *On Painting*, from the point of view of the artists, and not that of mathematicians.[33] We can recognize that Peruzzi's perspective accepts distortions to its geometric order, and that these distortions can assist the function of the stage design. In this sense, the drawing (*qua* scenographic drawing) emphatically affirms that set design has its own intrinsic processes, goals, and functions.[34]

Theatrical spaces are expressive.[35] The stage communicates a setting – the spatial location of the fictive action. *La Calandria* takes place in

Rome, and it is logical to assume that Peruzzi's design represents the Eternal City. The collection of monuments carefully described by Peruzzi in his drawing leaves no doubt of this setting. Yet the design presents Rome, and not a view *of* Rome or a location *in* Rome. We understand the set design as Rome, but in order to *see it as* Rome we need to think of Rome in a way that does not correlate to the reality of the city. To make us think of Rome as a whole, Peruzzi has created a physical impossibility.

In *Civilization and Its Discontents*, Sigmund Freud engaged in a conceptual exercise. Freud, addressing the issue of mental preservation, imagines Rome not as a space of human habitation but as a psychical entity "in which nothing that has once come into existence will have passed away."[36] In this imaginary Rome, ancient monuments and later buildings would coexist in one space, and the observer could call up one view or another by shifting his glance or his position. Freud calls this Rome an unimaginable fantasy, and concludes, "If we want to represent historical sequence in spatial terms we can only do it by juxtaposition in space."[37] It is unlikely that Freud knew Peruzzi's design; what is more likely is that Freud and Peruzzi shared a concern regarding the nature of spatiality and the human condition, and that we are here encountering a notion inherent in the consciousness of European culture, namely a diachronic and synchronic synthesis of Rome. The product of this project, Freud alerts us, would be absurd. Indeed, we may agree: Peruzzi's design is visually absurd. But absurd can be understood not as ridiculous or inane but in its etymological sense, from the Latin *absurdus* (meaning "out of tune"), since the non-perspectival sections of Peruzzi's space are dissonant and spatially divergent, in turn calling into question the harmony of the stage as a whole.

Peruzzi's Rome brings with it a Zeuxian aesthetic model. It is not so much Rome as "a certain idea that comes to mind" about Rome, to extrapolate a phrase by his friend and colleague Raphael.[38] Peruzzi's drawing is not unique in its spatial synthesis: Jessica Maier has shown that early modern renderings of Rome collapse geographical and temporal distance.[39] The movement away from the tangible Rome into a conceptualization of the city raises the question of Peruzzi's philosophical ideas, some of which he might have shared with Raphael, especially in regard to Neoplatonism. This philosophical school, cultivated within Peruzzi's circle, is significant as it befits the aesthetics of the drawing better than the chronologically problematic notion of Aristotelian spatial unity. Moreover, certain fundamental concerns for Aristotle – such as that order and size are essential factors of beauty – are clearly at odds with Peruzzi's design, complicating an Aristotelian interpretation of the drawing.[40] Writing on the topic of Peruzzi's knowledge of Neoplatonism, Manfredo Tafuri has argued that, though the artist may not have been fully aware of the theoretical implications of the philosophical system, he nevertheless absorbed a profound assumption of this philosophy, namely that "the absolute does not rest within itself but is an active force that proceeds by duplication."[41] In this light, the traditional interpretation of Peruzzi's design in terms of urban ideality and unity of place becomes increasingly difficult.[42] The drawing for *La Calandria* would then visually articulate the (technical and sublime) conditions of possibility inherent in the act of doubling. The Rome in the design is neither a perfect idea of Rome nor a dream of Rome "abstracted from the hazards of time."[43] However synchronic, the Roman ruins attest to the realities of temporal downfall: Peruzzi shows the abandoned state of landmarks like the Colosseum of the Torre della Milizie in the drawing, notably dotted with overgrown vegetation. Rome is therefore neither complete nor idealized. It is an aestheticized double visual encounter that operates sensorially with and for the spectators. The Rome in the design exists in between the real city and the space of the theatrical performance: it brings us beyond the latter, but it never becomes a simulacrum of the former.

In its act of replication, the drawing distorts its mimetic value and stipulates its own artificiality. One can imagine how much this subversion would have been palpable in the actual performance through the juxtaposition of three-dimensional elements with the flat, painted backdrop. The mimetic reality of the monuments comes to be negated in order to present Rome as an idea, destabilizing the immanent attestation of perceptual experiences. The drawing takes away the possibility of topological orientation: the visual communication of Rome emerges from an active disruption of the audience's phenomenological experiences of the city. What is more, the possibility of orientation itself becomes artificial: it is an orientation that, unrelated to distance and scale, is predicated on the artificiality of linear perspective.[44] Rome thus appears on the stage as an artifice, not as a simulacrum.

Wonderment

Salvatore di Maria has argued that a stage setting, "tends to define and contextualize the dramatic action, reinforcing it visually and conferring upon it specific meaning."[45] Yet Peruzzi's work does more than contextualize and reinforce. Its visual approach is not one purely in the service of the play but one that deserves to be understood as autonomous to a significant degree. Set design can do something that the text cannot. The independent function of the set would be codified in the work of the influential writer and theorist Giovanni Battista Giraldi (1504–73), commonly known by his sobriquet Cinthio. His *Discorso intorno al comporre delle commedie e delle tragedie*, written in 1543 and published in 1554, analyses the aims of scenography and reflects his own experiences as a playwright and producer.[46] Cinthio postulates that the stage fulfils a double function by establishing a definite indication of the place of action and by captivating its audience.[47] Though this text is of a later date than Peruzzi's drawing, it is relevant because of Cinthio's capacity to articulate crucial ideas about scenography in the sixteenth century.

Peruzzi's design conveys an unmistakable idea of the city. It is a definite indication, to use Cinthio's concept. No other place in the world could encompass the monuments therein. In other words, Peruzzi's indication of place is more authoritative and unmistakable than any actual view of Rome could be. It may be for this reason that his drawing seems concerned with a concept of monumentality that can only be accomplished by distilling the real Rome down to its greatest monuments. Peruzzi's is a self-expressed, triumphal and contrived, hypermonumentality – a surplus associated with Rome above all other cities.

Compare the design for *La Calandria* (figure 1.1) with Baldassare Lanci's (1510–71) set for *La Vedova* (figure 1.2), a play by Giovan Battista Cini performed in 1569 in the Salone dei Cinquecento, Florence.[48] The spectators of Lanci's design would find themselves standing in the Piazza de la Signoria, between the Loggia dei Lanci and the Palazzo Vecchio with Giotto's campanile and the dome of the cathedral towering over the horizon line. Although Martin Kemp has called Lanci's drawing a "drastic realignment of Florentine topography," it attempts to produce a naturalistic point of view that would have been utterly familiar to its original audience.[49] Given the difference in dimensions between the ample space presented in the design and the measurements of the Salone dei Cinquecento (54 x 23 x 18 metres), Lanci's cityscape would have looked strangely puny, especially in relation to the actors. Nonetheless, it is clear that his strategy towards space correlates to quantitative methods like surveying. In contrast, Peruzzi's visual tactics uproot the monuments from their geographical context. Altered in size, flattened, and repositioned, these are not buildings anymore: the absence of function foregrounds their artificiality.

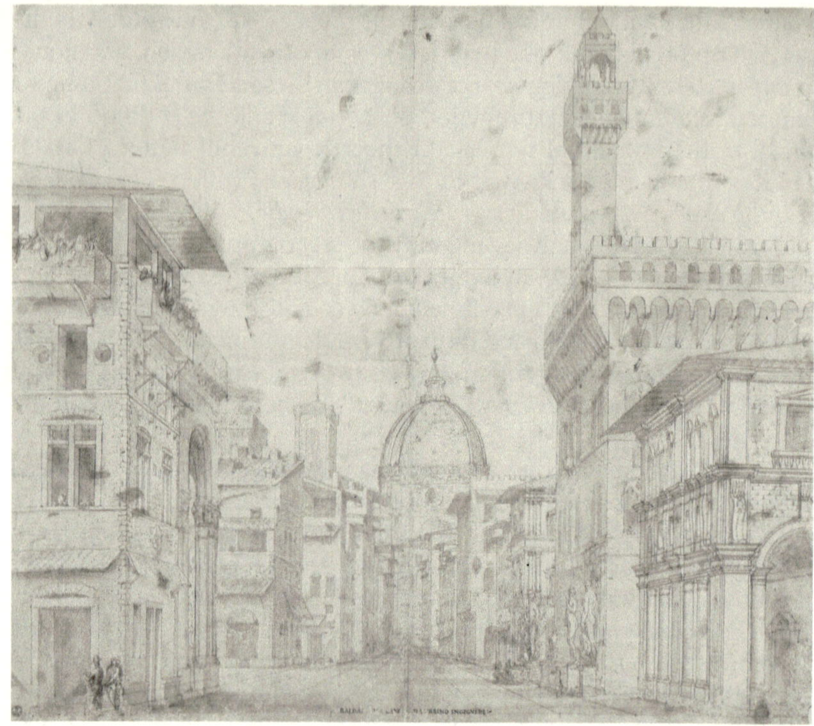

1.2 Baldassarre Lanci, theatrical perspective for *La Vedova*, c. 1569. Pen and ink drawing. Florence, Uffizi, Gabinetto Disegni e Stampe. Image from Artres.

Peruzzi's pavement conveys a space to live and move in (and, we must remember, Peruzzi's scenographic fame is due to his integration of acting and setting in the staged "piazza"). Yet the monumental Rome appears as an image of constriction where there is no possibility of movement, no breathing space.[50] It is likely that Vasari learned much from Peruzzi. In a letter to Ottaviano de' Medici, he explains the scenography he had conceived for the production of *La Talanta*, a comedy by Pietro Aretino performed in Venice in 1542. Vasari's written description of his design lists the following assortment of buildings: the Pantheon, the Colosseum, Trajan's Column, the Torre della Milizie, the Arch of Septimus Severus, the Templum Pacis, Santa Maria della Pace, Santa Maria Nuova, the Temple of Fortuna, Palazzo Maggiore, the Seven Hills, and the Pasquino.[51] To create a mental image of this scenography is, no doubt, an arduous task. This design is lost to us, but given Vasari's description and his praise for Peruzzi's inventive architectural capacities, the drawing for *La Calandria* offers us a visual referent. Peruzzi and Vasari experimented with the idea of invoking Rome's cultural and historical density as it stood in so many sixteenth-century minds.

The text of Aretino's *La Cortigiana* evinces a similarly busy cityscape. The Prologo describes the city: "there's the Palace, St. Peter's, the piazza, the fortress, a couple of taverns ... the fountain, St. Catherine's ... the Colosseum and the Pantheon, all sorts of things .... "[52] Though the exact date of its original production is not known, the play was written in Rome in 1525 or 1526. We will return to the significance of the subversions entwined in Aretino's text, which presents an unflattering portrait of the Roman court. For now, it is worth noting that the action of the play occurs in Rome, and that Aretino, by then a Venetian, nonetheless retained a vivid image of the Eternal City.[53]

"Baldassarre made during the time of Leo X two scenes that were wonderful (*maravigliose*)," wrote Vasari. Etymologically, *maraviglia*, from the Latin *mirabilia* and *mirare*, invokes not only looking and admiring, but also being amazed or surprised. The term can be directly related to *mirus*, wonderful. In early modern discourses, *maraviglia* is central for Cinthio, for whom the objective of the stage is not merely to convey a location, but also to create a sensation of wonderment by captivating the audience's attention.[54] *Maraviglia* gives prominence to the viewer's reaction – a delectable surprise deftly crafted by the unexpected. In order to provide something unexpected, it is necessary to create an anomaly. Burckhardt argued that visual engagement was so central to the aesthetics of the Renaissance that theatre designers aimed to make the stage "sufficiently captivating ... for the poetry to be forgotten."[55] Burckhardt's notion, it should be mentioned, has been challenged in recent years by Di Maria, who defends the idea that theatricality "in the Barthian sense of 'theatre minus the text' did not become so overwhelming as to suffocate the drama," and that, hence, visual art remained at the service of the narrative.[56] Yet, as Shearman indicates, sixteenth-century Italian art was "valued for its capacity to excite wonder," a quality that heightened the status of theatre and incited "the general tendency to admire the set piece' "[57]

Given that the theatrical principle of *maraviglia* only became prevalent around the middle of the sixteenth century, one might have some chronological reservations about Peruzzi's having consciously articulated it. Nonetheless, it is clear that his design established certain well-known aesthetic principles "that would later directly correlate to the aesthetics of wonderment. Values that were central to the period as a whole, and to artists working in his environment, are synthesized in his stage design for *La Calandria*. Peruzzi's visual deployment of a multiplicity of well-known monuments actively engages with the artistic value of quantitative and qualitative multiplicity (copiousness and variety) to beget an alluring, novel depiction of Rome. The aforementioned spatial disruptions and dissonances also relate to contemporary aesthetic discourses within Peruzzi's circle.[58] It is at this time that Castiglione defends a pluralist conception of artistic models, stressing the positive value of anti-normative "abuses" (*abusioni*). Tafuri summarized it as follows: "transgression is regarded as a condition of meaning."[59] As Shearman pointed out, the authority of Aristotle was also used to defend licence, especially his statement that "any 'impossibility' may be defended by reference to poetic effect, or to the ideal, or to current opinion."[60] It seems that *maraviglia* existed along with, and may have reified, a series of aesthetic values and practices anticipated by early Cinquecento artists like Peruzzi.

Sacred Resonances

In the eyes of Vasari, sixteenth-century stage designs were righteously modernized to forsake the performance of mystery plays. The writer is cautious in his engagement with Brunelleschi's mechanical contrivances (*ingegni*) for sacred plays, which he praises even as he promptly dismisses them as culturally extinct.[61] Vasari's stark distinction belies fundamental connections between sixteenth-century drama and the staging of mystery plays and religious events, as the Italian Renaissance theatre's engagement with transgression and wonderment resonates with earlier scenographic practices. Indeed, Vasari's argument that the text and set design for *La Calandria* had initiated a path away from mystery plays appears peculiar when juxtaposed with the period idea of artists as divine creators.[62]

Vasari's disruptive rhetoric notwithstanding, the relationship between religious plays and secular theatrical performances stands at the roots of late-fifteenth- and sixteenth-century stage design. As Thomas Pallen writes, "religious processions, mystery play productions, and theatrical performances all found a common denominator in the Florentine humanists and in the various brigades, companies, and confraternities that they formed."[63] Scholars have placed the popular Quattrocento mystery plays within the intellectual circles of Cosimo il Vecchio and Archbishop Antonio Pierozzi.[64] And Kristin Phillips-Court writes that the Florentine *sacra rappresentazione* "adopted epic's octave verse form, and incorporated an informative prologue like that found in the Greco-Roman drama."[65] The humanistic approach to these festivities may have justified or promoted a series of changes in the staging of mystery plays. In this sense, Luigi Allegri has differentiated the static, medieval mystery plays from Brunelleschi's designs for religious enactments, which incorporated "the entire space of the building in the theatrical dimension."[66] Yet these differentiations did not draw a sharp line. The Italian peninsula saw in the years between 1480 and 1508 (that is, between Poliziano's *L'Orfeo* in Mantua and the Ferrara representation of *La Cassaria*) a moment in which humanistic ideas came to develop from and through the medieval visual models found in sacred representations.[67]

The germ of Renaissance theatrical design has been traditionally traced back to Brunelleschi's innovative machinery for sacred performances (the famous *ingegni*). Brunelleschi's well-known works put miraculous events into action, by use of a series of mechanical apparatuses: the angel Gabriel flew across the church, Christ ascended to heaven, and circles of angels played music in a heavenly dome.[68] Brunelleschi's *ingegni* would directly influence Leonardo da Vinci's theatre designs.[69] Leonardo, who was critical of linear perspective, de-emphasized this pictorial technique in his scenographic projects in order to further explore the possibilities of engineering and machinery. "It is surprising that apparently no perspective scenery was built until the first decade of the sixteenth century," observed Kernodle.[70] But perhaps theatre designers simply did not conceptualize theatrical spaces in the same way as they did pictures.

The most lavish and ambitious of Leonardo's designs is the mountain of Hades: a construction that was capable of opening up to display its interior, as seen in the *Codex Arundel* drawings. By using this mountain, Leonardo was able to create a magnificent surprise for an audience who had visual access to the stage from the moment they entered the theatre (stages did not have curtains – an element that would be introduced later).[71] And while surprise became an artistic end in secular dramas, its origins are deeply rooted in the enactment of mystic events.[72] Is not the production of an unexpected, impossible spatial location a magical conjuring or even a miracle?

In their fictive creation of place, late-fifteenth- and sixteenth-century stages remained a space for wonder, awe, and surprise. Miraculous events became secular marvels. Artists like Leonardo encountered and explored this relationship between theatres and churches.[73] Tafuri has shown the visual and conceptual tensions that emanate from this juxtaposition of spectacle and liturgy: in Leonardo's architectural sketches, as the church is brought into a theatre, the priest becomes a mere actor.[74]

The relationship between theatrical spaces, their classical roots, and religious rituals became entangled in the fifteenth and sixteenth centuries. The Colosseum exemplifies this synthesis. Since the Middle Ages, the Roman amphitheatre had been identified as the Temple of Sol (*Templum Solis*), an interpretation that coexisted with the humanist notion of the venue as the exemplary theatre. In his 1536 edition of and commentary on Vitruvius's architectural treatise, Giambattista Capolari (1475–1555) explicitly invokes the sacred resonances of the Colosseum, which he calls a "round church" (*Chiese delle rotonde*).[75] Much as Cesare Cesariano had previously done in his 1521 edition of Vitruvius, Capolari uses the language of sacred architecture to describe the theatrical space: the stage is a pulpit (*pulpito*), and the senatorial seating in the orchestra is a double choir (*duplato choro*).[76] The Colosseum itself, much like other amphitheatres, was used for religious performances well into the fifteenth and sixteenth centuries.[77] This is the case with the Roman Gonfalone Company's Passion play, which served the priest Guiliano Dati to broadcast Florentine scenographic and literary developments. This popular production was staged in the Colosseum beginning in 1490 and was performed until 1539, at which point it was banned by Paul III after it incited an anti-Semitic outbreak of violence.[78]

The viewers of the Roman production of *La Calandria* existed in a world where sacred representation and religious connotations were the dominant theatrical form. Peruzzi appears to dispel such associations, bringing forth the Colosseum as a sign of Rome's classical past and as a trans-historical symbol of performance and viewership, rather than as the place of religious performances. In the design for *La Calandria*, the Colosseum is but one amongst many elements, a bantam fragment. Through its proliferation of buildings (sacred and secular, ancient and modern), Peruzzi's Rome dispenses with the notion of a singular architectural function while allowing for a number of resonances. In place of the type of visual miracle that occurred in sacred staging, the viewer of *La Calandria* encounters a secular miracle, a magical event. It is not the

Angel of the Annunciation that suddenly appears to the viewers, it is Rome as a whole (itself a physically impossible event).

In *La Calandria*, the Argumento states that the characters Lidio and Santilla "are both in Rome today," but that the audience should not imagine that these characters were suddenly transported "by necromancy," for it is Rome that has been brought forth and shrunken. The text, by explicitly stating that the relocation of the characters was not done by necromancy (*per negromanzia*), hints at the notion that the shrinking and transportation of Rome took place as a type of secular miracle. The rhetorical disclaimer of necromancy summons, if only to swiftly dispel, profane connotations, irreligious and forbidden. Within the context of early sixteenth-century artists, it reminds us of a lengthy passage in which Leonardo condemns necromancy as a superstitious and foolish activity that misleads its practitioners, promising the most impossible acts.[79] Whereas alchemy gives birth to simple things, he writes, necromancy adds unnecessary inorganic complications and does not produce real results. Peruzzi's scenography was not directly informed by Leonardo, but it is intriguing that the design does create something unnatural and intrinsically complex that is fundamentally impossible. The introduction of necromancy, especially given Peruzzi's nuanced description of ancient monuments, creates a curious connection with the period's archaeological enterprises, since unearthing activities had necromantic connotations.[80] The disclaimer that the sudden apparition is not conjured through necromancy may well formulate a comic, learned witticism flouting contemporary superstitions. Later in the sixteenth century, Benvenuto Cellini would again associate the Colosseum with sorcery, recounting his participation in a necromantic ritual performed in the famous Roman amphitheatre.[81] In a broader sense, the mention of black magic in *La Calandria* stipulates a logic of the imaginary, the fantastic, and the unnatural.[82]

The sacred and the secular should not be understood as diametrically opposed and mutually exclusive, especially in the case of Rome, where these two spheres are intimately intertwined. Indeed, this spatial duality is activated by the play, since Rome is the place depicted as well as the physical location of the performance. The Argumento states that "they are both in Rome today, and you will see both of them appear here. Do not imagine, though, that they were suddenly transported here from Rome by necromancy." The performance is taking place in

Rome, which means that no magic need be involved: theoretically, the play could have taken place in a street or on a balcony with a view of Rome. What the design (and not the text) creates is a Rome inside of Rome. Is the staged Rome a distilled rendering of the real city, or is it an irruption of the city's vital force? In either case, the doubling remains. Rome becomes a fantastic reality that is no longer a site. It is then perhaps not a miracle or an act of magic that creates Rome, as the text may connote, but above all a chimerical act of artistic creation. There is no reason, in any case, to embrace exclusionary models. Peruzzi is not presenting *either* a miracle, *or* a magic act, *or* an act of artistic creation; the design harnesses the simultaneity of these interwoven, yet dissonant, threads. These conceptual interactions become tangible on the stage as the artistic endeavour exposes itself and, subverting the goals of the miraculous and the magical, creates a synthetic, spurious view of Rome that can never become a simulacrum, a hyper-real imaginary, or a virtual locale.

Vasari praised the text and scenography of *La Calandria* because it represented a resurgence in classical dramaturgy that had been replaced by festivals and mystery plays during the Middle Ages; nonetheless, the boundary between secular and sacred spectacles was hardly hermetic in the Italian Renaissance. The theatre was not fully removed from the sacred and the magical, nor were religious celebrations sheltered from secular theatrical developments. The spirit of the Counter-Reformation brought with it a strategic approach towards images and a desire to capture the attention of viewers, in turn developing a spectacular and performative awareness that permeated religious celebrations. An attunement to the power of visual spectacles in the post-Tridentine church, as Andrew Casper notes, is palpable in the liturgical practice of the Mass as well as in public displays of relics – mostly famously the Veil of Veronica and the Turin Shroud – performative events that emphasized direct visual contact and bolstered belief in the real presence of the relics "through the performance of a visual spectacle."[83]

The dramaturgical world of the sixteenth century would also see a return to sacred festivities in the hands of the Jesuits, who found in the theatre a useful tool to communicate religious messages and induce emotive responses. Jesuit plays were performed as early as 1551. These stressed didactic dialogue and were performed within schools by amateur actors in order to establish virtuous habits and notions.[84] Towards the end of the sixteenth century, however, we see an increased interest in classical themes and Aristotelian structure, and the adoption of

Renaissance scenographic practices – which were nonetheless accompanied with severe arguments against secular-professional theatrical performances.[85] The interest in scenographic developments intensified in the early decades of the seventeenth century, which would encounter a growing taste for the spectacular and the complex. The 1622 production of Vincenzo Guiniggi's *Ignatius in Monte Serrato, arma mutans*, for example, added to the religious struggle and conversion of Ignatius of Loyola and Francis Xavier a series of secular and pagan elements: Indians, centaurs, chariots bearing personified continents, and battles on land and sea.[86] The incorporation of lavish costumes and sets would not go without criticism; nonetheless, the Jesuit stage continued to adopt the aesthetics of secular theatre in order to compete with such spectacles as well as to captivate audiences by using special effects and sumptuous scenography that appealed to the viewers' senses.[87]

The development of spectacular strategies in religious celebrations and sacred performances at the end of the sixteenth century shows deep connections between post-Tridentine religious celebrations and the early Renaissance developments by Brunelleschi. At the same time, the juxtaposition of theatrical spectacle and liturgy, cutting across the limits between magical ritual and artificial theatricality, implicitly generated tensions. Secular and sacred performances conjointly developed a taste for the theatrical and its visual potency while actively undermining each other.

Triumph

The magical qualities of the transformation in *La Calandria* are tangible in the Argumento, which proclaims to the audience, "The city you see here is Rome, which used to be so ample, so spacious, so large that, triumphing, it could contain many cities and towns and rivers. Now it has become so small."[88] The characters of the Argumento and the Prologo often introduced plays to the spectators, regularly uttering spatial clues to help the audiences navigate the stage.[89] The figures identify the geographic locations, even enacting fictive spatial displacements: sometimes spectators are described as being transported to a distant city; at other times, a foreign location is brought verbally to the audience.[90] The introductory function of the Argumento and the Prologo, which set the mood and provide spatial explanations, appears analogous to the figure of the interlocutor described in Alberti's *On Painting*: a figure whose outward gaze catches the attention of the viewer and "who admonishes and points out to us what is happening there … or shows some danger or marvelous things there; or invites us to weep or to laugh together with them."[91]

Bibbiena's Argumento in *La Calandria* proclaims a fictional displacement where Rome comes to the spectators. In Peruzzi's design, the abridged city activates a process where the triumphal essence of Rome comes to be part of the triumphal essence of the artistic practice. The notion of Rome triumphing in the text of *La Calandria* could be understood as what Tafuri has called the aesthetic "heroic," a notion that binds fragments and multiplicity into a cohesive entity.[92] Peruzzi's visual approach resonates strongly with the political circumstances of the performance. As Ronald Martinez has shown, both the 1513 performance of *La Calandria* in Urbino and especially the 1514 production in Rome have as a background dynastic events and festive celebrations that proclaimed Medici power (the spring of 1513 saw the death of Pope Julius II along with Leo X's ascension to power).[93] The exultant image of Rome, present in the text of the play (especially the Prologo), is further evoked in Peruzzi's design by the incorporation of the central triumphal arch – an architectural element associated with the theatre throughout the Italian Renaissance. The triumph of *La Calandria* then presents itself in terms of historical significance and contemporary political references, binding them together by presenting Rome as an active locale in which art, culture, religion, and politics are intertwined and self-reflective: "Rome's receptiveness is itself a topic of triumph, evoking the great triumphs of the literary tradition."[94]

Within the culture of early modern Italy, a rhetorical exaltation of a city is not unusual, nor is the idea of presenting a city as a generic assemblage or assortment of monuments novel.[95] To use a well-known example, the *View of Florence with the Chain,* commonly ascribed to Francesco Rosselli, emphasizes certain monuments by means of detail and size, generating a "vivid fabrication"[96] that nonetheless retains a sound topographical portrayal of the city. The notion of encomium that Thomas Frangenberg ascribes to the *View of Florence,* and that he uses to connect the woodcut to eulogizing texts like Bernardino da Firenze's *Le bellezze et chasati di Firenze,* correlates to Bibbiena's play and Peruzzi's designs, both of which celebrate the urban fabric of Rome and its history. We may consider additional parallels between the design for *La Calandria* and cityscapes of Rome (like Rosselli's now lost *View of Rome*) – cityscapes that amplify venerated buildings such as the Colosseum or the Pantheon.[97] In contrast to these city views, Peruzzi's design does not offer the rationale of topography, however imprecise, replacing it instead with the artificial, though only partially deployed rationale of linear perspective. And while city maps and views assumed that "a spectator had to invest prolonged time and thought,"[98] Peruzzi's Rome is deployed in an instant that overwhelms the viewer.

Bibbiena's text reads, "The city you see here is Rome," but the artifice of Peruzzi's creation indicates the contrary. If there were a place in the world where the spatial dislocations of Roman buildings would be noticeable, that place would be Rome. We must not forget that Peruzzi's design for *La Calandria* is almost contemporary with Raphael's 1517 appointment as commissioner of antiquities and the beginning of his project of creating an archaeological map of the city, a project that, though sympathetic to Peruzzi's stage design, is inherently divergent in its consideration of space. If the mapping and the surveying of urban topography are geographic attestations that aim at a commensuration of perception in relation to a place, we may wonder how Peruzzi's drawing attempts to ground its own visual discourse, an issue that deserves attention in relation to the text of the play.

Mimesis

Peruzzi's sacrifice of the specific location and of the viewers' phenomenological experiences allows him to visually convey something beyond sensorial information while retaining the specificity of Rome as a particular city. In its interest in both fiction and reality, Peruzzi's stage design and others like it exemplify a rather nuanced approach to similitude and artistic invention that cannot be reduced to mere "imitation." This visual and conceptual approach allows us to contextualize the design through discourses on mimesis, something especially significant given the aesthetic concept's lasting effect in Western thought.

The visual synecdoche of his design for *La Calandria* opens up notions about place and space in general, and about Rome with respect to its monumental cultural past. Peruzzi's design, through its experimentation, makes manifest central artistic concerns with regard to time, space, particularity, and universality.[99] If we were to interpret Peruzzi's work in relation to Aristotle's *Poetics*, it would be more logical to conceptualize the stage design not as articulating a unity of place that belongs to the second half of the sixteenth century but as operating alongside more general principles like Aristotle's prioritization of poetry over history.[100] The extent to which Peruzzi was informed by this Aristotelian valuation cannot be verified; nevertheless, the set design resonates with later scenographic theories like Cinthio's argument that the fictional and poetic are more verisimilar than the factual, and therefore more like the truth.[101] This notion clearly reminds us of Aristotle's thesis that history, being based on particulars, lacks the universal and broad nature of tragic drama.[102] Whether or not it was influenced by Aristotle, the design arguably conveys a "truer" notion of Rome's essence than a topographically accurate cityscape could.[103]

In forfeiting the particularity of perceptual reality and using linear perspective to override the natural need for spatial orientation, Peruzzi's design negotiates the potential tensions between the well-known and the unexpected – between the factual and the fictive. If Peruzzi's Rome can be understood to be more truthful in its scope, it is because the particulars of the stage do not operate as individual instances of monuments but as elements within a larger pattern.[104] Since true knowledge is general and conceptual, it is this composite synecdoche, this assortment of buildings, that communicates the significance and cultural gravity of the city. In a sense, there is a mimetic aspect to Peruzzi's city, in as much as monuments can be identified and named. We may recall Aristotle's acknowledgment of the positive philosophical qualities of mimesis, which are noted in the period by authors like Angelo Ambrogini, known as Poliziano.[105] Yet Peruzzi's design does not aim at a mimetic representation of place, or a mimetic deception in which the stage produces "the effects that are normally achieved by other means."[106] Rather, it creates a displacement where particulars become the means through which more universal values are disclosed. Resemblances function because viewers understand them, in a theatrical space, as a play on semblances, as something other than the constituents of topological space. In other words, mimesis is not a process of imitation, of making a product that matches the world the artist perceives.[107] Aristotle was quite aware of the tensions that artistic production generated. Mimesis is double-sided: art imitates nature (*he techne mimeitai ten phusin*) while additionally accomplishing or perfecting (*epitelei*) nature.[108] "There is then a general mimesis," writes Philippe Lacoue-Labarthe, "which supplements a certain deficiency in nature, its incapacity to do everything, organize everything, make everthing its work – produce everything."[109]

That verisimilitude is central to sixteenth-century stages is clear, just as it is a driving force in contemporary aesthetic treatises of the period. Torquato Tasso exemplifies this when he writes that no part of poetry "can be separated from the verisimilar."[110] But the aesthetic values of truthfulness and similitude do not imply a concern with the pictorial creation of a believable simulation of real place. Girolamo Fracastoro in his *Naugerious, sive de poetica dialogus* (written c. 1540, published in 1555), writes that poets must create nothing alien to truth (*veritate alienum*), though he quickly grants them freedom to create anything, whether it be truthful in appearance, meaning, allegorically, or in accord with what all or most men believe.[111] Universal truths, argues Fracastoro, are not to be left bare in their singular existence, but must be adorned:

> The poet is like the painter who does not wish to represent this or that particular man as he is with many defects, but who, having contemplated the universal and supremely beautiful idea of his creator, makes things as they ought to be ... The poet imitates not the particular but the simple idea clothed in its own beauties, which Aristotle calls the universal ... Therefore what the painters and the poets add to things for perfection is not extraneous.[112]

The Aristotelian concept of mimesis involves "a framing of reality that announces that what is contained within the frame is not simply real ... the more 'real' the imitation the more fraudulent it becomes."[113] This framing allows a truthful depiction of a city without topographic accuracy. And although in theatre resemblances are at their most elusive, mimesis is significant, vital, in fact, for stage designers who aim at evoking a specific location (e.g., to visually move from "a city" to "this city is Pisa"). But mimesis, as Jacques Rancière points out, is not how a copy resembles a model; mimesis is the means to make resemblances function within a set of relations that includes "modes of speech, forms of visibility, and protocols of intelligibility."[114] This is embedded in the notion of image in the Latin *imago* and the Greek *eikon* which denote "an abstract, general, spiritual 'likeness.'"[115] At the same time, as Hans Belting argues, the early modern artist of Italy "reevaluated the image as a work by an artist – that is, a product of art."[116] The creation of art becomes the domain of knowledge, but this knowledge comprises, in addition to geometry, mathematics, and optics, the capacity to invent (*"la inventione de le hopere,"* as Jacopo de' Barbari puts it).[117] Martin Kemp has in this very sense traced the Renaissance movement from a conception of the artist as *imitatore* (e.g., *di natura* or *degli antichi*) to *inventore*.[118]

With the loss of religious authority, the image, Belting writes, becomes "no more than an agreed-upon symbol,"[119] which in turn means that, "for an image to be accepted as proof, it was necessary to formulate rules by which to judge it."[120] Belting states that the parameters through which one judges an image shift over time, but that the necessity for rules of judgment is itself a constant without which there could be none of the above-mentioned agreed-upon symbols. I do not want to imply that Belting's stark differentiation of images made before and after the purported artistic turn of the Renaissance is without problems.[121] However, I want to retain Belting's accentuation of invention and artificiality, the collective capacity of understanding (the "agreed-upon"), and the notion of presence as an abstract and general arrangement. This leads not to the liberation of rules but to the liberation of the burden of proof. In fact, the "agreed-upon" need not be seen as a programmatic apparatus of imitation of optical reception. Rules of replication become rules of invention. This is what Castiglione upholds in *The Courtier* when discussing speech, and what we can extrapolate to visual encounters:

> Therefore, the habit of good speech, I believe, is instituted by talented men, who through the teachings of experience have obtained good judgment, enabling them to concur and accept those words that seem most fitting, which they recognize by means of a certain instinctive judgment, and not by any formula or rule.[122]

If resemblances function, it is because viewers understand them as something else, not as illusions. In a theatrical space, resemblances are collectively understood as a play of semblances, as something other than the topological space.[123] In the design for *La Calandria*, for example, the viewer is presented with well-known structures like the Colosseum, but the incorporation of carefully and accurately described buildings does not add up to a visually truthful whole. The setting of the play is unmistakable; *La Calandria* takes place in Rome. Yet the staged action remains fictive, and the accumulation of monuments, however identifiable, restates the ficticity of the drama. Mimesis, introducing an irreducible paradox between the factual and the artificial, is encountered with anxiety: Jonas Barish calls it "a kind of ontological malaise."[124] One may escape this disquiet, argues Lacoue-Labarthe, through admiration, "with the usual 'It's so real!' – which simply covers over the alteration."[125] And yet, despite rhetorical exhortations regarding the appearance of cities on stage, the additional, the ornamental, and the fictive, remain. In the theatrical stage, there are no simulations but only visual syntheses of recognizable buildings.[126] Even the more literal quotation from real spaces, like Lanci's design for *La Vedova* (figure 1.2), intentionally become "fraudulent."

Peruzzi's approach does not challenge illusionism merely because it reconfigures Rome but because it embraces a dramaturgical mode of representation that prevents reconciliation of the space into a believable whole: the viewers do not encounter the background as a continuation of their physical space. Vasari's praise of Peruzzi, in this respect, is of note. As Mark Rosen indicates, Vasari's *Lives* downplays or ignores city views and *vedute* as the outcome of a merely technical process of plotting, and as falling outside the laws of perspective and representational painting – while at the same time praising the urban scenographies created for theatrical performances.[127] Vasari's passages engaging with stage design indicate that he saw scenography as having a level of artistic merit that cannot be reduced to purely technical replication of optical experiences.

The reconciliation of the stage with our physical space, in any case, would remain an impossibility given the flatness of the edifices, the way they overlap one another, the internal distortions in size, and the external distortions created by the presence of actors on stage. From a historiographic point of view, it is interesting to encounter the long shadow of Panofsky's interpretation not only in the history of painting but also in the history of theatre and scenography. As has been noted by Elkins, interpretations of perspective are so zealous in the pursuit of perfect geometric coherence that scholars cover up perspectival errors, sacrificing irregularities to defend the presence of an ideal, illusionistic unity.[128] We can reiterate Burckhardt's insightful thesis: the aim of scene-designers was in no instance "illusion in our present sense but an appearance of festive splendor."[129] It would seem feasible for Peruzzi to conceive a space, especially in a drawing, that was fantastic yet illusionistic – or at least more coherent than his set for *La Calandria*. Lanci's scenographic designs, for example, show that a theatrical drawing, as a drawing, can imagine itself a limitless space unconcerned with the built stage. But Peruzzi's design remains fictive and rather concerned with the materiality of the stage. To be clear, I am not proposing that naturalism played no role in Renaissance theatrical developments – it certainly did. The representational forces that permeate fifteenth- and sixteenth-century painting and sculpture are certainly at home in the Cinquecento stage. Yet it would be misleading to presume that the

Italian stage sought to directly replicate perceived reality or that high naturalism was a final goal: sixteenth-century Italian artists and audiences continuously demonstrate a preference for style rather than for the reproduction of an aseptic simulacrum of the physical world.

To return to Elkins's point, the issue may rest not with the image but with the framework of interpretation. We come to the artworks with a mental set of preconceptions and assumptions: "a style, like a culture or climate of opinion, sets up a horizon of expectation, a mental set, which registers deviations and modifications with exaggerated sensitivity."[130] Gombrich reminds us that Boccaccio reacted with shock to his contemporaries' pictorial developments: "There is nothing which Giotto could not have portrayed in such a manner as to deceive the sense of sight."[131] The thrill of illusion, Gombrich proposes, exists in "the distance between expectation and experience."[132] It is easy to see why period audiences were taken aback by theatrical developments – why, for example, Castiglione praised the set of *La Calandria* for its mimetic qualities with words such as "the scenery imitated the ultimate street" or "the stage very naturally showed a reproduction of the city."[133] But to assume that viewers experienced pictorial space as a continuation of their physical reality requires perpetuating a historiographic mode of interpretation that neglects the ways in which early modern claims to illusion employed a specific rhetorical form that was not dependent on an absolute and objective framework. Let us take Castiglione's description of the set for *La Calandria:* "a very fine city with streets, palaces, churches, towers, true streets, and all in relief, but still assisted by excellent painting and very good perspective."[134] Even within this short description we already encounter the limits of illusionism. As Povoledo has noted, Castiglione's description clearly distinguishes between "streets" (depicted, fictive) and "true streets" (spaces for the actors to enter and perhaps perform).[135] Castiglione then commends the set design using common rhetorical terms to accentuate its naturalistic qualities, but neither the clear differentiation between real and fictive streets nor the large number of depicted urban elements can be read as an attempt to trick the audience into believing the space was a continuation of the auditorium.

Many of these issues are rooted in a notion of mimetic representation that permeates the history of painting and theatre. As David Summers writes:

> When we look from real space "into" a virtual space, we see an apparent space (and time) necessarily different from that in which we are standing;

> at the same time, as we recognize and complete virtual space and forms, they may become *as if* our visual experience, to the greater or lesser denial of our spatial situation. This reflection of the virtual into the real is only partially countered by the idea that what we are seeing is fiction … In general, virtual images make it possible to define the elsewhere as elsewhere … but given this detachment from present space and time, they also make it possible to bring some "elsewhere" into spaces of human presence and use.[136]

Rendering a space visible cannot negate the ambiguity of the experience. The illusion is but a playful manoeuvre – a playfulness intensified in the theatrical space. Summers continues:

> A theatre, a place for seeing, is, in the present terms, a place in which seeing is literally set at a distance from the seen and thereby made acceptable as merely apparent, on the level of which the "play" of the drama may proceed.[137]

In the sixteenth century, the fictive qualities of the theatre were never dispelled. Far from it, as the play introductions, the presence of *intermedi,* and even the internal spatial and material dissonances in the scenography all reinforced the ficticity of the dramaturgical event.

At the same time, the representational qualities of stages were celebrated throughout the sixteenth century. What we encounter in designs like Peruzzi's for *La Calandria* is then not a sense of illusionism as a continuation of our physical space or a *trompe l'œil* in which the artifice of the work is obscured. Rather, we encounter a space that hopes to maximize our recognition of its shapes. The representational qualities that show an attentive appreciation of Rome's monuments, along with the spatial anchoring made possible by linear perspective, produce a highly readable image. Again, the ease with which one may accept (at first) the design as visually consistent is a testament to Peruzzi's capacities. As Whitney Davis explains, the experience of properly seeing a projection that uses consistently proportional linear perspective creates a highly readable space regardless of "whether or not the proportions of these depicted things have the natural or 'correct' proportions of things in the real visual world."[138] We perceive what the picture intends to show regardless of whether the depicted things have the natural proportions of those things in the perceived real world; and our capacity to recognize shapes depends on the existence of the represented things.

If one were to talk about scenographic representation, it would be a representation of fragments of individual architectural elements. We have encountered this Zeuxian manoeuvre most clearly in Peruzzi's design. At the same time, those individual elements carry with them the burden of signification – in early modern theatrical designs as well as in our memories and imagination. In these encounters, withdrawal and introduction, distancing and approximation, semblance and truth disclose a ceaseless mimetic exchange.[139] Could the modern establishment of the theatrical as a regime of distance and passivity have been born out of the malaise, the discomfort, and the anxiety produced by mimesis?[140] As we are going to see in the next chapters, the artificial never truly leaves the stage. Above all, theatrical spectators are not the captives of Plato's cave, imprisoned since childhood, their heads and limbs constrained and physically forced to stare at the deceitful shadows projected on the wall in front of them.

Chapter Two

The Artificial City on Stage

Before the curtain opened, you probably thought it was the Tower of Babel back there, but instead it was Rome itself. Look: there's the Palace, St. Peter's, the piazza, the fortress, a couple of taverns … the fountain, St. Catherine's … the Colosseum and the Pantheon, all sorts of things….

Aretino, Prologue, *La Cortigiana*[1]

The comedies and tragedies of the Cinquecento take place in urban centres and one may feel compelled to state that, accordingly, the city is pervasively represented in early modern scenography. Yet, neither are real locations truly represented, nor are the diverse cityscapes easily generalized into the homogeneous category "the city." Such rhetoric has fomented a polarized interpretive framework that disjoins the general from the concrete, the categorical from the phenomenal. This dichotomy becomes increasingly unstable in the visual art that concerns us, where abstract ideas coexist with resilient material circumstances. Previously, we saw how Peruzzi introduced a conceptual notion of Rome by using an excess of uprooted particulars. As the above quotation from *La Cortigiana* demonstrates, this tactic was not an individual instance. In fact, the choice of presenting a broad cityscape saturated with monuments was already featured in the 1513 scenography for *La Calandria*, whose stage incorporated various streets, palaces, churches, and towers. The discussion in this chapter will proceed towards a contextualization of theatrical cityscapes in order to explore other cases of spatial dissonances, visual tensions, inquietudes, and internal inconsistencies that demonstrate the prevalence of a taste for playfulness achieved through aesthetic displacement. As this chapter shows, Cinquecento stages remained consciously artificial and ornamental – an artificiality only further intensified by the disproportional presence of actors' animated bodies, especially notable in stages decorated with painted people and animals.

As a result, we take further steps beyond commonly held notions of theatrical city views as conventional and formulaic presages of a perfect future.[2] Such interpretations are interrelated in the conceptualization of the utopian as a multi-media political machinery of social inscription – an interpretation that itself relies on the enduring scholarly conflation of theatrical city views, urban planning, and representations of cities. Before unsnarling those issues, it is profitable and sensible to continue engaging with the urban spaces as stage designs. Scenography encompasses "the focus of attention onto the spatial dynamics, the active presence of the performers in the given spaces, and the choices of materials."[3] We may then begin revising the assessment that the city is widely represented in early modern Italian stages. A more pertinent phrasing might be that constructions and depictions resembling urban environments are often presented on early modern Italian stages.

Scenography is concerned with audience reception and engagement. It creates a sensory, intellectual, and emotional experience.[4] As such, it is concerned with duration, narrative, and embodiment. Theatrical spaces do not wait to be uprooted from their circumstances of construction and presentation in order to be "looked upon as a kind of single 'picture.'"[5] Of these Cinquecento sensory-rich environments we have but vestiges: two-dimensional preparatory fragments of the ornate, lambent spectacles that were ultimately built on stage. It seems almost counterintuitive to think about drawings or prints as being anything other than images or pictures, but theatrical drawings and prints mediate between their own material physicality as objects and the potential, constructed theatrical space. Being more than merely architectural blueprints, stage designs materialize a future condition that oscillates between mediums and dimensions.

Artificiality

The scenographic design commonly known as *View of Pisa* (figure 2.1) was created by Domenico Beccafumi (1486–1551), probably for Alessandro Piccolomini's comedy *L'amor costante,* which was performed in Siena in 1536 for Emperor Charles V.[6] The drawing presents the city of Pisa, with its famous leaning tower, a bridge crossing the River Arno,

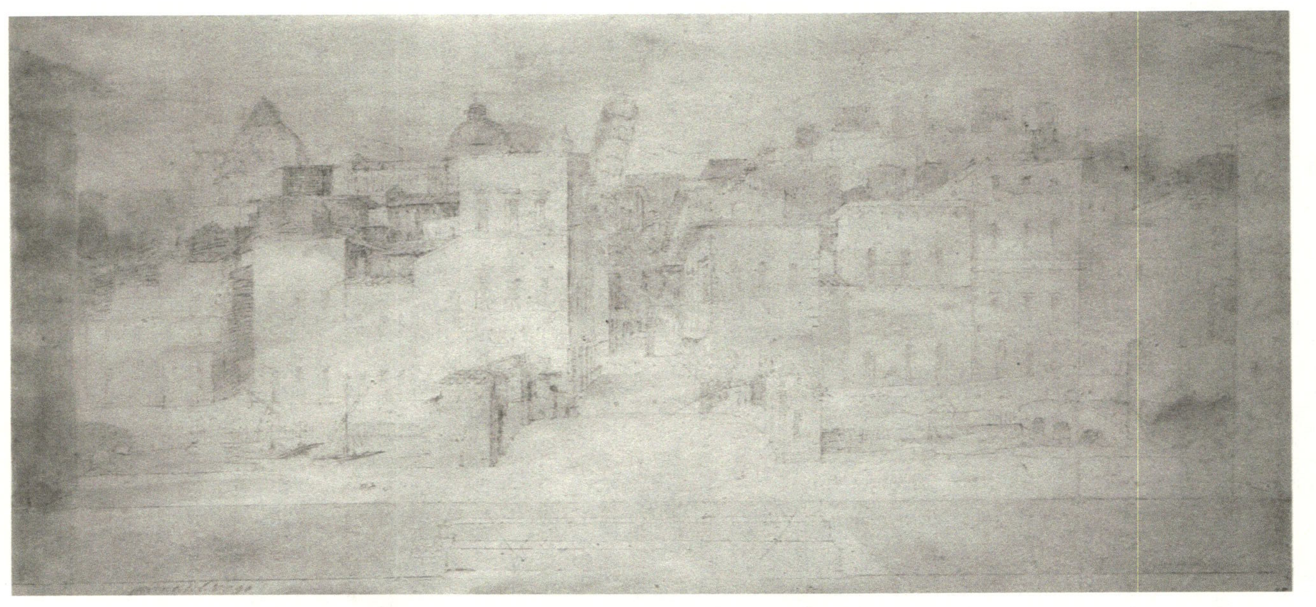

2.1 Domenico Beccafumi, *Scenographic View of Pisa*, c. 1536. Pen in brown ink on paper, wash, 18.6 x 38.8 cm. Image from akg-images.

and a main city avenue constructed using linear perspective. Much is original in Beccafumi's design, especially its approach to line and light – but its innovations appear to have had little influence in Italian Cinquecento scenography.

Born in Montaperti, near Siena, Beccafumi is most widely known for his unique painting style, a reaction against the popular, balanced classical style. Not much is known of Beccafumi's early artistic developments between 1508 and 1512, though he likely travelled to Florence and Rome. Resurfacing in Siena in 1513, Beccafumi introduced a heightened concern for intense and emotional contrasts of light and dark into his paintings, expanding upon Leonardo's chiaroscuro.

Much of this pictorial style must have transferred to his theatrical projects. Though *View of Pisa* remains a monochrome theatre design – a sketch of what was ultimately built – we can identify many of Beccafumi's aesthetic qualities in it: the contrast of light and dark, a noticeable articulation of linear perspective, irregular lines, and a hazy atmosphere. It is of relevance that Beccafumi, unlike so many contemporary stage designers, was primarily a painter, not a practising architect. Regardless of the tendency in the scholarship to define stage designs as made according to methods of painting, Beccafumi's *View of Pisa* is unique in its manifested concern with pictorial qualities – a concern that would not become conventional in the Italian stage.

In the drawing, the city appears resolutely. The buildings' facades, a harmonious rhythm of windows and doorways, pattern a tangible concreteness. A congealed aggregation of edifices materializes behind the facades. The urban fabric emerges as an indistinct resonance of silhouettes – constructions of diverse shapes and sizes rising as hatched shadows. If the buildings in the foreground, with their economical attentiveness to architectural detail, facilitate a view of a specific space, the indeterminacy of the unformed structures in the background asserts the expansiveness of urban growth. On the right side of the drawing, buildings clamber upon one another, relinquishing their individuality. The city bodies forth, muscular and dynamic.

The design's articulation of light and darkness is quite intriguing. We are familiar with scenographic drawings introducing shadows that confer a volumetric effect, but these generally tend to carefully and cleanly delineate architectural elements. Peruzzi and Lanci are remarkable exponents of this tendency, and subsequent designers will retain the value of clarity and descriptive outline found in those two artists. Beccafumi's drawing, on the other hand, swathes the city in darkness, evoking edifices through fluid lines. Behind the first row of houses, buildings are suggested without obtaining a definite form. John Pope-Hennessy, who once owned the drawing, described it keenly as "impressionistic."[7] The hazy effect does not hinder the identification of the city. We may name it with confidence. This city is Pisa.[8] The leaning tower protrudes into the central avenue, and the distinctive shapes of the cathedral and baptistry domes appear above the city's rooftops. Downstage centre, a bridge of odd dimensions arcs across the Arno, upon which a series of diminutive boats float.

The use of high-contrast shading recalls other preparatory artworks by Beccafumi, as his drawings and oil sketches continuously speak to his interest in chiaroscuro. We can compare Beccafumi's *View of Pisa* with his non-scenographic *View of Siena* (figure 2.2), drawn a few years later. The artist employs a very similar shading strategy in both drawings, as the towers of Siena materialize through shadows, conjured by a few fluid strokes of the pen. In both drawings, few edifices obtain volumetric solidity, and in both cases the city emerges as an amalgam of buildings. We perceive the urban space without being consumed by its architectural details. Much as he did in invoking the domes of Pisa with economical but effective detail, Beccafumi ensures that we perceive Siena's most distinctive buildings. The tower of the Palazzo Pubblico, lightened and carefully described, stands out from its surroundings. The documentary precision of the *View of Siena* is lost in the *View of Pisa*. In the latter, distance and proportion are forsaken, flaunting its *scenographic* essence.

The interest in disclosing the dramaturgical and fictive nature of the theatrical event is also present in the text of the plays. This is especially noticeable in the ways that characters such as the Prologo and the Argumento introduce meta-theatrical circumstances to the spectators.[9] For instance, Gigio Artemio Giancarli's *Cingana* is introduced with a rhetorical appeal to the audience to engage in an immediate (and factually impossible) act of self-deception:

> I would ask you to believe three things ... The first is that you should believe that these buildings before you are the city of Treviso. And although they do not altogether resemble it, you will deceive yourselves into believing it was like this at the time when the events which we are about to perform took place.[10]

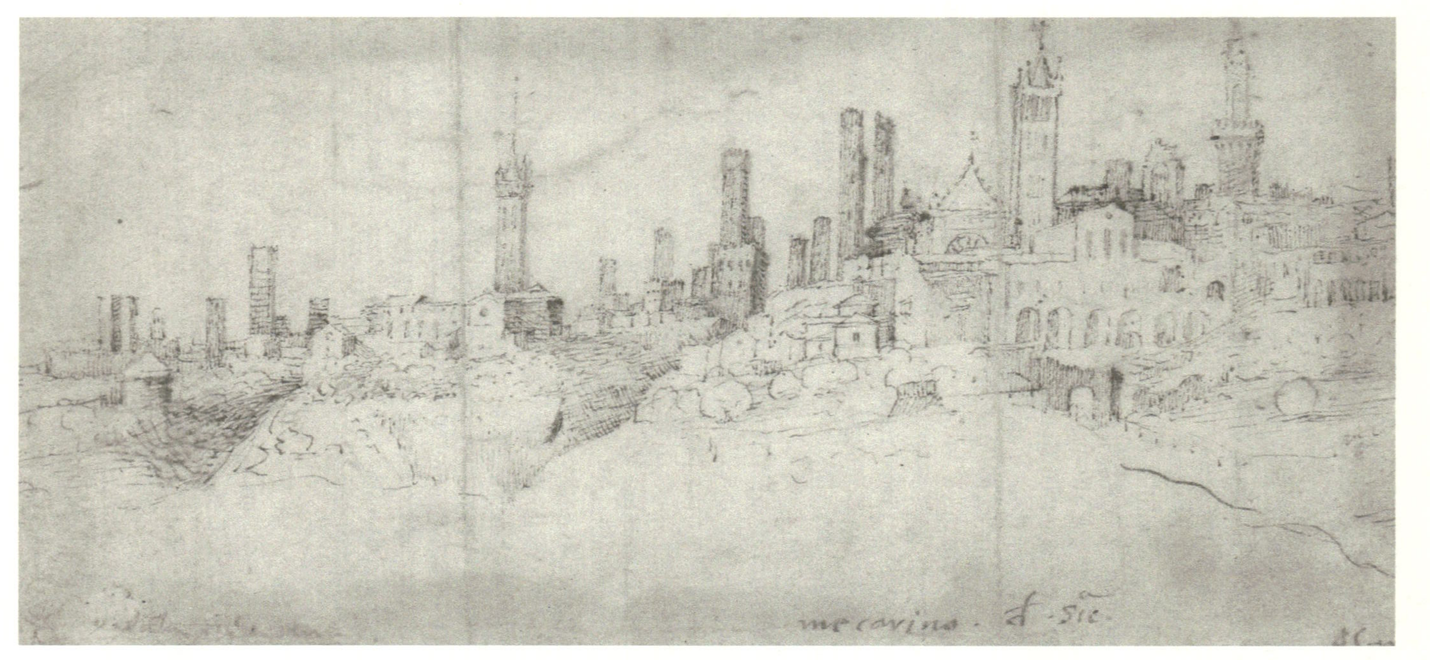

2.2 Domenico Beccafumi, *A View of Siena with Rooftops and Bell Towers*. Pen and brown ink, 1540s? British Museum, Department of Prints and Drawings, 1895-9-15-584. © Trustees of the British Museum.

The first lines of Piccolomini's *L'amor costante*, for which *View of Pisa* was made, explicitly acknowledge the fictional essence of the space and overtly endorse the discourse of wonderment. In this comedy, the character of the Spagnuolo (The Spaniard) introduces the comedy with the Prologo. The Spagnuolo begins the comedy speaking in Spanish – a fitting choice, given that the play was performed for Emperor Charles V, King of Spain:

> O come me spanto en ver estas maravillas! Que pueden significar estos aparatos y estas casas á qui? Y estos hidalgos con estas mugeres y donzella tan hermosas? Que quieren hazer estos señores? Todo sta muy bien, muy lindamente puesto.
>
> [I'm in such awe to see these wonders! What can this *apparato* and these houses here mean? And these gentlemen with these beautiful women and damsels? What do these men want to do? This is very well, very beautifully arranged.][11]

In this manner, the Spagnuolo mentions the wonderful stage (*maravillas*), the *apparato*, the buildings on stage (*casas*), and also either the audience or the actors (*hidalgos, mugeres, donzellas, señores*). Soon after this opening, the Spagnuolo states that he hopes to come across someone who could explain to him "all this wonderful occurrence" (*Pluguiesse a Dios que me topasse con alguna persona que me declarasse todo este magisterio).* It is at this point that the Prologo comes to his aid. The Spagnuolo quickly describes his state of confusion: he does not understand his current space, and asks what this *apparato* means (*vuestra merced me diga que quiere dezir todo este aparato*). The Prologo explains that he has stumbled into the performance of a comedy (*Qui s'ha da far una commedia*). Hearing these words, the Spagnuolo is pacified, and quickly becomes curious, requesting the Prologo to relate the plot of the play. Before commencing the story, the Prologo elucidates: the first thing the Spagnuolo needs to know is that "this city is Pisa" (*La prima cosa, adunque, avete da sapere che questa cittá è Pisa*).

Let us re-examine this introduction of spatial events. First, there is an exclamation regarding the wonders of the stage (*O come me spanto en ver estas maravillas!*). The Spagnuolo is taken aback by a feeling of fear or trepidation (*me spanto*), which is the result of seeing (*ver*) such wonders (*maravillas*). In this first sentence, we already perceive the significance of visual reaction, along with the introduction of the aesthetic notion of wonder. The Spagnuolo does not know where he is. He is utterly confused. His physical transition into the stage was a startling or portentous event. By stating that the stage is awe-inspiring, he is stipulating that the audience should experience awe as well. Subsequently, the Spagnuolo ponders the meaning of the *apparato* and the houses (*que pueden significar estos aparatos y estas casas á qui?*). Despite his confusion, the Spagnuolo correctly identifies that he is not experiencing a city, but an *apparato*. The Prologo explains to him that he is in a comedy, allaying the Spagnuolo's fears and inciting his curiosity. And it is then, finally, that the Prologo states, "this city is Pisa."

The naming of the city and, indeed, the presence of the city, ensue from an understanding that the space is fictive and wonderful, that it belongs to a stage, and that it is made for a comedy. The notion that the Spagnuolo has been thrown onto the stage mimics the experience of the spectators, who also have to negotiate with the staged space because it is dissimilar to their common experiences of the world. The utterance "this is Pisa" aids this situation. It replies to the polysemous, floating chain of signifiers that belong to the image, as Roland Barthes would put it, in order "to counter the terror of uncertain signs."[12] "This city is Pisa" anchors the image, but the assertion of wonderment, the acknowledgment of the space as a theatrical stage, and the genre of the play precede and condition the statement "this city is Pisa." But no stage is really a city, no less Pisa. The naming of the city is disclosed as a playful yet fraudulent christening ceremony. Viewers are explicitly invited to the semantic game inherent in the problem of images – a game that, as we previously noted, was described by Didi-Huberman as having a modern tone but defined classical roots. (Derrida reminds us, too, that a long tradition linking Plotinus, Martin Heidegger, and Jacques Lacan reverberates through the history of Western thought: the gift of the name gives that which the object does not have.)[13]

In turn, the immanent exchange between spectators and the stage trumpets the powers of the visual arts. Given the period *paragone* debates waged between visual artists and poets, the stage offers an implicit justification of the goals and means of scenography. This is the insurrection of the visual, a challenge to the idea that theatre is "first and foremost the space of visibility of speech."[14] Indeed, the concept of the Spagnuolo being "thrown" into the awe-inspiring world of the stage reminds us of Leonardo's retort against poets:

> If you say, "I will describe [in words] hell or paradise, or other delights and terrors," the painter will surpass you because he will place things before you which will silently tell of such delights or terrify you or turn your mind to flight.[15]

What rhetorical exhortations of illusionism and verisimilitude leave behind is the viewers' most basic experience: the location of the event is not a city but the theatre itself. Viewers create the distance between themselves and the stage. This is something that is understood as intrinsic to Renaissance scientific consciousness and artistic perception: that reality is known only when an observer establishes distance. But "distance" is a historically conditioned marker. Early modernity had no equivalent to our concept of distance, which has been intensified by the camera. Early modern life was an existence of proximity, of nearness. Acts of distancing are never separated from acts of engagement with one's environment, of bringing-near. In other words, the experience is never that of a detached retina: it is the *puissance* of the collective, embodied pulse of the audience, affecting and being affected.[16]

It has been said that the theatrical exists in an irreducible separation between the real and the unreal.[17] As Richard Schechner has argued, "Theater comes into existence when a separation occurs between spectators and performers."[18] Yet such putative separation is but a malleable limit. In fact, Beccafumi's *View of Pisa* has been readily identified as theatrical because of the spatial dislocations and moments of transition – the walls on the sides, and the stairs in the foreground.[19] The common presence of stairs at the forefront of designs is testament to the recurring movement of the actors from the auditorium to the stage, occasions that themselves shattered imaginary borders.[20] The creation of the "fourth wall" (the invisible yet absolute separation of stage and auditorium) is an Enlightenment notion. Such obliteration of the audience (Denis Diderot's "*think no more of the audience* than if it had never existed") was completely foreign to the early modern theatrical experience.[21]

A 1535–6 theatrical design by Bastiano da Sangallo (figure 2.3), known as Aristotile (1481–1551), corroborates that counter-factual and fictive depictions of cities were common practice.[22] Made for the celebration of the 1536 wedding of Alessandro de' Medici, Duke of Florence, and Margaret of Austria, Aristotile's set was crafted for the production of *Aridosia* by Antonio Landi. In this drawing, multiple sets of staircases in the extreme foreground lead up to an open, piazza-like

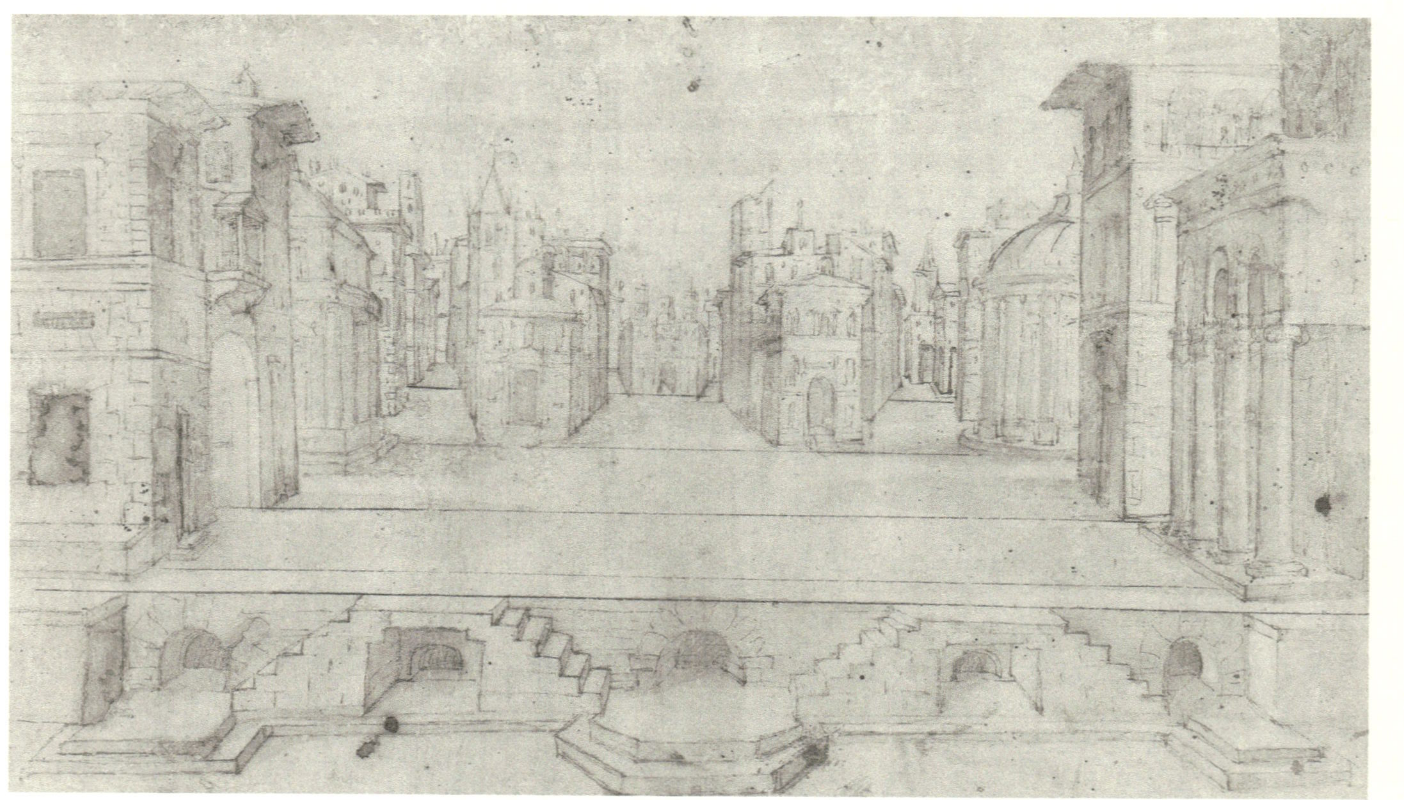

2.3 Bastiano da Sangallo, called Aristotile, *Scena urba*, c. 1535. Pen and brown ink, brown wash, over black chalk, on paper. 193 x 313 mm. The Morgan Library, 1982.75:600.

space between facades that flank opposite sides of the design. As the square recedes, it tapers into three narrow avenues lined by multi-story buildings. In Aristotile's design the first two downstage buildings on each side may have been constructed in three dimensions, the second line on the floor indicating the beginning of the backdrop. The solidity of the downstage buildings and stairs contrasts with the cityscape. Three streets recede into the distance, the middle of which bifurcates further on. This space is not unified through a single vanishing point, nor do the buildings' abrupt diminishing size create a homogeneous and naturalistic view. Marked disjunctions of scale appear as the viewer's gaze moves into the distance. Each of the three views has its own horizon line. Ratios are not consistent either. Despite the significance of its centrality, the building seen at the far end of the middle street appears surprisingly puny.

Aristotile's contemporaries praised him vehemently. Vasari notes that Aristotile was continuously improving and creating variety ("*semple migliorando e variando*").[23] In fact, if we believe Vasari, his sobriquet was given to him "because he appeared in truth to be in perspective what Aristotle was in philosophy."[24] What is more, his 1536 design is hardly the product of an inchoate talent. Aristotile was one of the first artists whose principal profession was scenography. He had collaborated in theatrical productions with Ridolfo del Ghirlandaio and Andrea del Sarto, and had been designing stages in Florence and Rome as early as 1518.[25] In Rome, where he worked for Leo X, he established a professional relationship with his uncle Giuliano and his cousin Antonio, and came into contact with Raphael and Bramante. It is quite possible that Aristotile witnessed the Roman production of *La Calandria*.[26] Aristotile appears to have been decisively interested in deploying technological advances in the theatrical arena, inventing movable machines that introduced the type of "machinery used in the religious plays onto the stage of the courtly theatre."[27] Given Aristotile's successful career as a theatre designer, it is likely that the spatial "imprecisions" in the drawing are intended, and that they are the outcome of a sophisticated understanding of scenography.

The scholarly interpretation of theatrical spaces as pictorial images is not one manufactured out of thin air. A mid-sixteenth-century interest in framing and one-point linear perspective is irrefutable. This demand is exemplified by designs such as Bartolomeo Neroni Il Riccio's scenography for the 1561 performance of Piccolomini's *L'Ortensio* (figure 2.4),[28] and the British Museum scenographic designs attributed to Francesco

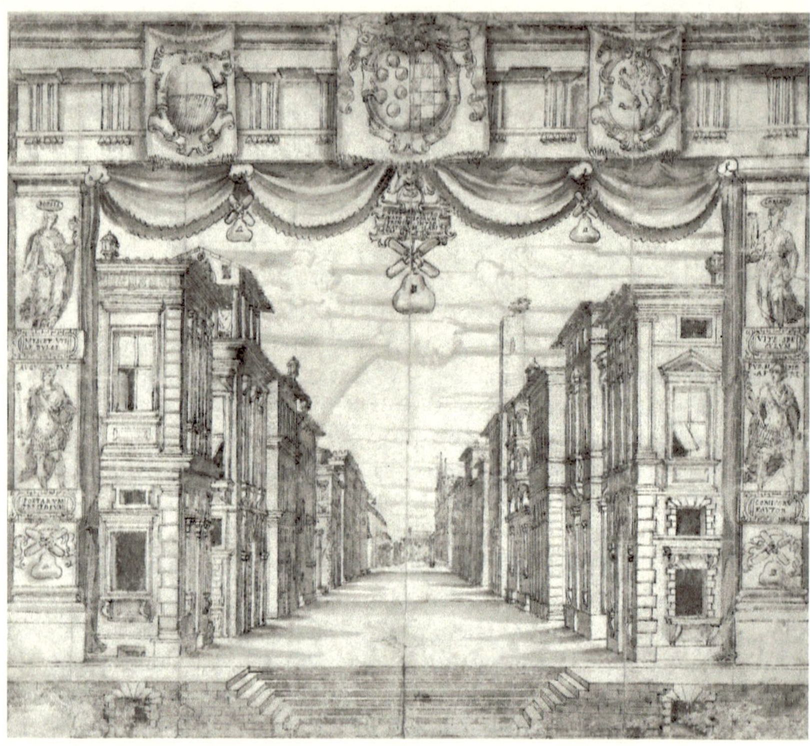

2.4 Bartolomeo Neroni, Il Riccio, scenography for Piccolomini's *L'Ortensio*, 1561. Pen and ink and wash. 28.89 x 33.66 cm. Victoria and Albert Museum, E.191-1954. © Victoria and Albert Museum, London.

Salviati for an unspecified production (figures 2.5 and 2.6). Even given the role of perspective in these drawings, it remains problematic to ascribe to the Renaissance an unswerving and homogeneous fascination with perspectival illusionism, much less accept that perspective held concrete epistemic gravity. And although the introduction of perspective certainly did institute an intense interplay between "theatre and life, actors and their spectators, virtual settings and actual places, illusion and truth,"[29] as Fabio Finotti recently put it, such intertwined relationships remain consciously resistant to visual resolution. After all, late-sixteenth-century permanent theatres like the Teatro Olimpico and the Teatro all'antica dispel or displace such devices, as we will

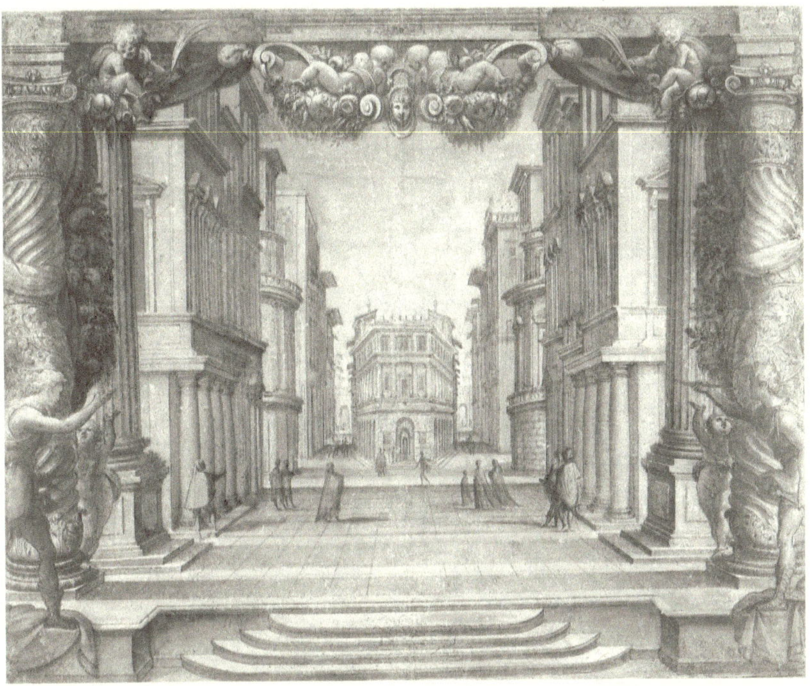

2.5 Attributed to Francesco Salviati, *Scenographic Design*. British Museum, Department of Prints and Drawings. © Trustees of the British Museum.

see. In many instances, the use of linear perspective is but one element among others.

Image and Identity

Riccio's 1561 scenography for *L'Ortensio* has been associated with Serlio's tragic stage.[30] As it is well known, Serlio illustrated the three classical types of scenographic designs in his 1545 *Secondo libro dell'architettura*, which, much like other treatises on theatrical spaces, follows Vitruvius's prescriptions in his *Ten Books on Architecture*.[31] Serlio's books on architecture, later important combined in 1585 as *Tutte l'opere d'architettura*, were immensely popular: his effective use

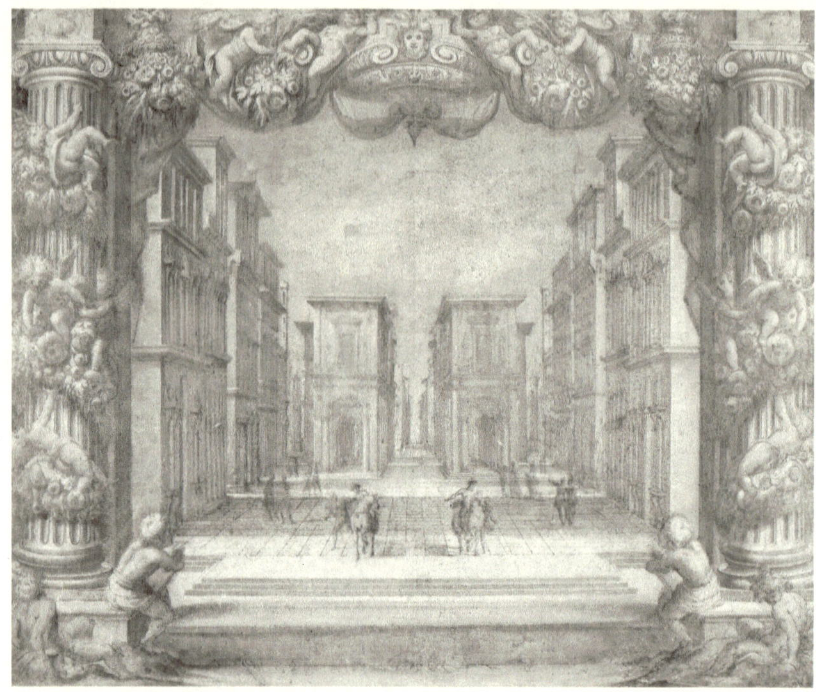

2.6 Attributed to Francesco Salviati, *Scenographic Design*. British Museum, Department of Prints and Drawings. © Trustees of the British Museum.

of Italian *volgare* and the novel incorporation of illustrations proved successful, in turn disseminating and standardizing the architectural orders.[32] In the passages on theatrical spaces, Serlio illustrates the three famous scenes: the comic stage (figure 2.7) shows a view into houses of private citizens such as lawyers and merchants; the tragic stage (figure 2.8) creates an aristocratic space; and the satiric stage (figure 2.9) portrays a rustic landscape. There are clear formal similarities between Serlio's stage and Peruzzi's designs. Serlio, after all, was a member of Peruzzi's workshop until the 1527 Sack of Rome. Serlio's stages and Peruzzi's design for *La Calandria* (figure 1.1) have intrinsically different approaches. Whereas Peruzzi's is defined by its specificity (of play, performance, and setting), Serlio's three designs are open-ended models that anticipate later modifications by other architects and designers.

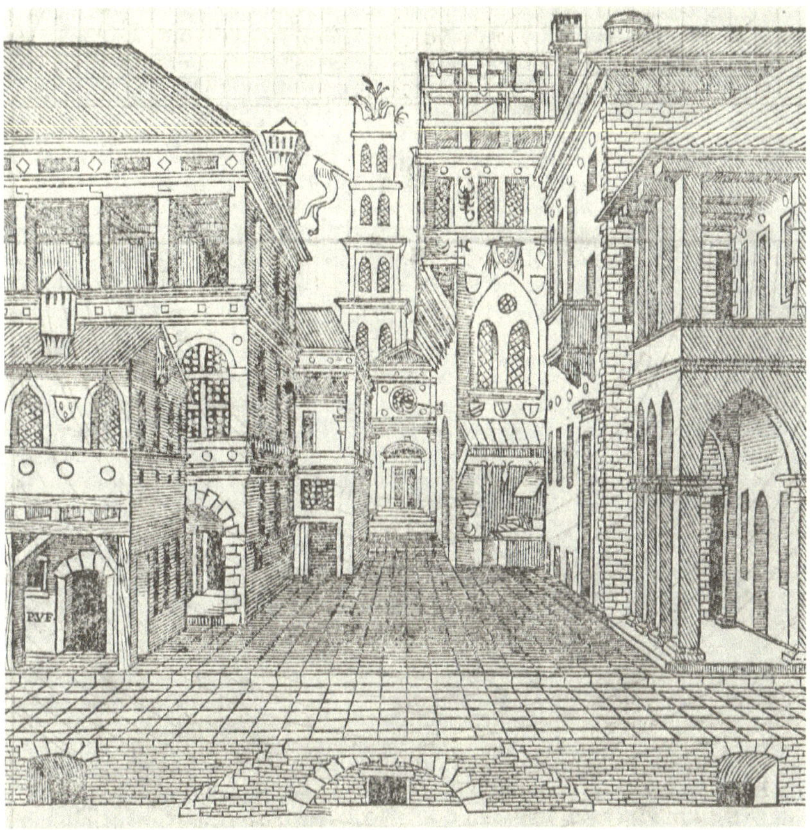

2.7 Sebastiano Serlio, *Comic Stage. Tutte l'opere d'architettura di Sebastiano Serlio Bolognese*. Venetia: Francesco de' Franceschi, 1584. Digitalized by Bibliotheken der Universität Heidelberg http://digi.ub.uni-heidelberg.de/diglit/serlio1584.

Further problems emerge, however, when comparing Serlio's tragic stage and Riccio's scenography for *L'Ortensio*. The latter, which was created for a production by the Accademia degli Intronati in Siena and performed either for Cosimo's entry into Siena in October 1560 or for his trip back to this city in January 1561, presents a view of Siena with the Duomo in the background.[33] However, it does not include the classical buildings that are so central to Serlio's tragic stage design. Riccio

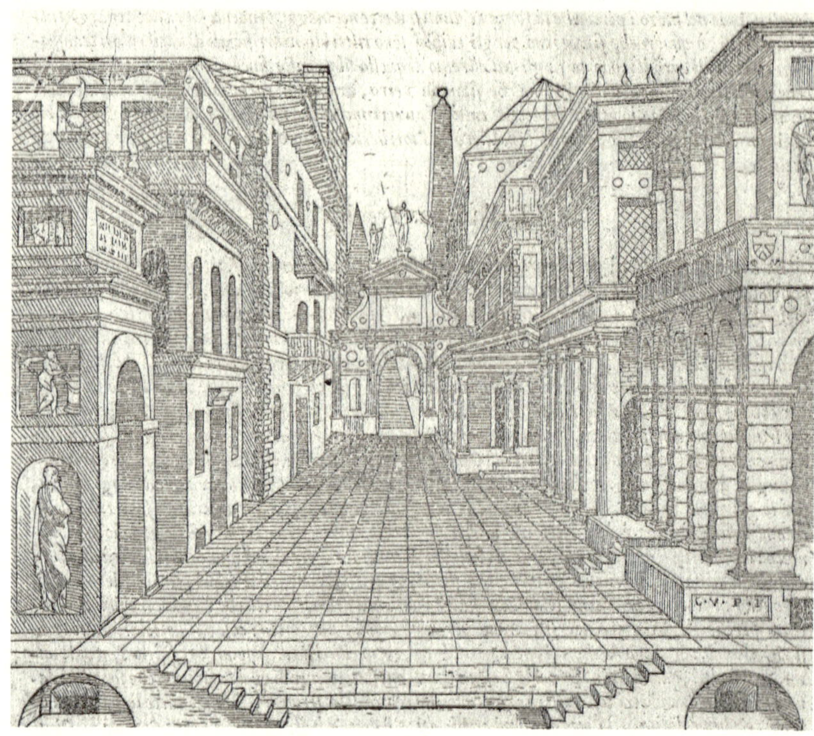

2.8 Sebastiano Serlio, *Tragic Stage. Tutte l'opere d'architettura di Sebastiano Serlio Bolognese.* Venetia: Francesco de' Franceschi, 1584. Digitalized by Bibliotheken der Universität Heidelberg http://digi.ub.uni-heidelberg.de/diglit/serlio1584.

remakes Siena as an impossibly flat city that does not correlate to the actuality of the undulating Tuscan city built on hills. The curved streets of Siena become regularized, which has the effect of displacing the audience's experiences of the urban fabric in order (perhaps) to beckon the idea of beauty as ideal planarity.[34] The most easily identifiable building, the cathedral, is relegated to the back, though other Sienese palazzi are subtly incorporated into the design.[35] The presence of palaces in the design deviates from Serlio's norms regarding the comic stage, as they are aristocratic buildings and not private domiciles and shops. Riccio's drawing partakes of the two Serlian modes, the comic and the tragic, further evincing the malleable nature of Serlio's prescriptions.

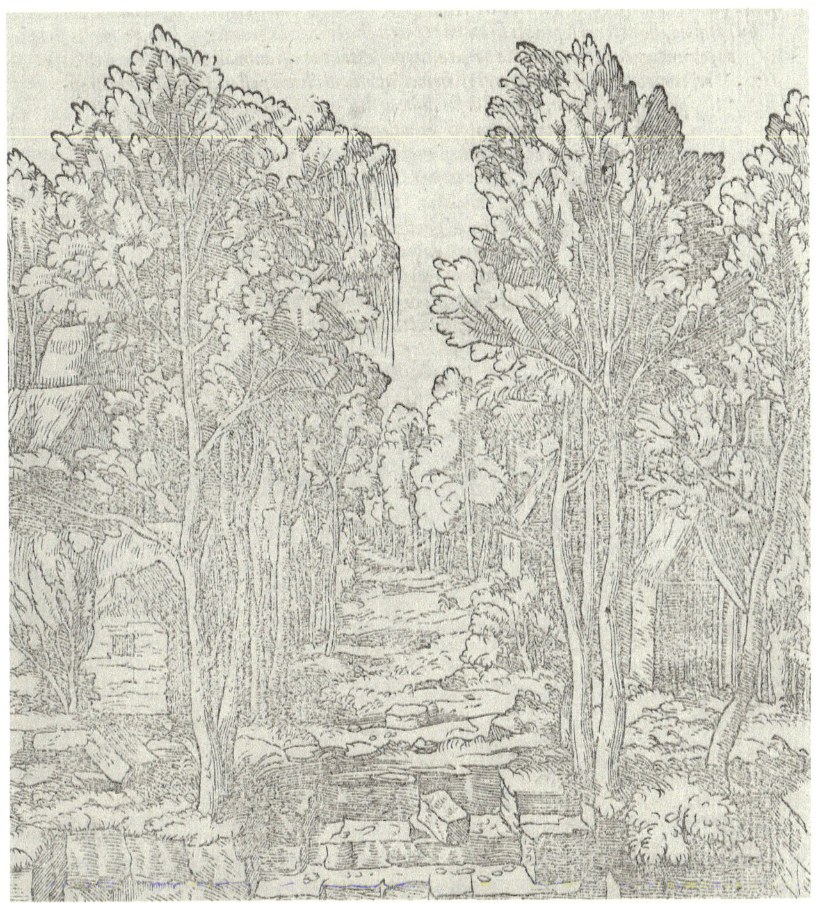

2.9 Sebastiano Serlio, *Satiric Stage. Tutte l'opere d'architettura di Sebastiano Serlio Bolognese.* Venetia: Francesco de' Franceschi, 1584. Digitalized by Bibliotheken der Universität Heidelberg http://digi.ub.uni-heidelberg.de/diglit/serlio1584.

Like Riccio's Siena, Beccafumi's *View of Pisa* also presents a dislocated cityscape, though here the impulse of regularization and orthogonal structure is understated. The central placement of the leaning tower, inclined into the perspectival central rachis decisively confers on this fictive space the description "this city is Pisa." The recognizable shapes of the Duomo's dome and the *lungarno* confirm this identification.

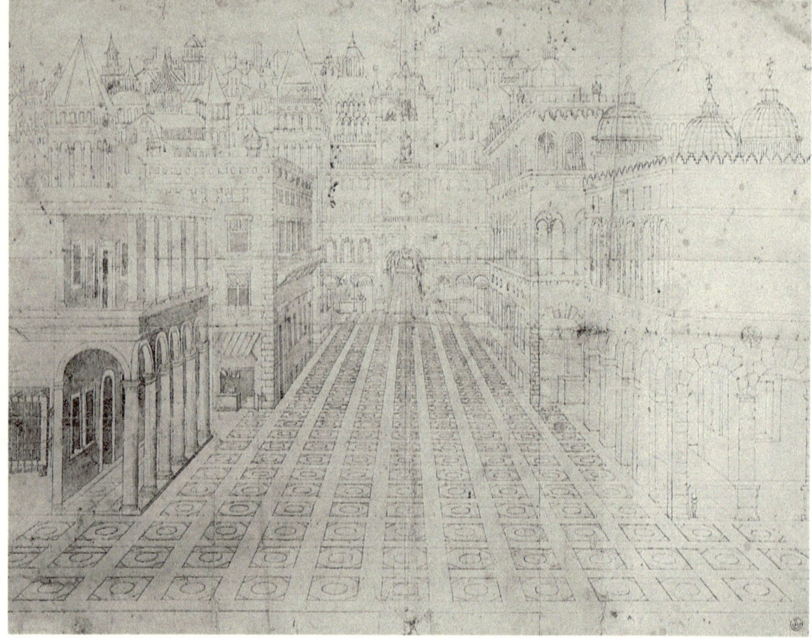

2.10 Sebastiano Serlio, *Theatrical Design*, c. 1532. Florence, Uffizi, Gabinetto Disegni e Stampe.

Nonetheless, disparities are immediately evident to anyone familiar with the Italian city. Most obviously, the space between the central (and later modified) Ponte di Mezzo and the Piazza dei Miracoli is, in Pisa, larger and less neatly aligned.[36]

As we consider the connection between Serlio's stages and Peruzzi's Rome, it is worth paying special attention to Serlio's *Scenographic Drawing Showing Venice* from the mid-1530s (figure 2.10). The design has often been connected to the process of reconstruction of the Venetian centre,[37] but in recent years Maria Ines Aliverti has connected the design with Nicholas Secco's *L'Interesse*, a play set in Venice and performed in Milan on 30 December 1548, during a series of celebrations honouring the future Philip II.[38] That one can immediately identify Venice is not a testament to the descriptive and illusionistic qualities of the drawing. On the contrary, this design proves how few indicators one needs in order to conceptualize and name a specific place even in extremely distorted conditions. Rather than perceiving an indeterminate space, we, the viewers, automatically place it in reference to a conceptual structure. The process of perception is a process of interpretation: we do not perceive abstract and disembodied sounds and images but concrete things. In the case of Serlio's design, we quickly see the drawing *as Venice* while simultaneously seeing it *as a stage design*. Indeed, it is because the drawing is understood as depicting a theatrical space that it becomes easier to accept its blatant distortions vis-à-vis Venice. In referencing Venice's Piazzetta, Serlio engages a space that has traditionally enjoyed a performative status. Later projects would help reify these theatrical associations: scholars have argued that Jacopo Sansovino, in designing the mint, library, and Loggetta (1536–8), sought to create a theatrical space as anticipated by Serlio's tragic stage.[39]

Serlio's scenographic square recalls the Venetian open area of the Piazzetta, though Serlio has synthesized the Piazza San Marco and the Piazzetta, manufacturing an unreal locale. A clearly identifiable element, the Torre dell'orologio, which is prominently placed in the centre, receives the pavement's orthogonals. The notion "Venice" is further buttressed by the presence of three structures: the later-destroyed tower of S. Giminiano (rather large, on the left), a shrunken Campanile placed next to the clock tower, and the domes of St Mark's Basilica (on the right). Unlike Beccafumi's Pisa, whose topographic alterations may only be noticed by someone who has visited that city, Serlio's displacements of Venice are not only more drastic but also more noticeable because of the visual fame of the Piazza.

The open space of the square contrasts with the city in the background. The houses assemble a rich pattern, creating the impression of a densely populated urban centre. This cityscape no doubt belonged to the backdrop, but it is nonetheless fascinating that Serlio, whose comic and tragic stage display salient organization, has here depicted Venice as a saturated amalgam of houses and churches. By stepping aside from the topographical actualities of the city, Serlio is able to contrive an impression of Venice's assemblage-like structure (its self-organization), rather than an idealized space dictated by ample avenues in perspective. The solidity of Venice in Serlio's scenography is remarkable. Its density reflects more the experience of navigating through the city than the experience of viewing the Piazza from the Bacino, the Giudecca, or San Giorgio Maggiore, across the canal. In Serlio's drawing, the monuments remain interlaced with the urban fabric and its fantastical mounded edifices. The buildings in the back rise above those in the front, as if they had been propped up on an imaginary hill. This deviation is consistent with Serlio's recommendations in his own treatise, where he argues that the buildings closer to the audience should be shorter than those in the back: "the most important thing of all is to choose smaller houses and put them to the front so that the other buildings appear above them … the result is that the greater height of the buildings behind gives an impression of grandeur."[40]

Serlio whimsically alters an environment he came to know well during his Venetian sojourn. The heralded value of verisimilitude is dissipated along with the unity of space. Nothing protects the appearance of fact. The clock tower serves as a centring force of the imagined piazza, a visual control made possible by the dwarfing of its surroundings, including the Campanile. The Basilica of St Mark, symbol *par excellence* of the city, is banished, and only its domes, uprooted and dissected, remain. We are reminded of Peruzzi's Rome, where the dome of the Pantheon and a section of the Colosseum also hover disengaged. In the Venetian scene, the Palazzo Ducale is absent, replaced by two generic buildings. An architectural insinuation: the building downstage left is decorated with crenellations that recall those of the Ducal Palace (a lingering, fragmentary quotation). Though this building also incorporates an arcade, it is one bereft of the actual portico's lithe, Gothic elegance, in contrast featuring round arches and thick, rusticated voussoirs. Behind it, the second building downstage left recalls the Palazzo Ducale's second storey – its double arches adorned with quatrefoils. Overall, there are noticeable similarities with Serlio's tragic stage (figure 2.8). In both cases, round arches dominate the design, a contrast with his use of pointed Gothic arches in his comic stage. The arrangement of the buildings downstage is comparable. In the tragic stage, a classic construction (in this case a triumphal arch) stands out against an opposite, rusticated, and heavier building.

In Serlio's stage design of Venice, the arch of the Torre del'orologio brings attention to the space of the Piazza (and likely refers to Roman triumphal arches). The focus on the urban fabric leaves no space for the canals and the water, vital to the city and its image. The Piazza as a public space is here the centre of the action. The visually recognizable qualities of the square allow for its identification, but the landmarks around the Piazza, and not the space of the Piazza itself, ascribe a location. Serlio has done away with the distinctive shape of the conjoined Piazzetta and Piazza. Buildings representative of church (Basilica) and state (Doge's Palace) are carefully dismissed or, at least, put aside. Location may be easily conferred, yet very little of the actual city persists.

If one is to trace the scenographic development from Peruzzi to Serlio, it is necessary to underscore their shared concern with excess, saturation, and displacement. A study of unity, verisimilitude, and perspective will not suffice. Rhythms and resemblances do flare up: visual quotations, architectural paraphrases, and designs that deliberately neglect the configuration of actual urban spaces. The theatrical visual mode was not committed to respecting the image of the city, carefully tracing its spaces. Donald Beecher has brought attention to a moment in Ariosto's *I suppositi* in which Erostrato goes in search of his servant and returns complaining that he has looked in the piazza and the courtyard, and that he has met almost every doctor and scholar in Ferrara. Beecher concludes, "the joke is presumably that he has been only to the edge of the stage."[41] Sergio Costola, studying the complexities of Ariosto's theatrical spaces, identifies a scenographic concern that anticipates postmodern concerns: "Ariosto relativised setting and world alike by showing the illusory nature of their means of production."[42]

The disclosing manoeuvre of sixteenth-century stages is a process of removal and adhesion. This is the resolute riposte of the dramaturgical, which took the city by force and disrupted the visual and topographical order to produce a festive, aesthetically powerful event. A theatrical space is not sequential or uniform.[43] Those searching for the germ of the hyper-real will have to look elsewhere.

Negotiating Vitruvius: Variability and Experimentation

Peruzzi and Serlio evince the period's interest in plural models, hybridity, and syntactical variability.[44] At the same time, Serlio's own codification of the three stages foments a partial understanding of how sixteenth-century artists conceptualized the theatrical stage. Today, the stage designs he published in his *Book of Architecture* have come to ubiquitously illustrate the period understanding of scenographic types, abundantly appearing in the scholarship as the *de facto* interpretation of Vitruvius's descriptions of the three canonical types of stages. The sixteenth-century reception of Vitruvius, however, was neither clear nor uniform. Artists reading chapter six of the Roman author's *Ten Books on Architecture* found a cursory description:

> The scenery itself is so arranged that the middle doors are figured like a royal palace, the doors on the right and left are for strangers. Next on either side are the spaces prepared for scenery. These are called *periaktoi*

> in Greek (revolving wings) from the three-sided machines which turn having on their three sides as many kinds of subject ... There are three styles of scenery: one which is called tragic; a second, comic; the third, satyric. Now the subjects of these differ severely one from another. The tragic are designed with columns, pediments and statues and other royal surroundings; the comic have the appearance of private buildings and balconies and projections with windows made to imitate reality, after the fashion of ordinary buildings; the satyric settings are painted with trees, caves, mountains and other country features, designed to imitate landscape.[45]

Throughout the sixteenth-century, Italian artists would have to negotiate with Vitruvius's descriptions, often arriving at divergent visual interpretations of the material – some put into practice, others remaining purely conceptual exercises. We can consider three distinct examples that demonstrate the sixteenth-century heterogeneous exchange with the Vitruvian canon: Giovanni Battista da Sangallo (1496–1548), Giovanni Romolo Cincinnato (c. 1540–c. 1595), and Ercole Bottrigari (1531–1612).

In the 1530s the Italian architect Giovanni Battista annotated his edition of Sulpizio's Vitruvius with translations and drawings (a book now known as the *Corsini Incunabulum*).[46] Under a brief marginalia discussion on rotating *periaktoi*, Giovanni Battista sketched the three Vitruvian stages (figure 2.11). Much like Peruzzi's design for *La Calandria*, Giovanni Battista's tragic stage incorporates an array of classical Roman architecture and a centralizing triumphal arch. Unlike Peruzzi's design and Serlio's tragic stage, which incorporate contemporary structures, Giovanni Battista's downstage buildings are classical, temple-like edifices with carefully delineated columns and pediments. Although Giovanni Battista's tragic stage reflects Cinquecento scenographic practices,[47] his drawing appears more concerned with following Vitruvius's descriptions than with contemporary dramaturgical interests or necessities. In contrast to the antiquarian space of the tragic scene, the comic stage illustrates an enclosed, early modern square. Much like his tragic stage, it is an imaginary space that evinces little concern for the limitations of staged constructions, with towering houses and an elongated central piazza populated by citizens and animals. Most unexpected is the bird's-eye landscape view in the satiric stage, a space that seemingly disregards the previous fifty years of scenic invention.

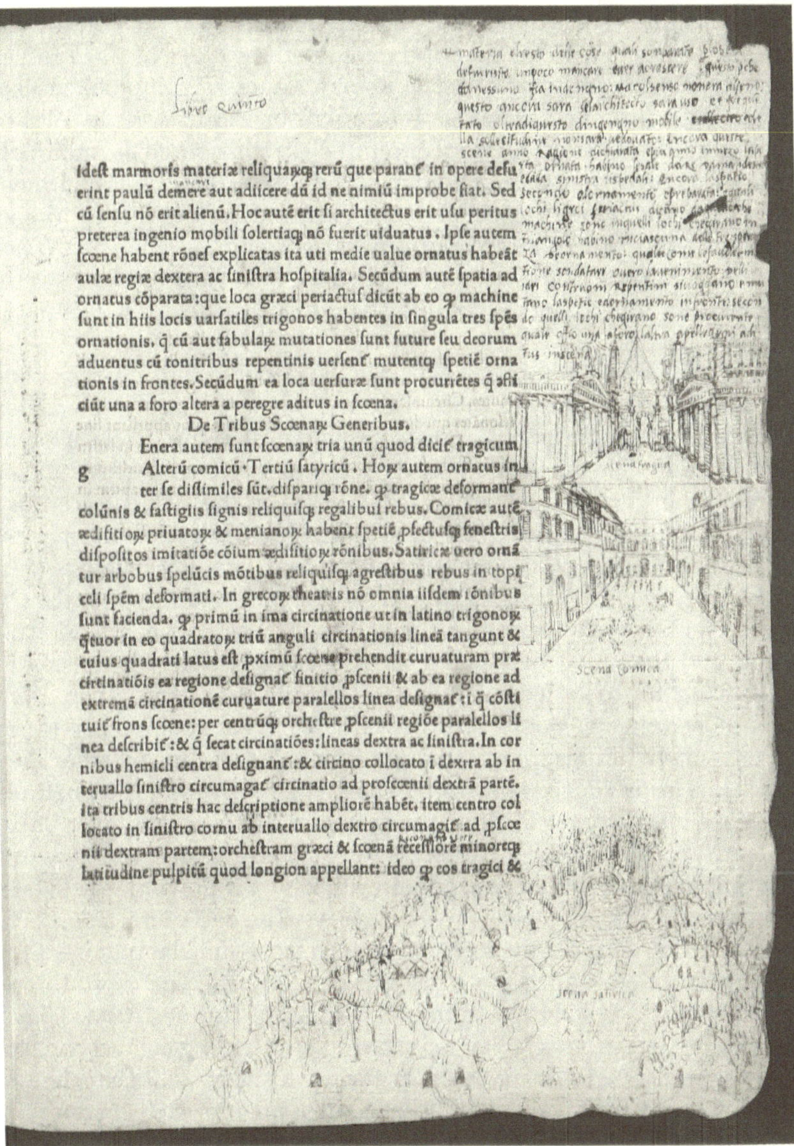

Ideſt marmoris materiæ reliquaꝝq; rerũ que paranť in opere deſuerint paulũ demere aut adiicere dũ id ne nimiũ improbe fiat. Sed cũ ſenſu nõ erit alienũ. Hoc autẽ erit ſi architectus erit uſu peritus preterea ingenio mobili ſolertiaq; nõ fuerit uiduatus. Ipſe autem ſcœne habent rõneſ explicatas ita uti mediæ ualue ornatus habeãt aulæ regiæ dextera ac ſiniſtra hoſpitalia. Secũdum autẽ ſpatia ad ornatus cõparata: que loca græci periactuſ dicũt ab eo ꝙ machine ſunt in hiis locis uarſatiles trigonos habentes in ſingula tres ſpẽs ornationis. q̃ cũ aut fabulaꝝ mutationes ſunt future ſeu deorum aduentus cũ tonitribus repentinis uerſenť mutentq; ſpetiẽ ornationis in frontes. Secũdum ea loca uerſuræ ſunt procurrẽtes q̃ efficiũt una a foro altera a peregre aditus in ſcœna.

De Tribus Scœnaꝝ Generibus.

Genera autem ſunt ſcœnaꝝ tria unũ quod diciť tragicum Alterũ comicũ. Tertiũ ſatyricũ. Hoꝝ autem ornatus inter ſe diſſimiles ſũt. diſpariq; rõne. ꝙ tragicæ deformanť colũnis & faſtigiis ſignis reliquiſq; regalibus rebus. Comicæ autẽ ædifitioꝝ priuatoꝝ & menianoꝝ habent ſpetiẽ pſpectuſq; feneſtris diſpoſitos imitatiõe cõium ædifitioꝝ rõnibus. Satiricæ uero ornãtur arbobus ſpelũcis mõtibus reliquiſq; agreſtibus rebus in topi celi ſpẽm deformati. In grecoꝝ theatris nõ omnia iiſdem rõnibus ſunt facienda. ꝙ primũ in ima circinatione ut in latino trigonoꝝ quatuor in eo quadratoꝝ triũ anguli circinationis lineã tangunt & cuius quadrati latus eſt pximũ ſcœne prehendit curuaturam præ circinatiõis ea regione deſignať finitio pſcenii & ab ea regione ad extremã circinationẽ curuature paralellos linea deſignať: i q̃ cõſtituiť frons ſcœne: per centrũq; orcheſtre pſcenii regiõe paralellos linea deſcribiť: & q̃ ſecat circinatiões: lineas dextra ac ſiniſtra. In cornibus hemicli centra deſignanť: & circino collocato ĩ dextra ab interuallo ſiniſtro circumagať circinatio ad proſcœnii dextrã partẽ. ita tribus centris hac deſcriptione ampliorẽ habẽt. item centro collocato in ſiniſtro cornu ab interuallo dextro circumagiť ad pſcœnii dextram partem; orcheſtram græci & ſcœnã receſſiorẽ minoreq; latitudine pulpitũ quod longion appellant: ideo ꝙ eos tragici &

2.11 Giovanni Battista da Sangallo, *Stage Drawings* from Vitruvius Pollio, *Ten Books on Architecture: The Corsini Incunabulum with the Annotations and Autograph Drawings of Giovanni Battista da Sangallo*. Biblioteca dell'Accademia Nazionale dei Lincei e Corsiniana, Roma, 50.F.1.

It is clear that sixteenth-century artists, in their interpretations of Vitruvius, engaged with his description of the three types of stage rather than his account of what classical Roman stages actually looked like. In fact, it is striking that neither set designs by Peruzzi, Serlio, Aristotile, Ricco, and Beccafumi nor conceptual exercises like Giovanni Battista's included the famous Roman *scaenae frons*. This omission must have been intentional, since Vitruvius clearly describes this feature as a facade with two or three floors and a central doorway. The *scaenae frons* was known in the Italian Renaissance, and Eugenio Battisti has argued that Alberti not only wrote about this structure, but also put it into practice. [48]

Although surviving set designs from the period ostensibly disregard the *scaenae frons* in favour of an open urban space, Carmen González Román has brought attention to a surviving drawing by the Florentine Romulo Cincinnato that sheds some light on how artists incorporated the Vitruvian-Albertian *scaenae frons* in the sixteenth century (figure 2.12). [49] Cincinnato, who travelled to Spain in 1567 at the request of Philip II, depicts a scenographic model that carefully follows Vitruvius's precepts. His design shows a *scaenae frons* with two levels. On the upper floor we encounter a row of balconies between Doric columns and triangular pediments: the artist seems clearly interested in displaying his knowledge of classical architecture. Beneath the two central pediments, doors open inward to reveal rooms beyond, in which stately figures mingle, though it remains unclear whether they are actors or privileged spectators. The first level shows, between three Ionic columns, an urban cityscape drawn in linear perspective. Vitruvius had prescribed the inclusion of three gateways on stage, of which the central portal should be especially imposing. Following this dictate, Cincinnato's design depicts three doorways. The two lateral thresholds are closed off in the drawing by ornate screens with slat blinds – they may have offered alternative views when opened. The central gateway appears divided by a central Ionic column. This obstructive pillar blocks the spectators' view of a city beyond, restricting a direct engagement with the vanishing point. A character in shadows appears within this lower threshold, awkwardly set against the projected space of the city. As we conceptualize how this design would have translated onto an actual stage, we notice a dissonance between the cityscape beyond the central portal and the architectural *scaenae frons*. This incites suspicions that the central city view is but a painting, or perhaps two *periaktoi*: certainly the framed urban space looks less volumetric than the

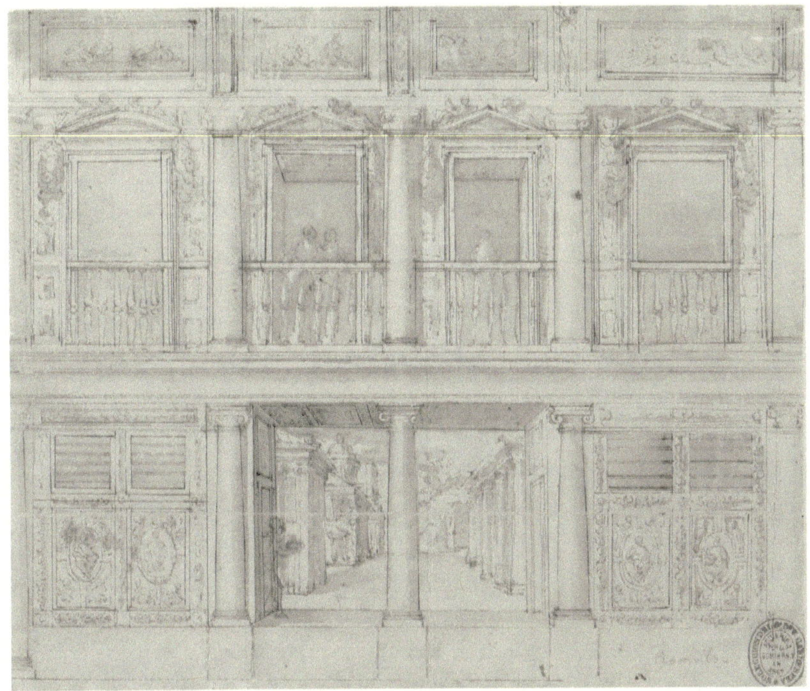

2.12 Giovanni Romulo Cincinnato, *Theatre Scene*, c. 1567. Image property of the Biblioteca Nacional de España.

architectural detail in the stage's facade, and the figure set against it does not aid the illusion.

Plurality of models is present even at the end of the Cinquecento, as evinced by the comic stage (figure 2.13) and the tragic stage (figure 2.14) in Ercole Bottrigari's (c. 1596) manuscript *Maschera, overo della fabbrica de' teatri*. Bottrigari's never-published text shows an acute awareness of Serlio, Daniele Barbaro, and other perspective theorists.[50] In spite of this, Bottrigari's stages clearly deviate from, and may even explicitly challenge, the so-called Peruzzian mode. The tragic stage presents an enclosed piazza rather than a projected street, "a theatre in a theatre" whose edifices have unclear dramaturgical purpose.[51] And the comic stage introduces a system of two-point perspective likely inspired by Jean Pèlerin Viator's 1505 *De artificiali perspetiva*.[52] With its abnormal hovering point of view, unclear ratios without unity of size, and impossibly

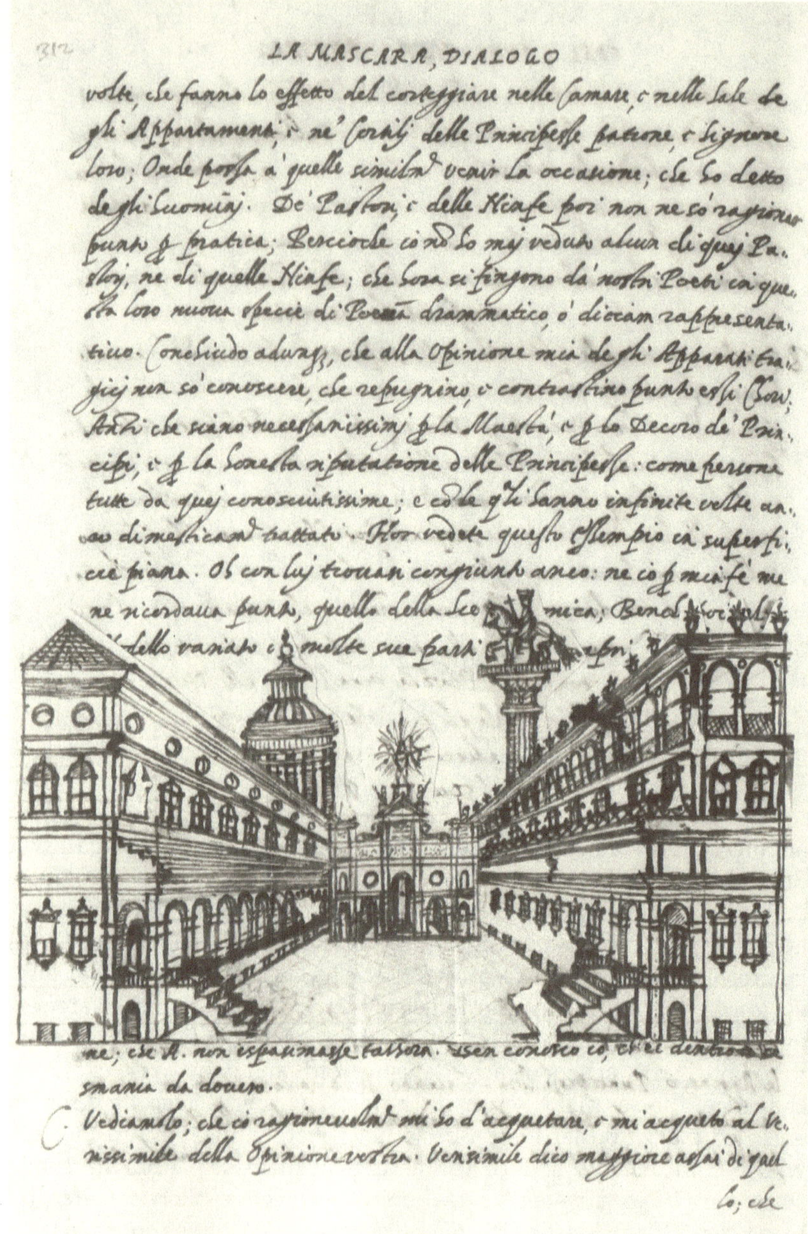
LA MASCARA, DIALOGO

2.13 Ercole Bottrigari, Tragic stage, *La Mascara*, 1596. International museum and library of music of Bologna.

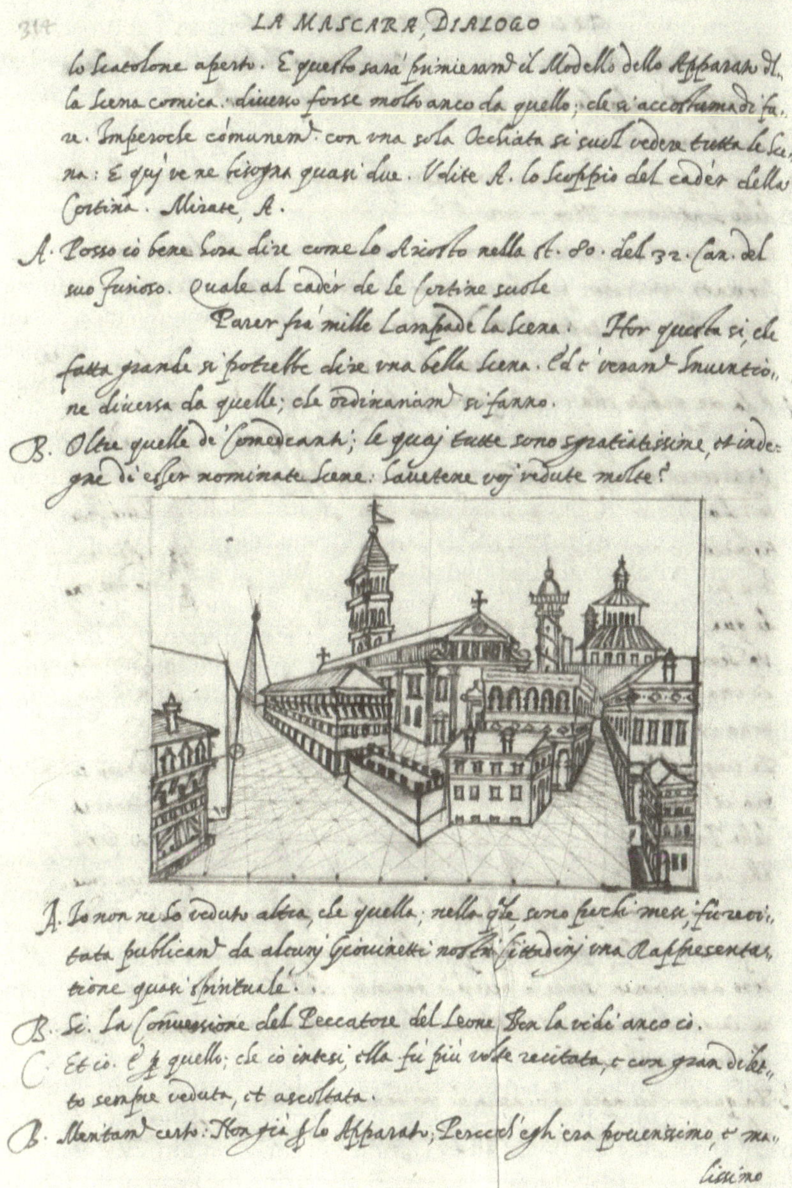

LA MASCARA, DIALOGO

lo Scatolone aperto. E questo sarà primieram.te il Modello dello Apparato della Scena comica: diverso forse molto anco da quello, che si accostuma di fare. Imperoche comunem.te con una sola Occhiata si suol vedere tutta la Scena: E qui ve ne bisogna quasi due. Udite A. lo Scoppio del cader della
Cortina. Mirate, A.

A. Posso ciò bene hora dire come lo Ariosto nella st. 80. del 32. Can. del
suo Furioso. Quale al cader de le Cortine suole
Parer fra mille Lampade la Scena. Hor questa sì, che
fatta grande si potrebbe dire una bella Scena. Ch'è veram.te Inventione diversa da quelle; che ordinariam.te si fanno.

B. Oltre quelle de' Comedianti; le quai tutte sono sgratiatissime, et inde-
gne di esser nominate Scene. Havetene voi vedute molte?

A. Io non ne ho veduto altra, che quella; nella quale sono pochi mesi, fu recitata publicam.te da alcuni Giovinetti nostri Cittadini una Rappresenta-
tione quasi spirituale.

B. Sì. La Conversione del Peccatore del Leone Ben la vidi anco io.

C. Et io. E per quello; che io intesi, ella fu più volte recitata, e con gran dilet-
to sempre veduta, et ascoltata.

B. Meritam.te certo: Non già per lo Apparato; Perciochè egli era poverissimo, e ma-
lissimo

2.14 Ercole Bottrigari, Comic stage, *La Mascara*, 1596. International museum and library of music of Bologna.

wide avenues, it is altogether unclear how the design would have been integrated with the physical stage. Although Bottrigari's approach was dismissed by his contemporaries and later seventeenth-century designers, his comic stage visually anticipates Ferdinando Bibiena's (1657–1753) development of the *scena per angolo*, a type of scenography that shows corners of interiors or courtyards by using multiple vanishing points.[53]

Ornament

Typology is central to Serlio's treatise, but the notion of typology in Serlio's stage designs demands a distinct approach. Though a new design for a comedy may have used Serlio's codified model as a source, it would ultimately have been the product of a series of practical engagements with the place of production, the patron, and other logistic conditions. Stage designs like Riccio's for *L'Ortensio* relied on Serlio without directly copying his designs. This was not a disservice to Serlio: his three stages were never blueprints meant to be followed with exactitude. In them, we discern an invitation for modification.[54] We may even say that Serlio's stages demanded interpretation and alteration.[55] Theatrical designs underscore the fluid and diachronic architectural practice of the period. As James Ackerman writes, "the character of Renaissance architecture owes much to the fact that its monuments started, not from a complete idea, fixed in the symbolism of the blueprint, but from flexible impressions constantly susceptible to change."[56]

Serlio's own scenographic view of Venice attests to this open situation. A different backdrop would alter the location quickly, as there is nothing inherently Venetian about the four downstage "houses." We read the space as the Piazzetta because of the domes of St Mark's and the Torre dell'orologio, but these are additional, ornamental features, since actors would not have physically used them. Location is connoted by the supplemental. I am here referring to ornament in the Derridian sense: a surplus that brings up a question about its own necessity; a manifestation of "a lack, which can only be remedied by its supplement."[57] The Renaissance's own concern with ornament can be traced to Quintilian's influential *The Orator's Education*, where "ornate" is defined as whatever is more than merely clear and acceptable.[58] The issue of ornament is nonetheless notoriously complex in early modernity. Leonardo, following Alberti, admonishes against obscuring the form of the figures and objects by adding too much ornament.[59] Ludovico Dolce would concur. Italian Renaissance artists and theorists, as Hellmur Wohl remarks, were attuned to the question of ornamentation, which can easily become a hindrance "to the imitation of nature, because it is not compatible with the truth of optical vision."[60] But for sixteenth-century scenographers, the presence of ornament and visual surplus need not detract from visual clarity, and richness and ornament were prioritized over verisimilitude.[61] The most ornamental sections of Serlio's and Peruzzi's designs are the areas most disassociated from the actors, making the space surrounding the actors easily legible. The same can be said of Beccafumi's Pisa, with its amalgamated houses heaped upon the upper section of the backdrop.

The monochromatic nature of theatrical drawings conceals what must have been a captivating, effulgent feat of artisanship – glittering and prismatic hues. The common description of sixteenth-century stages as glimmering jewel boxes attests to their vibrant ornamental qualities. Take, for example, Castiglione's description of the design for the 1513 performance of *La Calandria* recounts:

> Among other things there was an octagonal temple in half-relief … all made of stucco, with beautiful decorations imitating windows of alabaster, architraves and cornices of fine gold and ultramarine blue, and, in certain places, jeweled windows….[62]

Vasari, praising Peruzzi, applauds his arrangement and display of lights within a scenography that was itself saturated by architectural elements (as we saw, Vasari's own design for *La Talanta* was filled with an assortment of monuments).[63] And, in his treatise, Serlio's description of the wonders of scenography ascends to glimmering excess:

> There you can see in a small space, created with the art of perspective, splendid palaces, huge temples, multifarious buildings both near and far off, spacious piazzas graced with diverse edifices, long, straight streets crossed by other roads, triumphal arches, exceedingly high columns, pyramids, obelisks and thousands of other beautiful things adorned with infinite lamps – large, medium and small, depending on the type required – which are so skilfully arranged that they appear to be many dazzling jewels, as it were, diamonds, rubies, sapphires, emeralds, and the like.[64]

These aesthetic choices attest to the popularity of a style deeply rooted in Italian scenography that even gained momentum abroad, attracting the attention of the English architect and stage designer Inigo Jones.[65] But many of Vasari's Italian contemporaries would relocate the ornate and excessive outside of the stage.

As we saw before, the design for *L'Ortensio* (figure 2.4) presents a regularized and flattened version of Siena that seems to have banished the architectonic predilection for excess found in Peruzzi or Serlio. However, the decorative surplus has hardly disappeared from the experience of the set. A classically inspired proscenium arch decorated with triglyphs and metopes appears bedecked with sculptures elevating poetry and comedy. At the centre of the arch hangs a large, emblazoned banner with Cosimo I and Eleonora de Toledo's joint coat of arms. Flanking it are two emblems of Siena: the black-and-white *balzana* on the left and a rampant lion on the right. Below these political ensigns, a fabric garland is festooned with the symbol of the Sienese Accademia degli Intronati – a gourd with a hole made to store salt, symbolizing intelligence, and two crossed pestles – a symbol that also appears in the lower registers of the arch's pilasters.

Similarly, the British Museum design attributed to Francesco Salviati (figure 2.5) makes prolific use of visual saturation in the form of heavily decorated twisting columns, colossal sculptural figures, cherubs, and a central garland, all confined within the proscenium arch. In contrast, the staged city behind the arch is rendered more naturalistically, though its figmental symmetry and its vertiginous spatial recession retain a festive artificiality. In this drawing, the city emerges as a contrived mirror image. Framed by fluted columns, two buildings stand on left and right, of which the ones closer to the audience present colonnaded porticoes (perhaps recalling the Uffizi Gallery).[66] In between them, a checkerboard pavement likely delimits the actual built stage, in contrast to the receding ground, which lacks perspectival lines. The city bifurcates. Two projected avenues, depicted in forced perspective, lead towards two arched gates. Between the porticoes and the distant thresholds, the city appears as an ersatz vision populated by shadowy figures meandering over the checkerboard downstage and the symmetric avenues beyond.[67] Some of these choices also appear in another design associated with Salviati (figure 2.6), which further demonstrates artistic range, here decisively introducing one-point perspective.

These seemingly regularized and highly organized spaces of action are framed by (and placed in) a visual and social context of surplus, splendour, and magnificence. An aesthetic interest in excess destabilizes the assumed clear and organized system of linear perspective (a subject to which we will return). Immoderation reifies a visual economy of expenditure and desire-creation.[68] It is a concern that pervades sixteenth-century design: what Shearman calls "abundance in the sense of prolixity."[69] Writing about ornament and ambiguity in Renaissance architecture, Robert Venturi points at this relationship between "control and spontaneity," between "correctness and ease."[70] As has been noted, "the tasks which Renaissance architecture (not to mention Renaissance culture) placed before itself resemble a fusion of extremes: the reference to solid foundations and the appeal to subjective choice."[71] This tension can be further contextualized within the literary debates of the sixteenth century, which inform art production in general. Shearman points to Speroni's (c. 1562) *Discorsi sopra Virgilio*, where Virgil is criticized for not being sufficiently ornamental or florid and consequently becoming more of a historian than a poet.[72] In fact, many Italian authors challenged the idea that poetry should avoid complication,[73] a challenge that was also embraced in theatrical designs.

Immobility and Disproportion

Disproportional elements in scenographic designs were accentuated by moving human bodies on stage. After all, as Alberti stated, "all things are known by comparison, for comparison contains within itself a power which immediately demonstrates."[74] We may also recall Protagoras's dictum, which Alberti himself embraced: "Man is the measure of all things."[75] The presence and size of the actors on stage would have accentuated the fictive qualities of the buildings, both regarding size and solidity. For this reason, actors must stay away from the backdrop, closer to the audience. Scale divergences, however, were not likely an insurmountable problem for Italian audiences. Their own late medieval and early Renaissance artistic tradition stipulated a visual logic where proportional disjunctions between people and buildings did not hinder legibility. This is not to say that the Cinquecento stage was retrograde, but that there was a mode of expression in place that allowed for such divergences. Since we intuitively understand that "perceived size is related to perceived distance,"[76] disruptions on the presupposed coherence of nature are understood as non-natural events, an understanding that in turn creates a different mode of visual cognition, be it pictorial or dramaturgical. Stage environments inserted a mediating event, one that invited difference and dissonance.

As we will see in the next chapter, the artistic opening of the stage towards the auditorium was also an enclosing of space. But it is important to remember that despite the blazoned rebirth of the classical theatre, the sixteenth century saw the rise of the *commedia dell'arte* and theatre troupes performing on temporary or mounted stages, often in public spaces. Companies like the famous I Gelosi, managed by Francesco and Isabella Andreini, solidified the popular interest in the *commedia* while also reaching noble Italian audiences (as attested by the 1573 production of Tasso's *Aminta* at Ferrara).[77] Flaminio Scala's famous 1611 *Il teatro delle Favole Rappresentative*, which included scenarios along with two prefaces written by Francesco Andreini and Scala, respectively, further demonstrates the interest in the *commedia* at the turn of the century.[78] It is an interest that cannot be easily reduced to a singular value: Scala's preface demonstrates a multiplicity of uses by explicitly appealing to "the appetites and tastes of many different intellects, who take in such things either for recreation or in their profession."[79]

Whereas the scenography of involved academic court performances took months to conceive and build, the performances of *commedia* troupes were designed for quick installation, at times incorporating scenographic developments and machines but often remaining practical. It is impossible to create a unified vision of these productions since the performance locations were as varied as noble courts and public market squares, and troupes had very different economic resources. M.A. Katritzsky has categorized the multiple types of stages that coexisted in the late-sixteenth-century *commedia*: cleared spaces, natural stages such as terraces or loggias, unadorned raised stages, stages with curtain backdrops, architecturally enhanced curtain stages, and perspectival stages.[80] Because of the limited number of visual records documenting sixteenth- and early seventeenth-century *commedia* performances, as well as the questionable function of such records, it is not easy to draw conclusions. Nevertheless, it is clear that events incorporating linear perspective in their backdrops had to negotiate with the materiality of the stage, such as the pleating and folding of backdrops, forced recession, painted figures in the background, and other elements. Deviations were also made from the three Vitruvian models, with stages depicting hybrid sets, especially urban-rural scenes.[81] *Commedia* spectators were surely capable of appreciating the representational backgrounds without enjoying an ideal point of view or the illusion of being transported away. Such spatial and representational problematics, perhaps most evident in *commedia* performances, were also present in other sixteenth-century theatrical productions.

The fictitiousness of Italian Renaissance stages is exemplified by Serlio's emphasis that the houses closer to the audience should be smaller than the ones behind. This is itself a type of abuse, a challenge to naturalism and the optical order. Serlio's rationale ensures that the houses in the back would be easily seen and it also indicates social rank.[82] In his comic scene (figure 2.7), the house of the Ruffiana – a character who often used to be a prostitute – appears in a prominent position downstage, but it looks rather small in proportion to adjacent buildings.[83] Serlio's designs are interested not in perfect mathematical unity but in aesthetics and narrative.[84] His reduction of geometrical rules in his treatise signifies a movement away from the pedantries and regulations of analytic-axiomatic discourse.[85]

The fictitiousness of scenographic cities was further highlighted by the inclusion of painted figures. This pictorial introduction can be deceiving. Lanci's design for *La Vedova* (figure 1.2) incorporates three figures: two on the left of the drawing and another standing by the Palazzo Vecchio's statues. These figures grant a sense of magnitude to the depicted city, which appears to have a naturalistic scale that would not have been present when placed behind actors. Of course, the inclusion of figures in Lanci's drawing does not necessarily imply that they were actually painted on backdrops. They may be a playful addition to the sketch that was not transposed to the final scenography. Nevertheless, the presence of painted humans and animals in scenographic designs during the Cinquecento is not unusual. In the previously discussed scenographic drawings attributed to Francesco Salviati, for example, there are figures occupying not only the stage, but also the projected, painted avenues of the background (figures 2.5 and 2.6).

A further instantiation of this practice is a scenographic drawing of Ferrara, made circa 1550 (before the 1553 collapse of the Torre di Rigobello) and today housed in the Biblioteca Ariostea in Ferrara. The artist or group of artists behind the production and the drawing, as well as its date, remain debated in the scholarship: it has been ascribed to the circle of Girolamo da Carpi, Pellegrino da Udine, and even Raphael, and it was perhaps made for Ludovico Ariosto's *I suppositi*.[86] This drawing h[aving] been severely damaged, very little of it is legible today, though a hand-drawn copy was made and published in 1925 (figure 2.15).[87] The faithfulness of the copy remains unclear (the copy is itself somewhat smaller than the original, so the image was not traced). The 1925 drawing incorporates persons painted on what must have

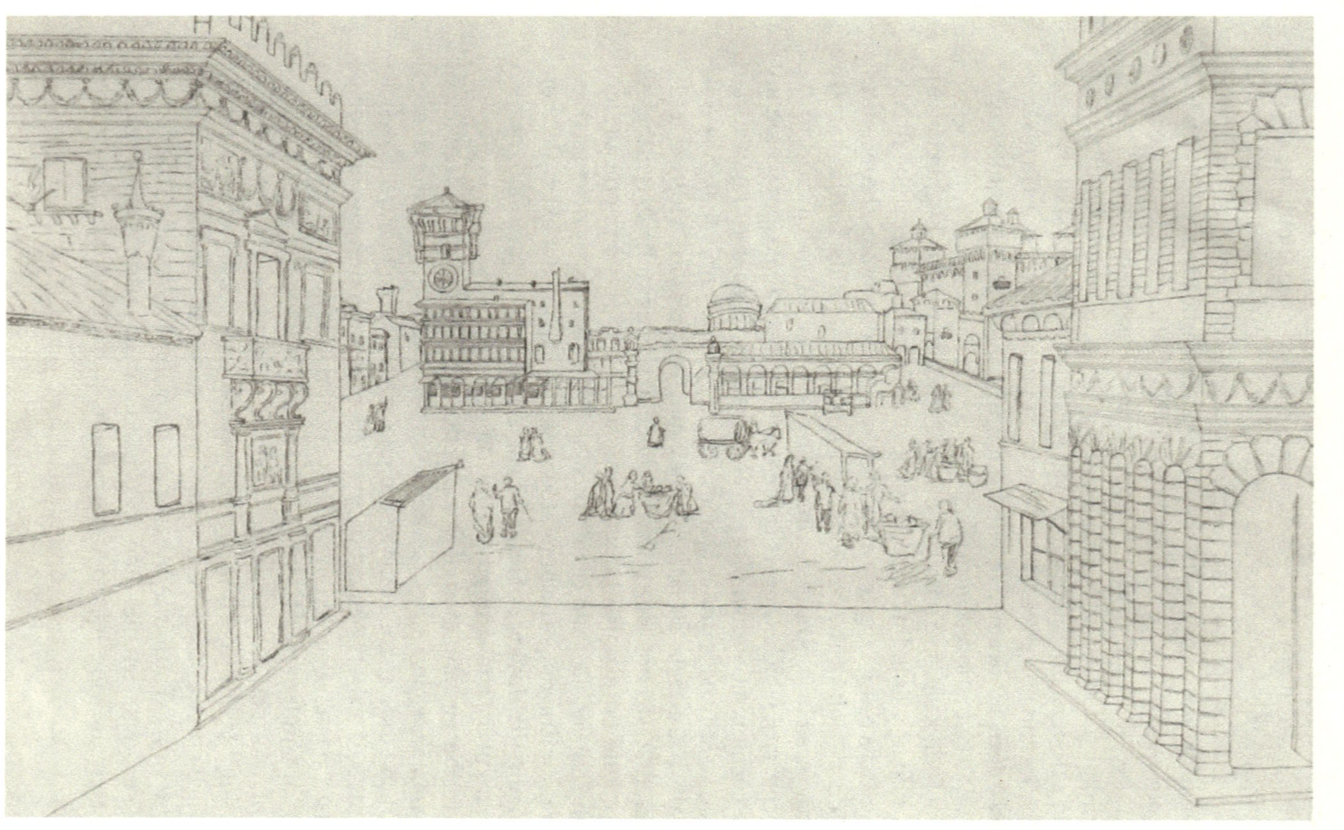

2.15 Circle of Girolamo da Carpi, *Scenographic Design*, c. 1550. Ferrara, Biblioteca Comunale Ariostea, H.5.1.60 (reconstruction).

been the backdrop: citizens shopping and walking around in an urban space resembling the central piazza in Ferrara, with the Castello Estense on the right. There seems to be little reason for the copyist to have populated the space if there were no figures originally in the drawing.

It is difficult to reach a conclusion regarding the presence of painted human figures and animals on stage, as drawings can anticipate actors or include playful sketches (Peruzzi's scenographic drawing housed at the Biblioteca Reale, Turin, for example, shows a cat craftily pilfering meat from a meat stall).[88] Nonetheless, such a practice must have been common enough, as Serlio explicitly condemns it:

> Although in scenerie like this some have painted certain figures to represent live people – such as a woman on a balcony or at a doorway, even animals – I would not advise you to do this since they cannot move, even though they are supposed to represent living things. On the other hand, a person sleeping or a dog (or other animal) sleeping would be suitable, as they are motionless.[89]

This criticism notwithstanding, Serlio himself clearly depicts birds in his satiric stage (figure 2.9), likely attesting that his proposal was not the banishment of animals from the stage but rather an appeal for their animation.

In scenographic cities we thus encounter the presentation of immobile fictions and fraudulent displacements. Their mercuriality, far from creating anxiety, introduces a playful degree of lightness that allows for a dramaturgical cognitive understanding.[90] In any case, scenographic buildings belong not to the world of the stage, but to the world of the theatrical *apparato*, which includes the auditorium and the experiences of the audience. It is to these visual and somatic engagements that the next chapter turns. As we do so, we may recall that, as Merleau-Ponty wrote, there is the inside of the outside and the outside of the inside, and that without such doubleness "we would never understand the quasi presence and imminent visibility which make up the whole problem of the imaginary."[91]

Chapter Three

Palladio, Scamozzi, and the Built Theatre as Enclosure

[Prologues] were only used for justification by the author or by the owner of the household in which the play was being performed. Tonight is one of those occasions, as requested by the author and your hosts. Those who have invited you to this house, the home of the lovely, kind, and generous Maria da Prato, ... have also thought to offer you some entertainment, music, and pleasant games

Anton Francesco Grazzini, Prologo, *Il Frate*[1]

With these words, Grazzini (1504–84) introduced the inaugural performance of his play on 6 January 1540–1. The location was neither a lavish academic theatre, nor a sumptuous temporary construction in an aristocratic palazzo. It was the house of Maria da Prato, a renowned Florentine courtesan who gathered in her circle a number of literary figures.[2] Performances in private rooms and courtyards were common, many without accompanying stage design. Dolce's *Marianna,* for instance, was first performed without music or scenography in 1565 in the house of the Venetian Sebastiano Erizzo for an audience of three hundred gentlemen.[3] Ariosto's *I suppositi* was performed in 1519 by candlelight in the apartments of Cardinal Cibo at Castel Sant'Angelo with a set design by Raphael, though it is unclear whether the set included three-dimensional scenery or merely a painted backdrop.[4]

Despite the plurality of theatrical practices, the discourse on theatrical spaces has traditionally been delineated through categorical demarcations according to medium. In this manner, the historiography proposes that while architecture aimed at the reconstruction of classical theatres, the goal of set design was the illusionistic representation of cityscapes using innovative pictorial techniques like linear perspective.[5] In this chapter, I move away from this dichotomy in order to engage with what period artists and theorists called the *apparato* – an inclusive term denoting the stage as well as the auditorium and its decorations. By avoiding the all-too-common tendency to focus on the phantom figure of the ideal viewer, and focusing instead on the *apparato*, I explore how sixteenth-century performative spaces were constructed with an invested concern for plurality and enclosure.

History contra innovation: this tension signifies the Renaissance's engagement with classical antiquity, an ongoing impetus of experimentation and interpretation. This is clearly exemplified by Michelangelo, who "retained essential features from ancient models in order to force the observer to recollect the source while enjoying the innovations."[6] The putative faithfulness of *imitatio*, which Gombrich appropriately called "elusive," is not a value in which theatrical spaces fully partake, in spite of the heralded rebirth of the Vitruvian canon.[7] Acts of recovery expose the limits of interpretation along with period concerns and anxieties. In truth, the impetus of faithful reproduction of antique form had neither viability nor vitality; instead, what we encounter are the effects of "refraction, experiment, and perpetual inquiry."[8]

The Reception of Classical Theatres

In explicitly addressing classical theatres, Antonio di Pietro Averlino, known as Filarete (c. 1400–c. 1469), exemplifies the imprecise state of knowledge in the Quattrocento: "I do not know what they looked like nor what end they served."[9] It must be remembered that, in the fifteenth-century, many surviving Roman theatres were used for prosaic purposes and *scaenae frons* had not survived. Quattrocento humanists reflected on the neglected state of Roman ruins. A clear example of this experience is Gian Francesco Poggio Bracciolini (1380–1459) and his 1448 *De varietate Fortunae*, in which he incorporates a meditation on Roman architectural remnants in the form of a dialogue between friends. Poggio, a passionate antiquarian, sought to explore, study, and document the vestiges of classical Rome, whether architectural ruins or literary texts. The book reflects on the evasive nature of fortune. Lamenting on the state of Roman ruins, Poggio complains that butchers were conducting business in the Theatre of Marcellus and that the Theatre of Pompey had become an apartment building.[10] The antiquarian tasks of reconstruction and identification was not itself an easy project. Poggio's attempts to identify Roman monuments were not always successful, often borrowing from incorrect pilgrim guides. As it has been noted, Poggio's failure to encounter physical evidence of the buildings mentioned in the imprecise descriptions of Pliny motivates the humanist writer to craft a glorious mental vision of Rome in which the lost city can nonetheless be retrieved through texts.[11] (Or artistic theatrical means, we might add, having in mind scenographic projects like Peruzzi's).

Resorting to their contemporary texts and language, Quattrocento authors often conflated the terms "theatre" and "amphitheatre."[12] Giovanni Rucellai (1403–81) refers to the Theatre of Marcellus as "*un altro culiseo o vero Teatro*" in his 1457 *Della belleza e anticaglia di Roma.*[13] Giovanni attempted to mitigate the confusion by calling it "a real theatre," though he employs "Colosseum" as a generic term denoting a place for spectacles.

Reading classical sources did not necessarily clarify the situation. Both Filarete and Flavio Biondo (1392–1463), author of the 1444–6 *Roma instaurata*, are puzzled by Pliny's descriptions of prodigious theatres in his *Natural History*. These are spaces like the perplexing tripartite theatre commissioned by a wealthy citizen named M. Scaurus: "The lowest storey of the stage was of marble, and the middle one of glass (an extravagance unparallel even in later times), while the top storey was made of guilded planks."[14] Or there was the extraordinary theatre of Curio, which actually comprised two separate theatres constructed with a contraption that allowed them to pivot, forming one large amphitheatre.[15] And exploring the classical Roman theatres as presented by Pliny was a double-edged sword in which the performative spaces appeared as architectural marvels and examples of opulent decadence. As Peter Fane-Saunders notes, Biondo not only remarked on the grandeur of Scaurus's theatre, but also cited Pliny's criticisms of the use of glass (i.e. mosaic) as an unnecessary luxury while also recommending scepticism about whether such a building ever existed – following also with a condemnation of Curio's rotating auditorium and Pompey's costly theatre.[16]

Even well into the sixteenth century, after humanists better understood what Roman theatres looked like, their dramaturgical purpose in antiquity would remain somewhat unclear, often embodying venereal connotations. The word *theatrum* itself survived in the Middle Ages without a concrete signified, referring to any place of entertainment, including brothels.[17] Pirro Ligorio (1510–83), an accomplished architect for Paul IV and Pius IV, writes in his 1553 *Delle antichità di Roma, nel quale si tratta de'circi, theatri, & anfitheatri* that the theatre in antiquity was "like the house of Venus, overrun with lasciviousness."[18] The association between actresses and sex workers, rooted in classical times, had a long-lasting effect, persisting across Europe through the early modern period.[19]

The Question of the *Periaktoi*

But it was not merely a question of what the theatre was as a building that generated interpretive problems in fifteenth-century Italy. Much confusion was also raised by the classical *periaktoi*, a device consisting of painted, rotating triangular prisms that allowed for a quick change in scenographic setting. Alberti in his 1452 *On Building* mentions the *periaktoi* without explicating them: "There would be rotating machinery, therefore, capable of presenting at an instant a painted backdrop or revealing an atrium, house, or even a wood."[20] This passage replicates Vitruvius's texts without explaining how to incorporate linear perspective into such mechanical devices – a chief problem being whether the horizon line on the *periaktoi* would (or even could) correlate to the horizon line in the backdrop.[21] In any case, the lack of understanding regarding such triangular revolving elements, in any case, continued throughout the century. Francesco di Giorgio Martini (1439–1502), for example, imagined in his (c. 1482) *Trattati di architettura* an amphitheatre in which a single, colossal *periaktos*, placed in the centre of the orchestra, would rotate in order to display each of the three Vitruvian stages.[22]

The solution for the problem of the *periaktoi* apparently had to wait until the mid-sixteenth century. In Ignazio Danti's 1583 edition of Vignola's *Le due regole delle prospettiva pratica*, the role of reviving the rotating mechanism is ascribed to Aristotile da Sangallo, who made use of it in 1543 in a theatre for Duke Pierluigi Farnese at Castro. Later, Danti narrates, it was adopted by Lanci for his 1569 scenography for *La Vedova* (fig. 1.2) – an intriguing reference, as the scenographic designs for *La Vedova* seem to present a rather naturalistic point of view and do not visually incorporate *periaktoi*.

Villa Madama

Conundrums regarding the form and function of classical theatre architecture were mostly resolved by the early sixteenth century. This is palpable in the theatre design planned for Villa Madama. The villa, prominently located on the slopes of Mount Mario west of Rome, was commissioned by Pope Leo X and later continued by his cousin, Cardinal Giulio de' Medici (who became Clement VII in 1523). Raphael began the design of the villa but, following his death in 1520, Antonio da Sangallo the Younger designed the final plans and supervised the construction. From the early stages of the design, it was clear that Villa Madama was meant to revive the palatial sumptuousness of the Caesars, with clear referents in classical villas, palaces, and gardens such as Pliny's villa or the Domus Aurea.[23] Construction of the villa was intermittent, with halts after the deaths of Raphael and Leo X and the 1527 Sack of Rome, and the proposed built project was never fully finished.

Villa Madama was designed to include a theatre, which would be built into the slope of Monte Mario, imitating actual Roman models like those showcased by Fabio Calvo in his (c. 1514) translation of Vitruvius (a book that Raphael had hoped to illustrate).[24] Christoph Frommel enthusiastically praises the design, calling it "the most important event [in theatre architecture] preceding Palladio's Teatro Olimpico."[25] Tafuri considered it the first attempt to reconstruct a classical theatre.[26] The design of Villa Madama's theatre certainly presents antiquarian concerns, visible especially in its grand semicircular auditorium and its stage. Its historicist commitment even neglected contemporary scenographic developments. Such a narrow stage would render the display of intricate sets unfeasible, and it is clear that the design bypasses the development of perspectival backdrops. But the interest in imitating classical models found in Villa Madama's theatre is also partial. Though Sangallo's plan incorporated a Vitruvian structure, the design lacked a true *scaenae frons*, presenting instead a columned loggia with a central opening offering views onto the villa's courtyard.[27] Perhaps more importantly, the planned theatre existed within the interior of a private villa. Unlike classical models, the theatre involved neither the construction of a freestanding building nor the integration of the space within the urban, public fabric of the city. In any case, this highly praised classicizing theatre remained but an academic reverie.

Villa Madama typifies period academic exercises: classical theatres were rigorously studied and avidly praised but not reconstructed – an issue often neglected in the scholarship.[28] The lack of classicizing theatres is often understated and explicated as the result of aristocratic patrons' practice of sequestering the humanist theatre. By appropriating performative spaces, and placing them within their palaces, educated elites seized the cultural prestige of the classical public theatre.[29] But the antiquarian reconstruction of theatres faced a more direct challenge: classical theatres would not have satisfied the artistic values of the period's designers and spectators.

Inventiveness

Precedents are significant. Cinquecento dramaturgical interests had been influenced by the theatrical practices of previous centuries, even if those practices were not explicitly called "theatrical." As Umberto Eco points out, medieval Europe "had the real experience of theatrical performance but had not a working theoretical net to throw over it."[30] Many theatrical innovations, especially in respect to technological advances like trap doors and concealed machinery, had their roots in the *sacra rappresentazione*. Alessandra Buccheri goes so far as to declare, "In Aristotile's setting, the most important innovation was the extensive introduction of the machinery used in the religious plays onto the stage of the courtly theatre."[31] For an audience of commoners, a clear point of reference for an enclosed spectacle would have been the religious space, in which multiple layers of meaning, levels of interest, and spatial resonances intermingled.

Sixteenth-century audiences expected imaginative, unique spectacles. Designers and artists found a justification for innovation in studying classical text. The value of inventiveness (*inventio*), which humanists took from authors like Cicero and Vitruvius, actively called for novel answers. In Kemp's words, "the tone for the Renaissance was set by Vitruvius who indicated that the inventive architect cleverly arrives at an original and correct solution to a new or old problem."[32] The classical world stood as a referent, but the artistic process was predicated on innovation. ("Antiquarian history itself degenerates from the moment it is no longer animated and inspired by the fresh life of the present," as Nietzsche would later put it.)[33] In humanist plays, the interest in antiquarian authenticity was often rhetorically introduced only to embrace independence from classical models.[34] The Prologo of Annibal Caro's *Gli Straccioni* (1543) explains that deviations are fundamental because "change is inevitable, since actions and the laws of actions depend on the times and fashions, and these change with every age."[35] Caro explicitly justifies his relativist position against antiquarian zealots as follows:

> The constipated traditionalist may take offence at the triple plot, because the ancients never went beyond a single or double one. But don't forget

> that although there are no existing precedents for our procedure, neither are there prohibitions against it ... There's no such thing as an established set of rules for comedy. The models are legion. Everyone has his own head, every head has its own ideas, and every idea has its reasons.[36]

Nostalgia never stood in the way of innovation; more often than not, it was either at the service of innovation or it was politely brushed aside after a genuflecting remark.

The Theatre as Place of Viewing

A theatre is determined not so much by the action on stage as by the actions that occur in the auditorium in relation to the stage. Theorists nowadays posit that the theatre is defined not by limits but by gaps, silences, pauses, and openings – that the theatre is a space that generates a communitarian, dynamic process of communication.[37] And although those terms are palpably modern, their core ideas have a lineage that expands from the birth of dramatic spectacles in antiquity and through early modernity. Etymologically, "theatre" descends from the Greek *theatron*, "place for viewing" (from *theasthai*, "to behold"). The theatre was the place from which spectators (*theates*) viewed. "*Thea*" (from *theomai*, to contemplate or see with admiration or bewilderment) along with "*theatron*" denoted the visual characteristic of theatre.[38] In the theatre, viewing itself is the medium for the spectator's participation. This is something that the theatre, as a building, has communicated since classical times. And this is the meaning of "theatre" that permeated through the sixteenth century. To pick one example among many, Cesare Cesariano understood the Greek word "theater" as "the people's ability to see what is going on" in his 1521 edition of Vitruvius.[39]

The notion of a theatre as a space for spectators is patent in the frontispiece woodcut for the 1497 Venetian edition of Terence by Lazarus de Soardi for Simon de Luere, an engraving later reused for the 1510 edition of Plautus's *Comedies* (figure 3.1).[40] Its epigram, "*Coliseus sive Theatrum*" (Colosseum or theatre), corroborates the ambivalence of these terms and asserts the depicted space's performative essence. The woodcut illustrates a semicircular auditorium as viewed from an elevated point over the stage (which itself displays two small set pieces). Let us focus on the audience – without a doubt the true protagonist of this engraving. Seven robed men populate the foremost row, absorbed by the action on stage. Hands in repose and torsos facing forward, their gazes intently

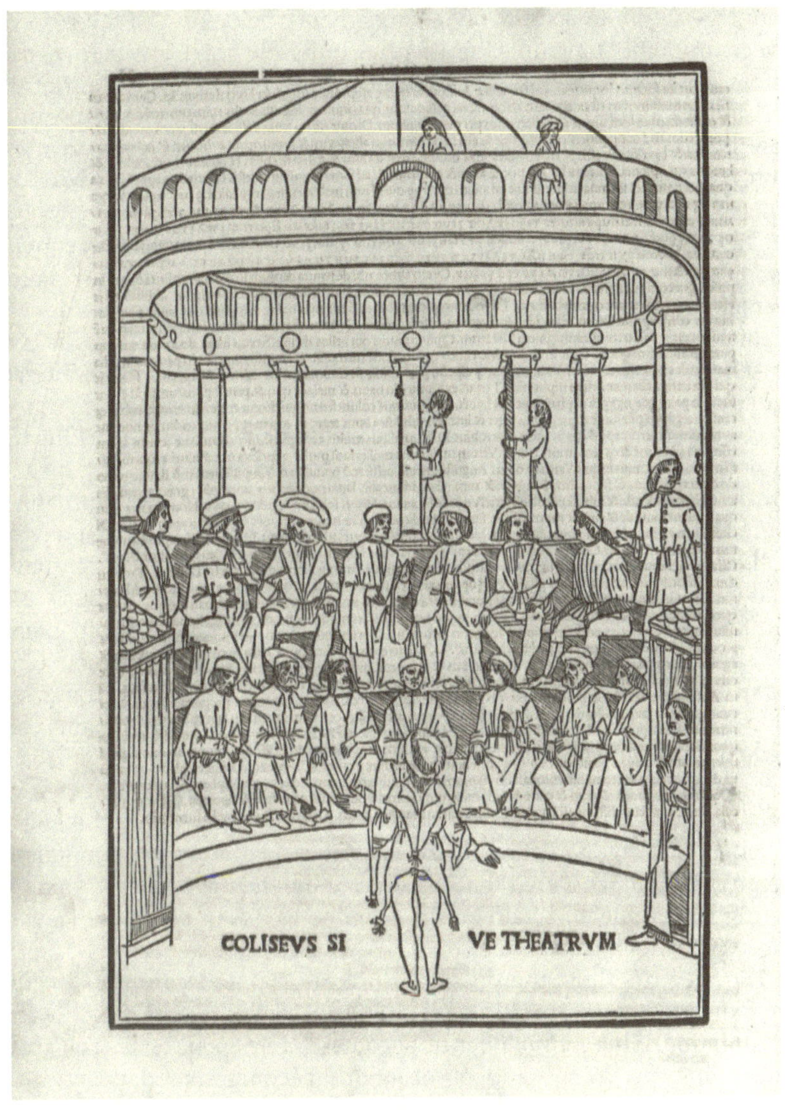

3.1 Plautus (Titus Maccius), *Linguae latinae principis comoediae XX*. Venice: Lazarus Soardus, 1511, 10v. Image from Bayerische Staatsbibliothek (1783033 Res/2 A.lat.a. 192 urn:nbn:de:bvb:12-bsb10195815-6). The woodcut had previously appeared in Soardi's 1497 Venetian edition of Terence.

converge upon an actor. Only a single hand, belonging to the man on the centre right, interrupts the attentive quietude of the lower-row spectators. And even then, it is a restrained indication: a discrete lilt of the wrist; the subdued declarative suggestion of a pointed index. The upper row, by contrast, effuses activity. The action on stage receives no attention. Viewers are distracted, engaged in conversation. Their torsos are rotated towards one another. Hands are active. Intellectual discussions are underway. At the far right of the top row, a viewer stands in conversation with a colleague whose profile barely emerges from the image's frame. Are they entering the space, or have they risen to discuss the architecture that surrounds them? Dialogue and contemplation: the contrast between the upper and lower rows illustrates two ways of interaction that are nonetheless bound together by the theatrical space.

The extent to which this image serves to document an actual theatre or performance is unknown. Even if the image does not register specific practices, the depicted spectators demonstrate the ways that humanists were thinking about classical theatres, and how they were visualizing and conceptualizing performances. The woodcut certainly accentuates that viewing a play was not a solipsistic act. Alberti had previously recommended artists to understand the plural nature of viewership: painters should aim to satisfy the opinions of the multitude of viewers.[41] This point remains just as valid for dramatic events, where plural viewership is *condicio sine qua non*. Throughout his treatise, Serlio remains concerned with the entire audience as a plural entity (*i spettatori*). This is clear when he writes that faux flat statues should be placed "far enough away such that the viewers cannot see them from the side."[42] Likewise, a Venetian envoy reporting on the construction of the 1576 Buontalenti theatre in Florence stated that the floor of the theatre's hall "is going to be higher on one end than on the other so as not to block the view of those who are placed further back."[43]

The theatre grants the possibility for an enclosed communal activity that incorporates multiple conditions of visibility and multiple foci of attention. This independence becomes interdependence. The spectators' interpretations and observations become shared experiences through conversations – before, through, and after the performance. Personal interest and opinions burgeon and interact. Rebecca Zorach challenges the assumption that linear perspective exists in relationship to a single viewer: "It's worth emphasizing that in early modern Europe the viewer was *not alone* – with all the comforting and potentially menacing implications of that phrase."[44]

Artificiality and Multiplicity in the Teatro Olimpico

The Teatro Olimpico in Vicenza (first performance 1585) has come to epitomize the Cinquecento passion for the theatrical. Designed by Andrea Palladio and later modified by Vincenzo Scamozzi, the Olimpico was constructed for the Academia Olimpica, a local sixteenth-century group of intellectuals. The Olimpico, though frequently trotted out as exemplary of theatre design in the Renaissance, is just one model amongst others, many of which remain physically unavailable to us. This vacuum is severe: a small number of accounts, either visual or textual, exist of what was once a fertile theatrical world. Even leaving aside performances in private domiciles, there are few surviving records of the multiple theatres that were successfully built in the mid-Cinquecento: Ferrara circa 1530; Rome 1545; Mantua 1549, by Bertani; Bologna 1550; Siena 1561, by Riccio; Venice 1565, by Palladio; Florence 1585, by Buontalenti.

The visual qualities of the Teatro Olimpico transpose viewers into a fascinating world. Spectators sit in a curved auditorium crowned by a colonnaded portico with classical statues. On stage, an imposing *scaenae frons* is profusely decorated with classical columns, pediments, sculptures, and reliefs. Five portals punctuate the stage facade, of which the central one evokes a triumphal arch, dominating the space. The thresholds grant visual access to projected avenues, within which a scenographic city has been meticulously constructed. In order to augment the impression of expanded depth, the built passageways heighten the illusion by using forced perspective.

Palladio designed this Roman-inspired auditorium inside an abandoned fortress. Working within the constraints of an existing building forced the architect to make concessions. The round auditorium and the *scaenae frons* attest to Palladio's antiquarian knowledge, but unlike in Roman theatres, Palladio's seating area follows an elliptical curve rather than a semicircle. Neither are the construction materials true to Roman architecture: Palladio and Scamozzi worked with wood, plaster, and stucco to create the effect of white, polished marble.

Today, contemplating the stage, one may even remember why perspective was once so enthusiastically lauded (figure 3.2). Central as the projected passageways are to the experience of the theatre, their genesis remains uncertain. Palladio never lived to see the theatre's opening production, and up to his death he assumed that the inaugural performance would be a pastoral comedy by Fabio Pace. This has led to some

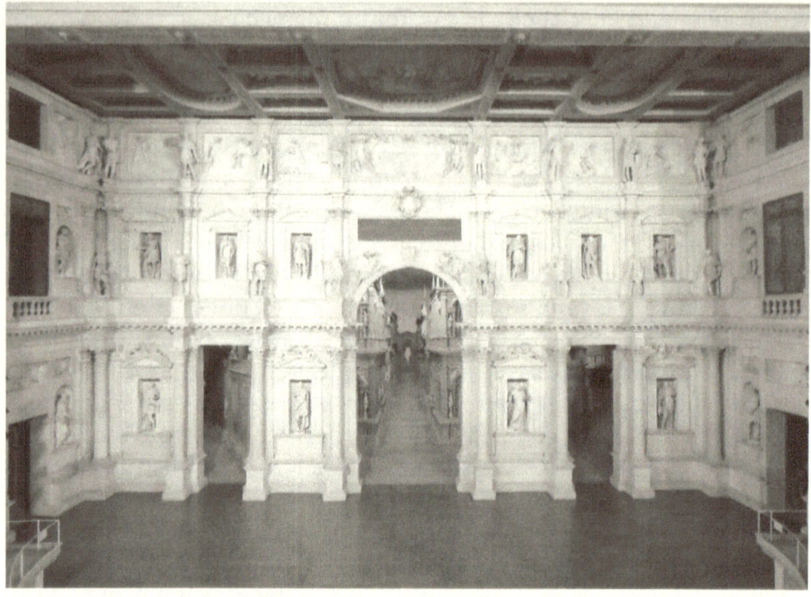

3.2 Andrea Palladio and Vicenzo Scamozzi, Teatro Olimpico. Author's photograph.

speculation on whether Palladio may have planned for a panoramic landscape view that would show through the *scaenae frons*.[45] It was in 1583, three years after the architect's death, that the members of the Academia changed their minds, deciding instead to perform Orsatto Giustaniani's *Oedipus King*. Following this modification, the Academia raised the funds to purchase the additional real estate required for the projected avenues.[46] Vicenzo Scamozzi completed the construction of the auditorium and added the stage design. It remains unclear whether the projected avenues were designed by Scamozzi, followed an original plan by Palladio, or were the result of a series of drawings produced by Silla, Palladio's son.[47]

The addition of the projected avenues to an otherwise classicizing structure demonstrates the commitment to innovation and experimentation that characterized Cinquecento theatre, taking precedence over purist and antiquarian reconstruction. The perspectival passageways required additional disbursement for what was becoming a costly project of dubious viability. The planning and construction of the Olimpico was a long, arduous process during which multiple complications arose, even up to the eve of the inaugural production on 3 March 1585. Many of these challenges involved the financing of the building and the inaugural play, a monetary complication that required the Academia to enforce supplementary payment by its members – a request not altogether successful.[48]

Beyond its fascinating history and aesthetics, the Olimpico has come to play a vital role in the scholarship, where it resolves the conflict between two divergent but fundamental practices. On the one hand, stage designs are seen as disguising the stage's materiality to fabricate a believable illusion deploying linear perspective. On the other, the space of the theatre appears as a self-aware architectural model: the theatre as a fixed, classical place of performance.[49] In this paradigm, the scenographic (pictorial) apparatus dematerializes while the building is reified. Because the Olimpico seemingly offers an elegant and arresting resolution to this tension, its aesthetic and intellectual qualities can easily achieve a final exegetical gravity.[50] This resolution, however, is more theoretical than experiential. In the Olimpico, the visual and haptic qualities of the auditorium and *scaenae frons* contrast with the projected hallways, and the possibility of a synthesis remains achievable only in thought: colouring, materials, scale, and other elements articulate a disjunctive space.

The issue of photography is especially problematic here, for the Olimpico is consistently portrayed in ways that foment the idea of unity. Reproductions of the Olimpico magnify the potential illusion by placing the photographic camera directly in front of the vanishing point. It is with the single eye of the camera and the steadiness of the tripod that perspective truly functions. If we were to take up Walter Benjamin's concepts, we could say that it is through the mechanical photographic medium that a certain aura is given to the Olimpico as an exemplar of theatrical unity.[51] Hence, the Olimpico exists in the scholarship as a hyper-real version – a technologically perfected chimera in which the camera, not the embodied perception of a plural audience, is the ideal viewer. Photographs that artificially highlight linear perspective forcibly impose the vanishing point as the punctum – a gateway to the infinite staring back at us. As a consequence, the finite existence of the viewer is collapsed into a generic and static suspended eye. This is the mythical authority of perspective invoked by Norman Bryson, who interprets the gaze of the painter as contemplating "the visual field from a vantage-point outside the mobility of duration."[52] But both creation and

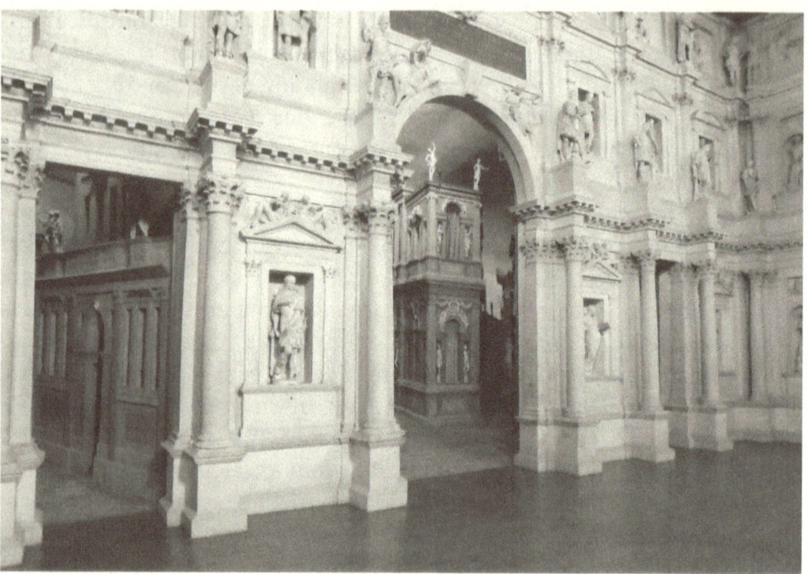

3.3 Andrea Palladio and Vicenzo Scamozzi, Teatro Olimpico. Author's photograph.

contemplation remain intrinsically temporal activities, and the images of the Olimpico are accredited with a quiet, independent truth that is foreign to the actual space.

Challenging the seemingly unitary character of the theatre, the projected streets incite multiple disruptions (figure 3.3). The introduction of divergent pathways on the stage backdrop was anticipated by previous stage designs, like that of Aristotile (figure 2.3) and like the drawings attributed to Salviati's (figures 2.5 and 2.6) drawings, both of which incorporate plural perspectival avenues. Even Kernodle, who praises the Olimpico as a three-dimensional adaptation of the pictorial tradition of linear perspective, had to negotiate the fact that it is a plural space with multiple projected hallways. Kernodle manoeuvres these problems through a deflationary interpretation in which he argues that the side projections remain accents. David Rosand, in his brief engagement with the Olimpico, faces similar problems in trying to integrate the projected streets with the *scaenae frons* and the stage. Rosand argues that the stage and the auditorium remain unified, whereas the perspectives, although fabricated, "remain essentially pictorial spaces, disassociated from the structurally organic unity of the main body of the theatre."[53] In Rosand's view, in order to enforce unity, Palladio replaced the proscenium arch with a triumphal arch. As a result, performers and audience shared a common space:

> Neither actor nor spectator is actually invited back into the perspective streets. Yet during the performance itself those vistas do indeed become an integral part of the spectacle – when the forestage and the perspectives are united by lighting effects, and this common illumination finally distinguishes the illusion of the drama from the reality of the audience.[54]

In Rosand's position, we find a way to negotiate with the Olimpico's spatial dissonances but at a high price: the projected spaces lose their alluring physicality. This position is paradoxical, as the perspectives in the Olimpico, given their three-dimensional nature, actively seem to invite the eyes of the viewers. Indeed, it seems impossible to stand in front of its stage and not let your eyes wander into the distance. But there is no (single) distance: only distances. If we were to apply the regulations of perspective to the Olimpico, we would conclude that, since there is only one vanishing point that perfectly correlates to a single individual, and there are seven vanishing points, at most only seven people in the audience could truly see a correct perspective. And even then, such a position would have to admit to the fact that a perfect alignment with a side street in the Olimpico implies a discordant experience of the other perspectival views. This concern, in any case, seems more appropriate to our modern expectations than to the then contemporary experience of the space.

The Olimpico was created for a diverse and plural audience of two or three thousand spectators, who began entering the building in the late morning and early afternoon and would be entertained with wine and fruits until seven thirty in the evening, at which time the curtain fell. The Academia made concrete plans with regard to the seating for the opening performance: Academicists and their wives sat in the orchestra, and the first *gradi* was reserved for aristocratic ladies, whose entry was a spectacle in itself.[55] Proximity to the stage rather than spatial orientation with regard to the city views was prioritized, perhaps to ensure the seeing and hearing of the action on stage. Neither the multiple perspectival views nor the lack of unification seem to have raised criticisms. Quite the contrary: a letter by Filippo Pigafetta written the day after the inaugural performance stresses that the perspectival views were "very well understood and seen."[56]

The early modern British architect Inigo Jones greatly admired the Olimpico, and his experience of the space sheds light on how the Olimpico can be better understood as a dramaturgical space rather than as an adherent to the mathematical rules of perspective. Praising its design, Jones jotted down a note stating that its "chief artifice was that whear so ever you sat you saw one of thes Prospects [sic]."[57] In this laconic observation, Jones did not report the theatrical unity or spatial synthesis commonly described by modern scholars. What he found fascinating is that every person would always see a projected street, regardless of where they sat. His position is absolutely plural, which means that it is not the perfect contemplation and adjustment to a vanishing point that matters but having visual access to a projected street. Hence, the Olimpico is exceptional because everybody has visual access to a view, despite the lack of an absolute, unitary point of view.

Under the Eyes of the Duke

The Teatro all'antica (figures 3.5 and 3.6) was commissioned by Duke Vespasiano I Gonzaga of Mantua, designed by Vincenzo Scamozzi, and constructed between 1588 and 1590 in Sabbioneta, a town founded by the Duke in the sixteenth century as his residence.[58] Scamozzi, who had supervised the construction of the Olimpico after Palladio's death, no doubt found in the Teatro all'antica a formidable commission: to create, for the first time since antiquity, a permanent, freestanding theatre built as an entirely new structure.

Compared to the imposing magnitude of the Olimpico, the Teatro all'antica could be described as cosy and intimate. Scamozzi's design, though retaining elements from the Olimpico, deviates from Palladio's ideas. The Teatro all'antica does not incorporate a classical *scaenae frons* or a proscenium arch. The narrow, elongated space presents a single and short perspectival street (the current stage being a twentieth-century reconstruction following the original plans). The theatre presents a space of compromise: its diminutive size demands a scale not true to life. The buildings on stage are notably dwarfed in relationship to the actors, and the built perspective is shallow and encompasses only a couple of houses. Beyond these constructions, a painted wall further fractures the illusion by presenting a massive mountain on the right and a tower on the left.

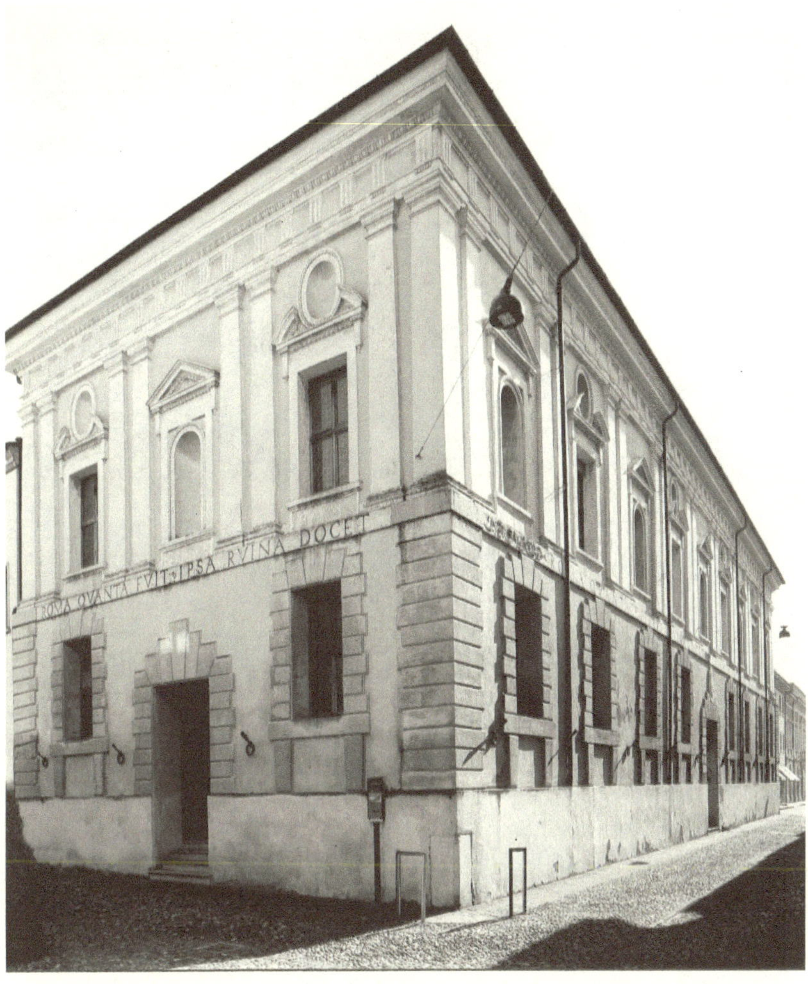

3.4 Teatro all'antica, photograph by Danilo Malacarne – Istituto Centrale per il Catalogo e la Documentazione (ICCD) – Ministero per i Beni le Attività Culturali e il Turismo (MIBACT).

The auditorium of the Teatro all'antica combines two separate seating areas. Five tiers of curved, bell-shaped benches nestle at ground level. Above, a classically-inspired colonnade encases a semi-circular balcony. The structure of the auditorium reveals a hierarchical seating

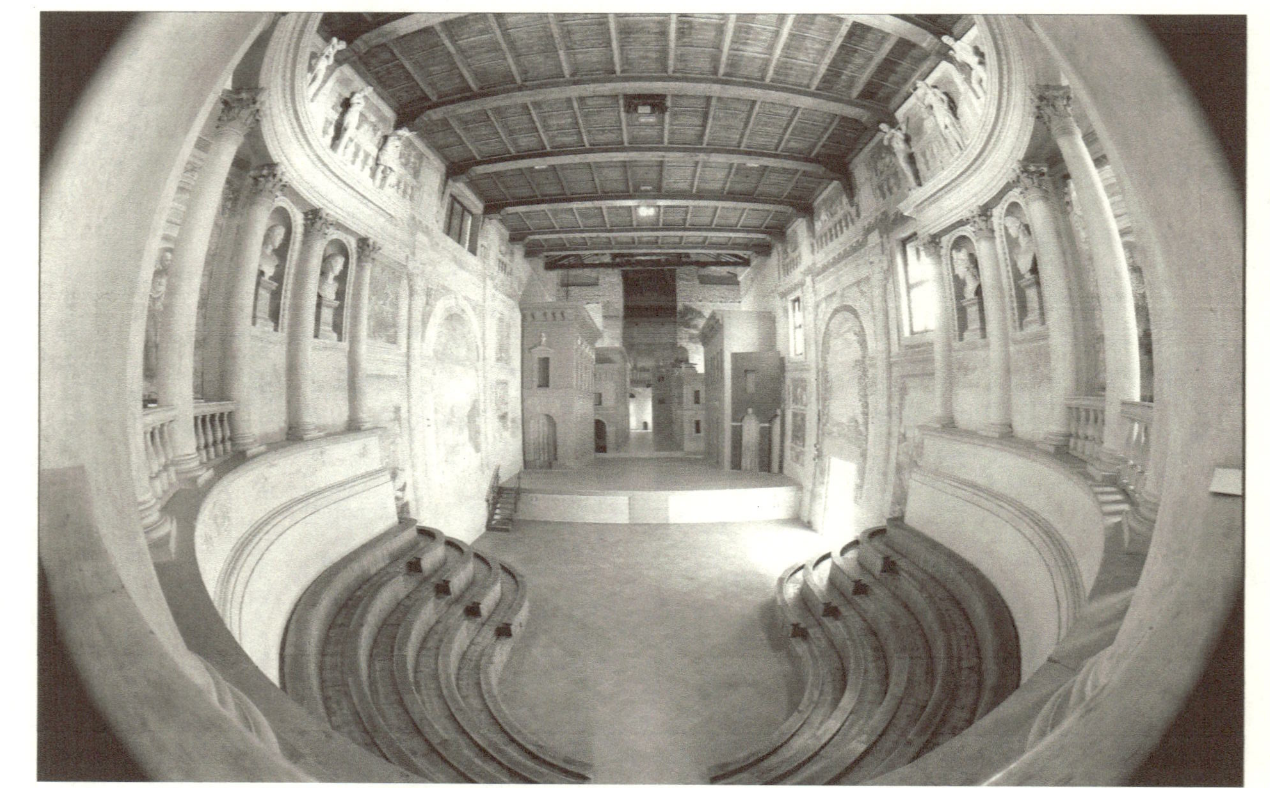

3.5 Teatro all'antica, photograph by Danilo Malacarne – Istituto Centrale per il Catalogo e la Documentazione (ICCD) – Ministero per i Beni le Attività Culturali e il Turismo (MIBACT).

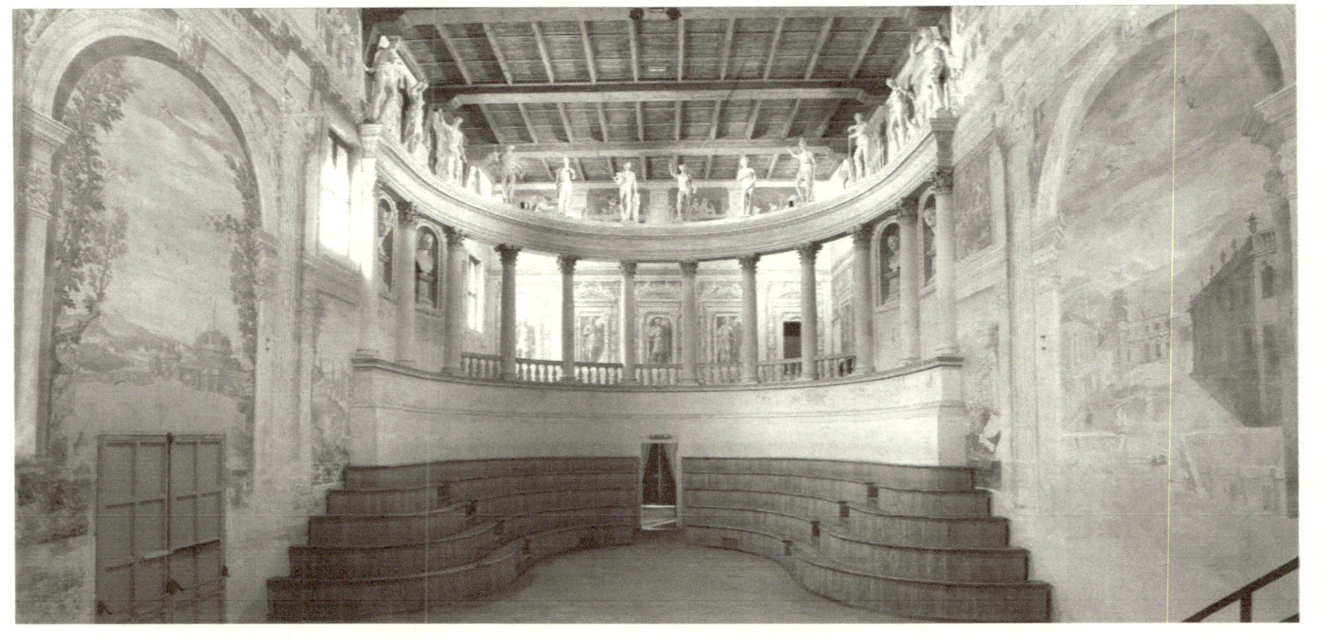

3.6 Teatro all'antica, photograph by Danilo Malacarne – Istituto Centrale per il Catalogo e la Documentazione (ICCD) – Ministero per i Beni le Attività Culturali e il Turismo (MIBACT).

arrangement. Duke Vespasiano and his innermost coterie enjoyed the stage from a privileged position in the upper balcony, where they sat on individual chairs, framed by golden frescoes portraying sculptures of Roman *viri illustres*. The remainder of the spectators sat below the Duke, in the communal rows that had oblique views to the stage. In contrast to the white sobriety of the colonnade, the auditorium integrates a colourful and complex fresco program: the wall sections between the seats and the stage envisage fictional views of Rome, while a register, wrapping around the top of the auditorium, depicts theatre audiences disposed in an imaginary upper balcony.

Because of the positioning of the Duke in relation to the perspectival set design, the Teatro all'antica has been seen as a technological triumph constructed so Vespasiano would perceive the illusion on stage. Elena Povoledo describes the theatre as centralizing a single focal view and, in recent years, Ann Marie Borys, developing from Kurt Foster's seminal study of the theatre, has even called the space a camera obscura built "to create the illusion of an ideal city in a box."[59] This interpretation follows the pervasive notion that theatrical stages enact a break from reality, enclosing the staged action in a fictional, autonomous universe – a scenic space liberated thanks to linear perspective. From George Kernodle to Roy Strong and more recently Dorothee Marciak, scholars have argued that stages were designed so only the aristocratic ruler would have access to the illusion – the prince's seat being the only position from which the perspectival stage design could be properly seen. In this view, linear perspective is a technique that materializes an organizational principle, asserting an ethical and political structure. A more recent instantiation sums it up: "perspective painting builds on the idea of a privileged viewer ... who contemplates the universe from the perfect seat, and like the prince in a theater whose entire architecture builds a symmetry around the noble viewer."[60] Hence, the absorption of Aristotle comes to imply the absorption of a system of representation in which the theatrical stage becomes a stage of visibility for an orderly world that is ruled by a hierarchy, and which visually expresses that hierarchy, shifting a democratic medieval paradigm (where all viewers had equal access to the stage) into a monarchical one.[61]

Nonetheless, it cannot be surmised that, because festivities and performances had symbolic capital, scenographic spaces categorically became *instrumentum regni*. Neither can it be assumed that princely intentions were successful. What is more, the notion of an ideal point of view contrasts with the empirical reality of seeing, as the two eyes of any spectator (including those of the prince) always move, and aligning oneself with a perspectival view is a rather artificial exercise. As Damisch stresses, there is no such thing as a "perfect" point of view; a more central position may be better than others, but the viewers (including the prince) still have to come to terms and negotiate with the stage.[62] Despite the common presence of a privileged spectator, the art historian must account for the experiences of all viewers, including those seated at "disadvantaged" positions. Should we think that those viewers had no visual access to the space? That their experiences were ignored by the designers? The popularity of theatrical productions indicates the contrary.

To make my position clear, I am not arguing that the location of the Duke in the Teatro all'antica had no symbolic capital. Nor I am in contention with the premise that the theatre was gestated with a hierarchical sociopolitical program in mind, as Foster has convincingly demonstrated.[63] After all, the two separate viewing areas, with their respective separate entrances, clearly differentiate between classes. And the central position in the balcony presents a fresco of the Roman emperor Vespasian as if he was lowering a laurel wreath onto something below him, an image that would have been "completed" by Duke Vespasiano sitting under the fresco and virtually receiving the wreath on his own head (figure 3.7). Yet, the stage and the auditorium are not extrinsic to the rest of the viewers. The experiences that are set up by the Teatro all'antica gather the viewers in relationship to the stage, but also to one another. And although no contemporary descriptions of the space remain, we can conceptualize how the Teatro all'antica, as a space and not a mere point of view, convened the audiences in the lower rows.

We must presume a definite atmosphere of participation. For those sitting down in the lower sections, an immediate encounter with others is tangible. There are spectators all around you: viewers sitting right below or above you, to your left and your right, even facing in your direction. Your eyes meet those of others. You nod politely, with a gracious smile. These are people you know well: associates, colleagues, acquaintances, and even a few rivals. Likely, you have chosen to congregate amongst your friends. While spectators wait for the production to commence, conversations are pervasive. Probably not enough to create tumult – this is a civilized occasion – but sufficient to engender a noticeable undercurrent of exchange and scholarly banter. It is, after all, a festive event. A glimpse of the stage becomes a lingering examination. Swivelling, you make a comment about it to a friend, praising its refinement. You also overhear bits and pieces of other conversations around you: intellectual

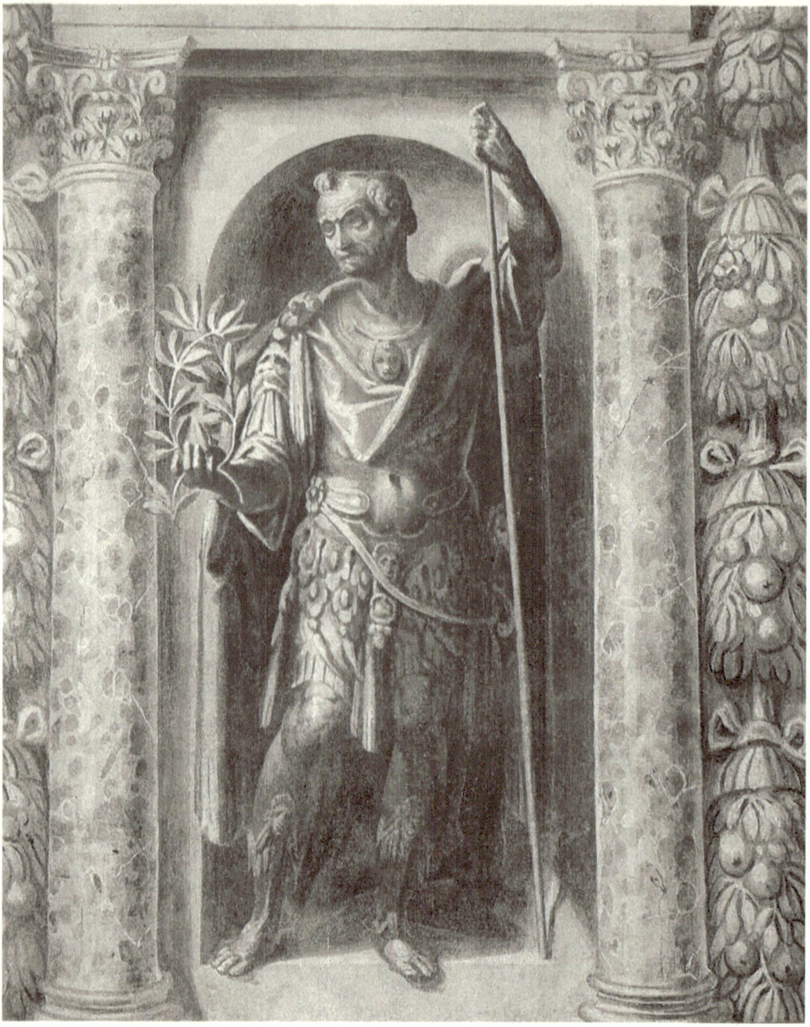

3.7 Teatro all'antica, photograph by Abrizio Buratta e Fausto Valente – Istituto Centrale per il Catalogo e la Documentazione (ICCD) – Ministero per i Beni le Attività Culturali e il Turismo (MIBACT).

remarks about classical theatres, about how magnificent the space is, about the restored glory of antiquity. There may even be some louder-than-necessary comments about the glory of the Duke, who has granted this splendid opportunity. Does Duke Vespasiano acknowledge such comments? Do those seated in the upper loggia look down, or do they remain completely isolated, ignoring the lower section?

The place of the Duke (today marked by the presence of a solitary chair) reveals its limitations, and he remains detached from the collective exchange below. An awareness of the complexity inherent in these visual and social relationships challenges the notion that dramatic logic invites the spectator to see the stage as a complete, unitary, and absolute world that exists independent of the viewers.[64] But the materiality and physical circumstances of Cinquecento performance events remain. We may consider the 1542 Venetian production of *La Talanta*. As Vasari, who designed the stage and the room, grouses, "so many people attended that, between the lamps and the crowding, one could not withstand the great, suffocating heat."[65] Dolce, in a letter regarding the 1565 performance of his *Marianna*, complains that the first performance of the play "was hindered by the unusually large audience."[66] It is hard to imagine those spectators remaining absolutely silent, beholding a stage that relocated them to a world beyond their spatial reality. Awkward positions, oblique angles of vision, and unpleasant temperatures attest to the viewers' basic phenomenological experience, namely their presence within a theatrical space among other viewers. After all, as explicitly expressed in period works like Pellegrino Prisciani's (1435–1518) manuscript *Spectacula*, a treatise dedicated to Ercole I d'Este, Duke of Ferrara, the theatre has always been a place to see and to be seen.[67] The auditorium is the stage in which the social drama is performed – a stage for obsequious gestures and critical expressions.

The Teatro all'antica's Frescoes

The interior of the Teatro all'antica is richly decorated with frescoes. These paintings are not included in Scamozzi's architectural plan for the theatre, but they appear to be integral to the experience of the space, and were likely planned at the time of construction.[68] The painted program is comprises the loggia's *viri illustres*, fictional views of Rome, and frescoes of elegantly dressed spectators populating an imaginary third floor. As a result, entering the theatre opens up a prismatic experience where viewership is dramatically intensified, and the auditorium becomes a fictional stage emplaced physically, albeit fantastically, within Rome.

One finds in the painted upper balcony a conspicuous variety in costume, posture, and physiognomy. Some playgoers are paired, other spectators stand solitary, while still others are regaled by musicians. As one may expect, a number of the frescoed figures are quite attentive to the stage, but for others the stage is not a focus of interest, as they survey the auditorium or engage with objects, animals, or other spectators (figures 3.8, 3.9, and 3.10). Looking up to the back wall, behind the loggia, one notices two men pointing, directing the attention of their respective female companions (figures 3.11 and 3.12). Their gesture and accompanying body language suggests that they are conversing about something specific within the theatre, yet it remains unclear whether they are pointing at each other, the Duke below, or at some feature of the auditorium. A viewer of the period, partaking in a tradition that harkened back to Alberti's *On Painting*, would have understood the connotations of the painted figures that were looking and pointing, and would have discerned in those figures objects of imitation, justifying their own motions and shifts in attention.[69] The sculptural program crowning the loggia further incorporates an active inclusion of the audience. For example, from the lower-left seats, viewers look up at the Olympian sculptures that appear to return their gaze – Poseidon even points his trident down towards the viewers. Each seating area in the Teatro all'antica grants access to a unique view.

On the right and the left walls, between the audience and the stage, there are large paintings presenting an imaginary view of Rome. Seen through painted arched thresholds are well-known structures, including the Castel Sant'Angelo and the Capitoline Hill (figure 3.13 and 3.14). The pictorial presence of Rome parallels the repeated inscription in the building's facade, "ROMA QVANTA FVIT IPSA RVINA DOCET" ("How great Rome was, its very ruins tell").[70] Certainly, a fictive view of Rome's monuments has a theatrical pedigree. The fictional image of Rome in the frescoes may relate to designs like that of Peruzzi for *La Calandria*. The depiction of the Campidoglio also conveys theatrical resonances because of the historical presence of the 1513 Capitoline theatre, and because Michelangelo may have been influenced by Vitruvius's tragic stage in the design of the piazza.[71] As the viewer stands in front of the Campidoglio fresco, the eyes of the viewer move upwards following the *cordonata* and the two ascending figures, who are engaged in conversation. The fresco itself seems to adopt a theatrical mode: the buildings are conveyed with a high degree of flatness, perspectival orthogonals recede formulaically rather than realistically, the space behind the Palazzo Senatorio appears as a backdrop, and the scale of

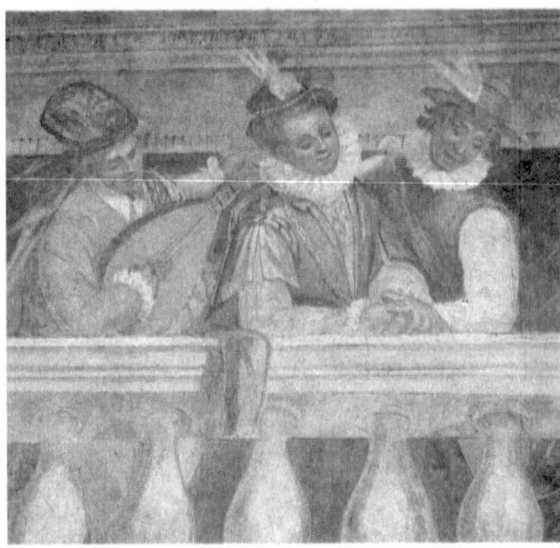

3.8 Teatro all'antica, photograph by Abrizio Buratta e Fausto Valente – Istituto Centrale per il Catalogo e la Documentazione (ICCD) – Ministero per i Beni le Attività Culturali e il Turismo (MIBACT).

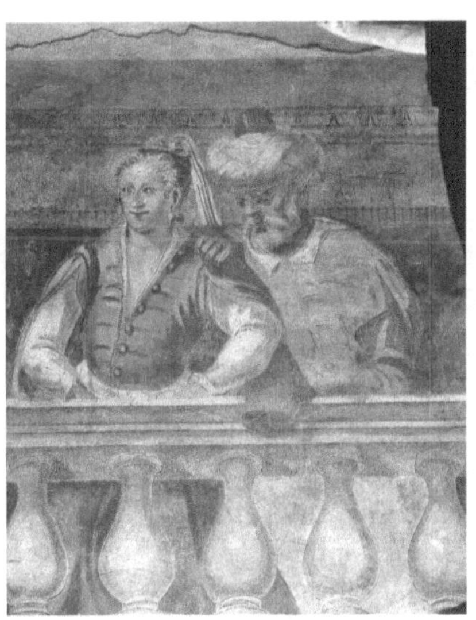

3.9 Teatro all'antica, photograph by Abrizio Buratta e Fausto Valente – Istituto Centrale per il Catalogo e la Documentazione (ICCD) – Ministero per i Beni le Attività Culturali e il Turismo (MIBACT).

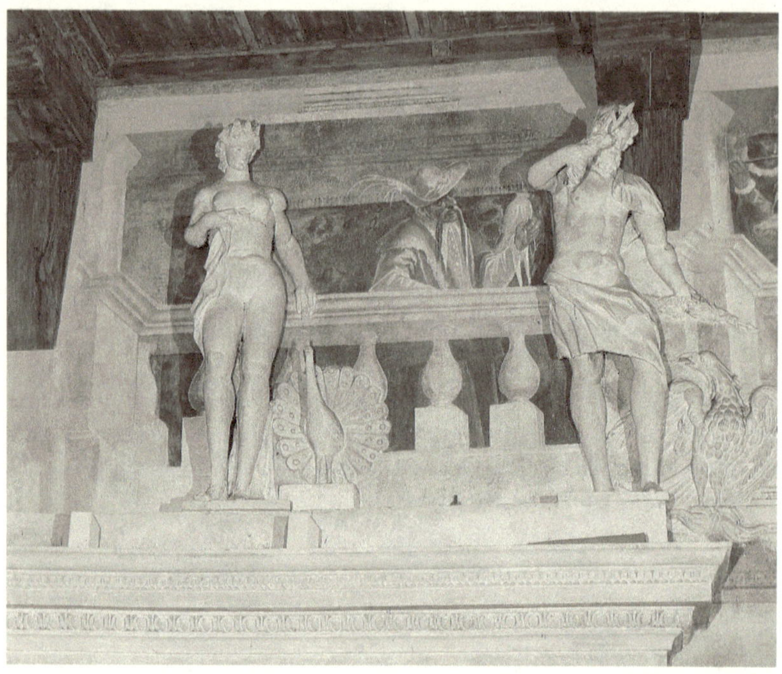

3.10 Teatro all'antica, photograph by Abrizio Buratta e Fausto Valente – Istituto Centrale per il Catalogo e la Documentazione (ICCD) – Ministero per i Beni le Attività Culturali e il Turismo (MIBACT).

figures and buildings is not unified. But it is not really Rome: Foster observes that Sabbioneta's square appears behind the Capitoline, and the Gonzaga fortress behind the Castel Saint'Angelo.[72] The rhetorical intention of the frescoes is to praise Duke Vespasiano as a Cinquecento emperor. The Duke would sit on his chair and contemplate the theatre as the rebirth of a new Rome.

The frescoes of the Roman cityscapes generate a geographical and historical fiction, underscored by their lack of naturalism. As a whole, the pictorial program of the Teatro all'antica celebrates not just the Duke but also the theatre itself as an artistic mode of expression that foments communal gathering. Much like the two figures ascending the stairs in the Capitoline fresco and the pointing couples behind the loggia, the spectators of the theatre enjoyed a plural experience.

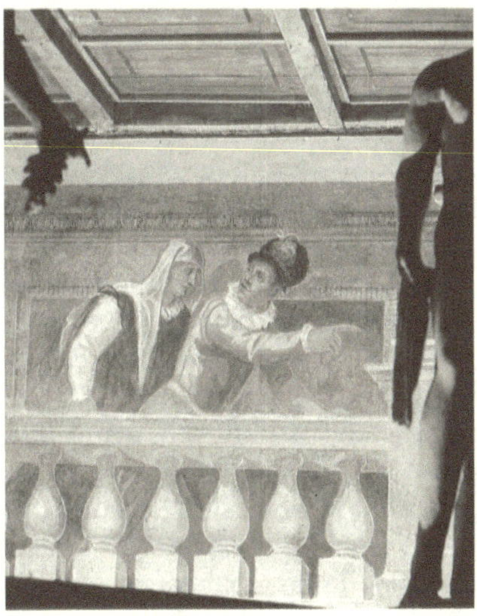

3.11 Teatro all'antica, photograph by Abrizio Buratta e Fausto Valente – Istituto Centrale per il Catalogo e la Documentazione (ICCD) – Ministero per i Beni le Attività Culturali e il Turismo (MIBACT).

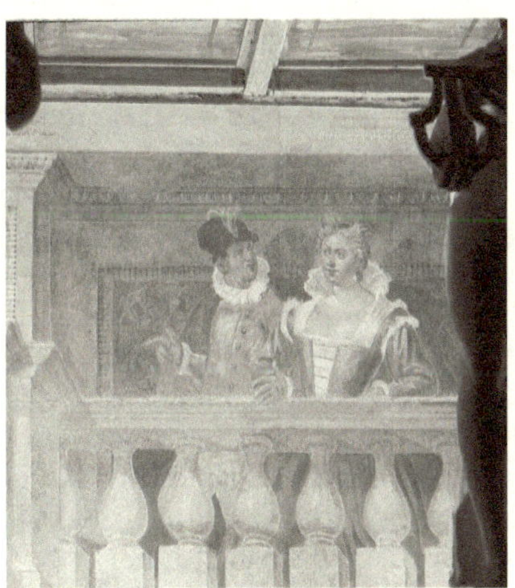

3.12 Teatro all'antica, photograph by Abrizio Buratta e Fausto Valente – Istituto Centrale per il Catalogo e la Documentazione (ICCD) – Ministero per i Beni le Attività Culturali e il Turismo (MIBACT).

Interiority and Enclosure

Both the Teatro Olimpico and the Teatro all'antica demonstrate antiquarian concerns, even if these concerns are commingled with contemporary aesthetics and politics. Notably, it is the unique interiors of these theatres that render them so significant in the history of theatre architecture and scenography. Early modern architects and artists copied, drew, and revered the classical theatres, but they did not replicate their exteriors and facades. It was the interior space of the theatre that concerned contemporaries, stipulating a distinction between what is seen and what is not.[73] As previously mentioned, it has been argued that this enclosure is the outcome of a political manoeuvre – that aristocrats appropriated the public, humanistic concept of theatre and transformed it into a private spectacle for their own glory. And yet, attitudes of the period drifted towards ideas of enclosure. At a general level, the concern with interiority is not limited to theatres: studios, cabinets, alcoves, closets, and other small, private spaces define a noted architectural concern associated with the psychological interior space of the self.

From private domiciles to court theatres, the Renaissance theatrical space manifested this engagement with interiority and enclosure. Even the most physically open spaces, such as the Campidoglio and the Piazza degli Uffizi, were used as theatres because of the enclosure inherent in their design.[74] The use of secluded spaces, such as courtyards, for theatrical productions had a long tradition. The interior facades of the *cortili* were used for performances, as their layered porticoes were seen as referents to the Vitruvian scene and the theatrical lineage of the Colosseum.[75] Scholars have found in the transition from medieval street festivities to private courtyards a germ of the Renaissance theatre. This transition is exemplified by the mid-1480s performances by the Roman Academy of Pomponius Laetus (1427–98). This group enacted plays by Seneca and Plautus at Cardinal Raffaele Riario's residence, also performing a play about Emperor Constantine in a courtyard of the Pontifical Palace with Pope Innocent VIII enjoying the performance from his window.[76] The use of courtyards for theatrical performances would continue in the Cinquecento. For example, the 1554 Loggia Cornaro, designed by Giovanni Maria Falconetto, not only resembles a *scaena frons* but was used as such in courtyard performances.[77] And it is significant that for the 1539 celebrations of his wedding with Eleonora, Cosimo I chose a courtyard that was "one of the many *horti interclusi* opportunely confined within high walls."[78] Evidently, its secluded

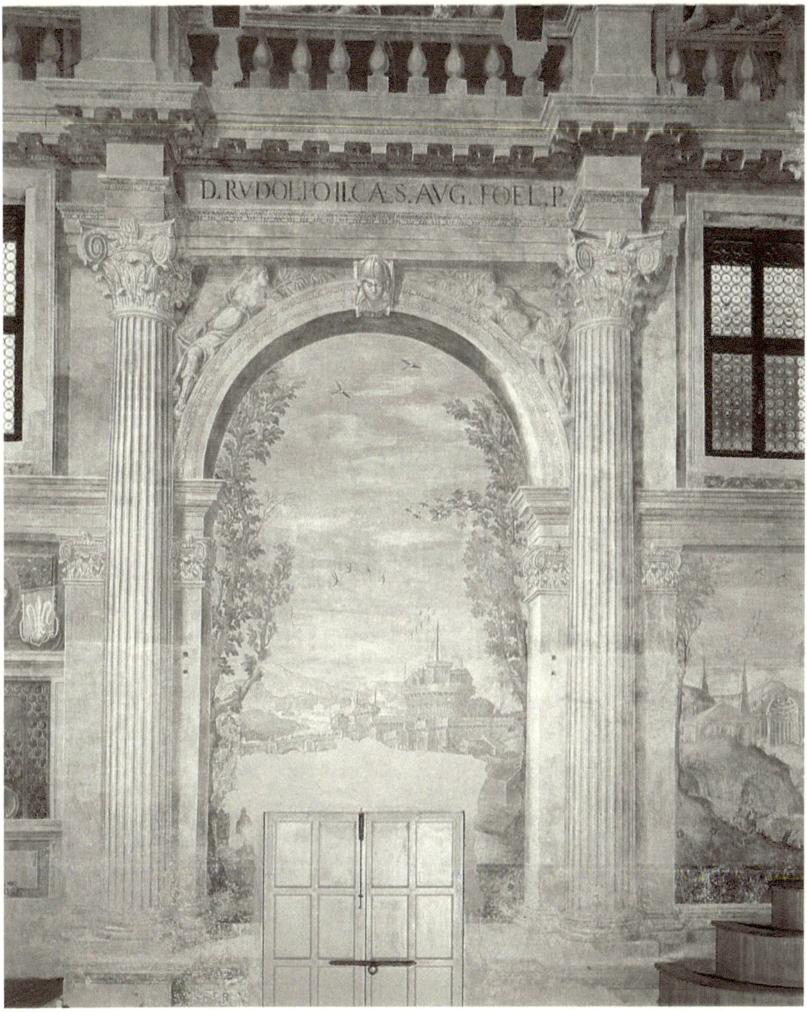

3.13 Teatro all'antica, photograph by Abrizio Buratta e Fausto Valente – Istituto Centrale per il Catalogo e la Documentazione (ICCD) – Ministero per i Beni le Attività Culturali e il Turismo (MIBACT).

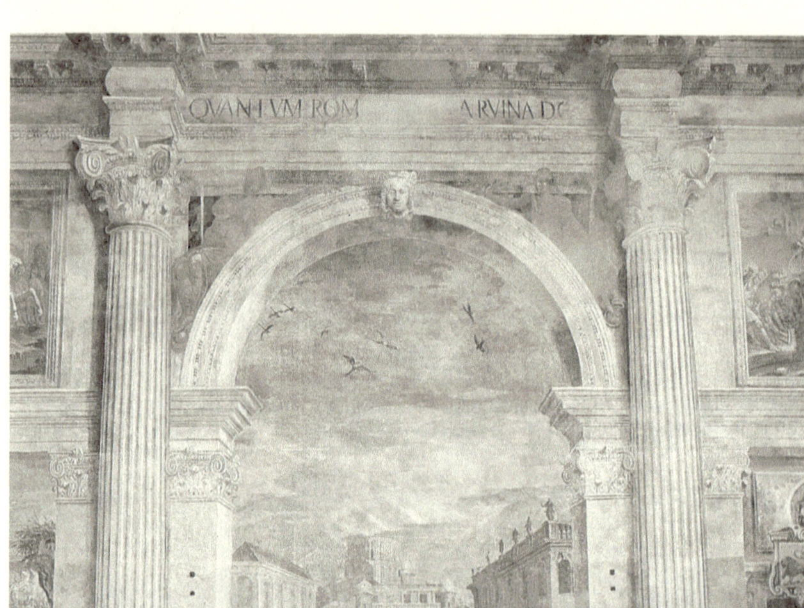

3.14 Teatro all'antica, photograph by Abrizio Buratta e Fausto Valente – Istituto Centrale per il Catalogo e la Documentazione (ICCD) – Ministero per i Beni le Attività Culturali e il Turismo (MIBACT).

qualities did not suffice, as walls and a roof were further constructed within it. It was then twice enclosed and twice removed from the fabric of the city.

Canopies and faux skies were often-used elements to signify theatrical enclosure, even in private domiciles. This practice may find parallels with antique *velaria*, but it cannot be reduced to purely antiquarian concerns, as it perpetuates a usage present in prior performances such as pageants and sacred representations. We know from Vasari that Francesco d'Angelo, known as Cecca (1447–88), covered the Piazza di San Giovanni in Florence with an azure cloth sky embellished with large fabric lilies and heraldic banners.[79] Similarly, Poliziano's *Orfeo* (c. 1480), which has been seen as demarcating a pivotal moment towards the Renaissance stage, incorporated an artificial sky adorned with zodiac signs.[80] In the previously mentioned academic performances at Riario's residence, a fabric was stretched over the palazzo's courtyard.[81] The 1501 temporary theatre built in Mantua likewise made use of a canopy ornamented with lights and astrological symbols.[82] Castiglione, in his description of the 1513 performance of *La Calandria,* states that "very large masses of greenery were attached to the ceiling of the hall, so that they nearly covered the vault."[83] Marin Sanudo was taken aback by a 1515 Venetian performance at Ca' Pesaro.[84] This event included a *commedia* that took place in Hell, a tableau of Paris and the Goddesses, a banquet, and a ball. Sanudo stresses that the performance was beautiful, praising the costumes but giving little account of the set design; he does accentuate, however, the presence of a canopy or awning that covered the courtyard with a "sky."[85]

The association of enclosure and theatricality is palpable in a series of autograph notes by Daniele Barbaro. Commenting on Augustine's *City of God,* Barbaro highlights that the separation of senatorial elites from the common people in Roman spectacles led to popular discontent and revolts. In turn, Barbaro praises Venice, "where senators, *cittadini,* and *popolani* still mingled on a regular basis as spectators in the courtyard of the Doge's Palace."[86]

In truth, the Venetian Republic had a difficult relationship with theatrical spaces, as exemplified by two Venetian playhouses built in 1580 and destroyed five years later. Eugene Johnson writes about the peculiar existence of theatre boxes (*palchi*) that could be closed off to hide their interiors from passers-by.[87] Johnson has brought attention to the potential sexual nature of the behaviour within the boxes, which would have led to scandal, though we cannot rule out that the acts on stage were themselves of an erotic nature.[88] A 1580 decree from the Council of Ten had in fact censored the comedies performed in the city for containing "many lewd lascivious and most unwholesome words and acts."[89] These private boxes present a dialectical experience in which the dynamics of social power are conceivably more palpable than in spaces such as the Teatro all'antica: privilege means anonymity; seeing without being seen. What was the function of the boxes? Were they used to protect the identity of privileged spectators? Or were the boxes used to receive sexual favours? These functions are not mutually exclusive. We must further imagine the experience of less privileged spectators who saw or knew about these enclosed boxes without having visual access to their interiors. Surely those theatre-goers jested and speculated about the occupants of the boxes, a dialogue that added a further layer of experience to the theatrical spectacle.

A beguiling Venetian project that sought to architecturally revive antiquity was Alvise Cornaro's (1484–1566) proposal to construct a fully classical theatre on an artificial island between the Dogana and the Guidecca.[90] Cornaro's theatre has been seen as the type of humanist space, public and democratic, that aristocrats appropriated.[91] But this project substantiated the conflict between classical and early modern spaces. It reclaimed a type of space that was antagonistic to the principles of enclosure in Renaissance theatres and, unsurprisingly, it was never built. Providing a contrast to other theatres, such as the Teatro Olimpico, the Teatro all'antica, or the one at Villa Madama, Cornaro's proposal celebrated the exterior of the theatre. Indeed, the theatre would have doubled as a space for performances and as a backdrop to be enjoyed from the Piazzetta, which in turn would have become an auditorium of sorts.[92] The theatre would have been a sign of the power of the arts and a triumph of culture over (perhaps) less cultivated spectacles (such as public executions) that might be witnessed in the Piazzetta.

It is tempting to conceptualize Cornaro's theatre not as an actual proposal but as a direct provocation and even as an exercise in resistance.[93] It must be remembered that in 1559 legal manoeuvres entrusted theatrical events to Jesuit hands.[94] Given that Venetian authorities incessantly attacked the moral qualities of the theatre, Cornaro's proposal challenged these attempts at restraint, even defending the theatre's autonomy. And yet, for all its humanistic values, its public emphasis, its openness, and its antiquarian interests, Cornaro's theatre was distant, symbolic, impractical, and completely unconcerned with popular interests and desires.

Perhaps it is in the Venetian theatres destroyed in 1585 that a real political provocation can be found. After all, secrecy was an unusual condition in Venice that not even the Doge enjoyed. Perhaps, in those theatres, individual agency and consciousness found a subversive means of expression. The demolished theatres illustrate the tension between political rulings, theatrical spaces, and human desires – a subject that the next chapter will explore. Although there were privileged points of view and antiquarian dreams, those provide but a partial foundation for an understanding of theatrical practices and experiences. The disappeared Venetian theatres stand in contrast to antiquarian never-built theatres, like that of Villa Madama or Cornaro's proposal, and other constructed, but little-used spaces, like the Teatro Olimpico or the Teatro all'antica. The material pull of what was ultimately constructed, even if less erudite and wholesome, disassembles the allure of the ideal space.

Chapter Four

The Medici Theatres, Political Aspirations, and Cognitive Autonomy

In short: let anyone say what he will ... Afterwards, everyone is free to censure or praise as he likes, because censure will not infuriate the Monsignori and praise will not make them arrogant.[1]

Cecchi, Prologo, *L'assuolo*

In addressing sixteenth-century Florence, Medici performances and propaganda are inextricably intertwined. Especially following Cosimo I's rise to power, a cultural policy was put in place with the objective of glorifying the Medici and embedding the dynasty into the socio-political fabric of Florence. Weddings, sacred holidays, and public festivals became intensified political spectacles. This chapter seeks to reevaluate the hermetic gravity often given to those politicized performances in order to disentangle political aspirations from the realities of theatrical productions.

Many of the questions central to this inquiry are inherently textual. Were playwrights concerned with the dissemination of political propaganda? To what extent did viewers of the period have autonomy to evaluate a dramatic plot? Other topics are integrated within art-historical discourse. The latter has shed much light on the aristocratic desire to deploy art as a means of self-promotion. As we saw in the previous chapter, much of the discussion of stagecraft as a political tool reverts to visual practices, especially linear perspective. The idea of a centralized princely theatre is compelling. But humanist culture was predicated on dialogue, on welcoming dialogical diversity and ambiguity.[2] And the dramaturgical amplified a culture in which polyphonic dialogue operated externally in the social world and internally in the individual's own mind. The issue at stake is not the political intent of performative events but whether such intentions encompassed all aspects of theatrical productions, from stage design to built theatres, and from texts to the audience's absorption of the putative intended message.

Oblique Points of View

As we saw in the previous chapter, no device is more associated with theatrical demonstrations of political power than the "prince's seat": the perfect location in the auditorium, directly facing the vanishing point of the stage. Yet of all the tools that an early modern ruler could use to promulgate a political message, the positioning of a chair opposite a vanishing point is a marginal and puny device. Political leaders in early modern Europe sought to impress upon viewers their authority by building palaces and commissioning public artworks. Renowned artists were called upon to design lavish banquets, fantastically choreographed parades, and triumphal entries. Medals were forged, poems written, and dedications to the glory of the leaders printed.

Despite the facility with which linear perspective makes its way into discourses on theatrical spaces, it is neither a straightforward nor a unified subject. Perspective is a pictorial device used to represent optical experiences. It is also a cultural signifier existing in a conceptual web where it becomes a means to explain causal connections: the vanishing point in Renaissance painting becomes the vanishing point of an age. Explanations of what linear perspective is or does are destined to remain instrumental – however inflated or deflationary – because it is a technique that retains significant artistic, social, and cultural resonance. At the same time, the historiographic addition of meanings to linear perspective leads to a distended system of signification in which individual instantiations are assumed to systematically reflect a fixed epistemological structure. The plurality of scholarly explanations, understandings, and interpretations of linear perspective, far from elucidating the subject, has transformed it into a behemoth of many heads: "artistic self-consciousness," a "way of envisioning," an "epistemological problem," and "a language of art."[3] Such diverse interpretations reflect the voluminous and notoriously divergent literature on the subject. Perspective appears as a cultural signifier (Panofsky, Bryson), and merely as an artistic means to represent an object in space (Gombrich); as a technique that can be studied and assessed by positivist means (Kemp), and as an irreducible and multifaceted way of thinking that exposes the phenomenology of the gaze (Damisch); as the means of ensnaring the subject and controlling nature (Merleau-Ponty, Jay, Harries), and as a way to think about observation (Battisti); as a way of "seeing through" a window (Panofsky), and as a way to present receding individual objects without necessarily crafting unified spaces (Elkins); as a flexible artistic tool where aesthetics takes priority over mathematical accuracy (J. White), and a rule-based language (Goodman, Saint-Martin); as a technical means to produce pictorial illusions (Grafton), and even metaphorical representations of God's grace (Edgerton, Moffit).[4]

The word "perspective" or *prospettiva* is a notoriously complex, polysemic signifier. Michael Baxandall has shown the dangers "of equating 'perspective' exclusively with systematic linear perspective constructions."[5] In theatrical spaces, the word obtained further meaning, as it denoted the scenography (in contrast to the *apparato*). This is a separation of terms that one encounters in Vasari. Giambullari, in his description of *Il commodo*, similarly associates perspective and the built set: "one can see how a sun emerges slowly from the *prospettiva*."[6] For other authors, perspective came to be associated with *scenographia*, a word that Vasari, despite his knowledge of theatre, does not use. This latter association is nonetheless clear in translations of Vitruvius: Fra Giocondo in 1511, Fabio Calvo in 1521, and Cesariano in 1521.[7]

The introduction of perspective into the three-dimensional theatrical space, needless to say, does not simplify the tensions of perspective as a word or a concept. A perfect alignment with the vanishing point, including that of the prince's seat, was hardly pervasive in the fifteenth and sixteenth centuries, including that of the prince's seat. In Serlio's influential plan for a theatre, the best viewing position appears to correspond to an aisle.[8] As Damisch points out, the aristocrats seated in the privileged first row "could doubtless hear very well but they'd see no more of the actors than their heads, and their view of anything happening on the inclined plane would be almost totally blocked."[9] In Serlio's plan, Damisch concludes, the best location with regard to perspective is the central seats situated right below a main aisle, a section designated for "women of quality."[10]

A seating arrangement can show consciousness of political dynamics without aligning them to the technical precepts of visual demands. The 1509 Ferrara production of Ariosto's famous *I suppositi* exemplifies this disconnection (the play would become rather popular, with later performances in Rome in 1519 and also by various *commedia* troupes). Throughout the Renaissance, Ferrara was a city thoroughly invested in theatre, spectacle, and public ceremonies, from jousts to religious performances. Such artistic investment was palpably political, for "Estense leaders were quick to realize the importance of public ceremony and spectacle in reinforcing their despotic but broadly popular rule."[11] It is therefore not surprising that the premiere performance of *I suppositi* was consciously framed by a strict social apparatus that defined the order of entrance as well as the seating arrangement within the theatre. At the same time, as Sergio Costola has demonstrated, the careful social performance of rank in the arrangement of the audience did not create a hermetic and unified structure. Two letters, one by the humanist Pencaro to Isabella d'Este and another letter by Isabella herself, demonstrate an acute awareness of spatial, socio-political relationships. "The thirteen tiers of the grandstands are built on the sides of the hall," writes Isabella d'Este, "the women sit in the middle while the men [sit] on the two sides."[12]

Costola illustrates the arrangement, which he aptly described as a "dialogue of gazes" (figures 4.1 and 4.2). The model shows how advantageous views of the stage did not necessarily correspond to rigidly controlled social and political systems, which can become destabilized in theatrical spaces. For this performance, the men's positions lined the side walls of the rectangular auditorium, while the women's designated location was along the back wall. And disregarding court etiquette, men and women could easily watch each other. Moreover, while the Duke's "privileged" position directly in front of the stage facilitated a more effective auditory experience of the production, the stage's width hindered his visual access.[13]

Rectangular auditoriums were common. Giuliano da Sangallo's 1488 design of a palazzo commissioned by Lorenzo de' Medici for Ferdinand of Naples incorporated a polyvalent central rectangular space surrounded by seats.[14] Such an arrangement along three walls (the so-called *Teatro da sala*) was likewise used in Ferrara during the 1491 celebration of the marriage of Alfonso d'Este and Anna Sforza (for which Plautus's *Menaechmi* and Terence's *Andria* and *Amphitrione* were performed on three consecutive evenings).[15] Likely, variations of this arrangement had already been introduced in previous performances in Ferrara: the 1486 performance of *Menaechmi*; the 1487 carnival production of Plautus's *Amphitrione* and Niccolò da Corregio's *Caephalo* in the Cortile Nuovo, with the participation of the painter Giovanni Bianchi (Trullo); and the 1489 celebration of Isabella's marriage to Francesco Gonzaga.[16]

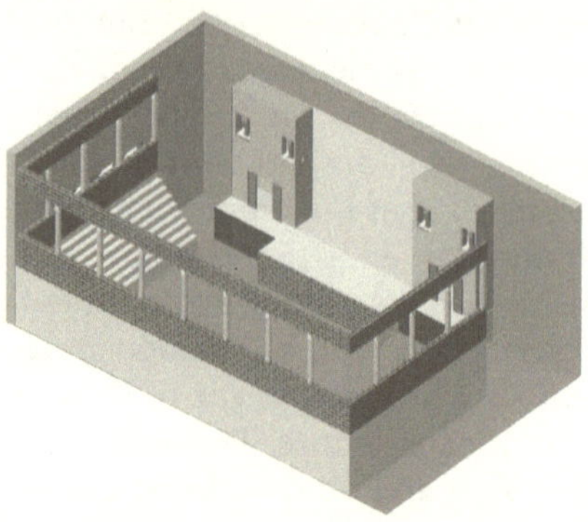

4.1 Auditorium for the 1509 Performance of Ariosto's *I suppositi*. Image originally appearing in Sergio Costola, "The Politics of a Theatrical Event." *Mediaevalia* 33 (2012): 195–228.

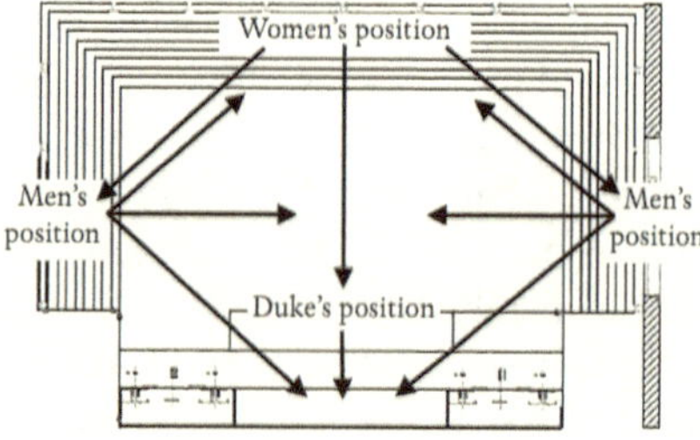

4.2 Auditorium for the 1509 Performance of Ariosto's *I suppositi*. Modified image for clarification with permission from Sergio Costola. See original in "The Politics of a Theatrical Event." *Mediaevalia* 33 (2012): 195–228.

Another space that followed the rectangular model was the temporary 1513 Capitoline theatre, erected in Rome for the celebrations accompanying Leo X's ascent to the pontificate.[17] The theatre, which measured thirty-five by thirty-one metres, was entered through a triumphal arch and had seating rows against its walls. The stage was decorated with five arcades, each framing a painting.[18] The space witnessed a series of events in which the secular and the sacred were intertwined: a Mass was performed, followed by the ceremonial dispensation of Roman citizenship to Leo X's grandson Lorenzo and to his brother Giuliano, then a banquet, allegorical representations, an eclogue, and, finally, a masquerade at two a.m. [19] The next day, there were various theatrical performances, including Plautus's *Poenulus*.

An atypical configuration was witnessed in 1501 for a temporary theatre commissioned by Francesco Gonzaga in Mantua.[20] The theatrical performances produced for this theatre show a clear interest in classical antiquity, with three classical plays performed in addition to a new, classically derived work. The theatre itself embraced a certain classicizing mode, recorded in a contemporary letter by Sigismondo Cantelmo, a Neopolitan in the service of Ercole I d'Este.[21] The theatre decorations connected the Mantuan court with Roman antiquity: the room was adorned with classical faux arches, framing Mantegna's *Triumph of Caesar*. In the words of Cantelmo, the space "represented to the mind a building eternal and ancient."[22] At the same time, and as Povoledo indicates, the rectangular auditorium hardly recalled ancient theatres – likely a conscious decision that shows divergences between humanist theory and theatrical practices.[23] Cantelmo's letter indicates that the stage was idiosyncratically placed in a corner of the room, a choice demonstrating that antiquity could be invoked without following its architectural models and that practical concerns, along with established practices, could take priority over antiquarian ideals (if the latter were even considered for this performance).

In Florence, the theatre built for the Medici wedding of 1539 also had a rectangular structure. And half a century later, the Uffizi theatre was remodelled for the 1589 Medici wedding. During the latter, women sat in two L-shaped, tiered platforms (*gradi*) along the back and side walls, whereas men sat on chairs on the auditorium floor.[24] The seating arrangements for the Medici weddings stipulate a distinct hierarchical social structure, incorporating *palchi* designated for the most privileged viewers to enjoy a central view of the stage. But this theatrical space also makes possible other positions and modes of viewing. Moreover, panegyrics often hide tensions and anxieties, and communicative intentions are never perfect.

The Theatre as a Murder Weapon

The Florence of the 1530s was notable for its political upheavals and uncertainty. In 1530, Pope Clement VII restored Medici rule after the republican faction had taken control of the Tuscan city following the Sack of Rome in 1527. The nineteen-year-old Alessandro was appointed duke – a title made hereditary by the Holy Roman Emperor Charles V.

From the start, Alessandro's rule garnered numerous detractors. His own cousin, Ippolito, was delegated to clandestinely voice his grievances to Charles V. Ippolito's sudden death before meeting the Emperor resulted in the propagation of rumours regarding Alessandro's role in the death.

It was during the infamous rule of Alessandro that Lorenzo di Pier Francesco de' Medici produced in 1536 his own play *Aridosia*, an episode illustrating how theatrical events embody political pressures. Aristotile created the *apparato* for this occasion. Regarding the production, Vasari tells us that Lorenzo wanted to relocate the musicians outside of the stage, asking Aristotile to build two platforms over the seating area, one for vocalists and one for clavichords and organs.[25] A dispute emerged between producer and architect regarding how these platforms should be supported. Aristotile wanted thick arches; Lorenzo requested a less sturdy construction on the premise that it would better distribute the music's volume. And here, Vasari tells us, Aristotile realized that the performance was a subterfuge by Lorenzo, who was plotting to assassinate Alessandro (and the three-hundred spectators) by having the musicians' platforms collapse onto those sitting below in the auditorium. Vasari himself then auspiciously appears in the narrative as an astute young man, mitigating the situation. He proposed a system of iron bolts to hold up the rafters, which Aristotile readily endorsed and Lorenzo reluctantly approved to conceal his intentions. Whether Vasari's anecdote is truthful or fabricated, the homicidal desires of Lorenzo were not ineffectual. He succeeded in assassinating Alessandro in 1537.

Cosimo and Eleonora's Nuptials

Lorenzo's attempt to claim power was unsuccessful, and the Medici faction would facilitate Cosimo's taking control of the Florentine government. Lorenzo fled to Venice, where he was eventually assassinated in 1548. Cosimo I de' Medici inherited an unstable Florence. Many intellectuals felt uneasy with his authoritative rule. Michelangelo would later write a madrigal where Florence appeared as a woman in bondage at the hands of a tyrant.[26] Cosimo sought to alleviate this circumstance by exercising a tight control on art production to promote his rule. His 1539 marriage to Eleonora de Toledo created the perfect occasion to broadcast his power to Florentine inhabitants and foreign dignitaries.[27] Its ephemeral street constructions, the triumphal entry, the poems and music composed for the occasion, and the lavish banquet reminded all present that the ruler was nothing short of ubiquitous in the cultural fabric of his domain.

A theatre was constructed in the courtyard of the Medici Palace on Via Larga. This performative space is discussed by Vasari in his "Life of Aristotile da Sangallo," and by Francesco Giambullari, who described it in a 1539 letter to Giovanni Bandini.[28] The similarities between the description of the stage design constructed for this occasion and the previously discussed Beccafumi's *View of Pisa* for *L'amor costante* (figure 2.1) are noticeable (to the point that a contemporary model of the theatre, housed in the Palazzo Medici Ricardi, has clearly, though probably incorrectly, incorporated Beccafumi's design). It is quite possible that Aristotile knew Beccafumi's design and may have imitated it – hence the similarity in the descriptions and the ensuing confusion. Despite the visual similarities between the two, Aristotile's design was technologically innovative in its introduction of mechanical contrivances, which included a mobile, shining sun. The 1539 theatrical space is quite germane to our discussion, first because two reputable sources describing the nuptials have survived, and second because the wedding was a paradigmatically festive occasion that embodied a political message. There is little doubt that Cosimo wanted the celebrations to have sufficient pomp and magnitude to reach the Emperor's ears; it seems reasonable, therefore, to think that the play and its set design would present themselves as profitable means to convey a positive message of his political prowess.

For the performance, the courtyard was transformed into an interior space by the raising of a massive tent that encompassed a theatre. The tent's ceiling and walls were decorated with a series of paintings made for the occasion by well-known artists, including Bronzino and Salviati. These paintings glorified Cosimo (on the west wall) and the Medici (on the east wall). Symbols of power were both pervasive and conspicuous: from *stemmi* and *imprese* to forty-eight allegorical figures representing the Tuscan land controlled by Cosimo. The presence of Pisa on stage may have spoken of how this city existed at the will of Florence, and thus of the Duke – though the choice of Pisa as a political gesture does not imply that the stage design itself was at the service of such a political message.

The most detailed account of the wedding comes to us from Giambullari, who was commissioned by Cosimo in a clear political manoeuvre, as his description is addressed to Giovanni Bandini, the Florentine ambassador in the imperial court. Giambullari's account is quite exhaustive. He even explicitly states, "I wish to give you a full and particular account of all the festivities."[29] He begins his narrative with Eleanora leaving from Naples on 11 June 1539, travelling through Pisa and Empoli, eventually arriving in Florence on Sunday, 29 June. Giambullari presents an eloquent and comprehensive description of the adorned and constructed elements that decorated the entry into Florence: from the triumphal arch to the ornamented city gates to an equestrian sculpture made by il Tribolo. He then goes on to chronicle the decorations in the palazzo. With much detail, he dwells on each of the sixteen lunettes in the corridor leading to the first courtyard, after which he continues to describe the many paintings, heraldic symbols, and insignia that decorated the second courtyard. Through this process, Giambullari diligently quotes and describes every inscription he encountered – this priority given to text is not negligible.

The second courtyard is where *Il commodo* would be performed on Wednesday, 9 July, and it is quite apparent that the set was already in place during the banquet on 29 June, since Giambullari mentions its beauty. Interestingly, in his brief mention of the space during this first banquet on the twenty-ninth, Giambullari writes about the *apparato* in relation to the eyes of the spectators (*gli occhi de' suoi spettatori*), and not just in relation to the Duke (despite the use of *periaktoi* and the presence of a special box for Duke Cosimo). Giambullari, so garrulous otherwise, finds himself suddenly without words: "I don't want to say any more about the stage setting for the comedy in order not to take away its beauty with my inappropriate words. Even those who saw it can hardly imagine it."[30]

The following Wednesday, Giambullari tells us, there was another banquet, this time in the first courtyard. After dining, everybody went once again into the second courtyard, where the play *Il commodo* was to be performed. Giambullari relates that there was only one additional element in the space: hanging cupids holding torches that illuminated the tent. Again, he does not write much about the set: "All the guests being seated here and admiring the stage setting, little by little from the eastern side they saw appear in the sky of the stage a Dawn."[31] Once more, Giambullari, otherwise so punctilious in his description of details, is quite unconcerned with the seating arrangements and the scenography. Cosimo and Eleonora sat in a loggia facing the stage, but Giambullari does not connect their position with the perspective view. The perfect alignment of the ruler with the vanishing point seems unlikely – at most, the concern was approximate. When his narrative reaches the commencement of the play, he casually refers the reader to his earlier account of the space, though this report bypassed the stage altogether, solely mentioning how the *apparato* was enjoyed by the audience.

In contrast to Giambullari, who is silent on the subject, Vasari's, in his description of the wedding, praises the stage's perspective and streets, commending the scenographic capacities of Aristotile to present "the most varied types of windows and doors," and many "inventive and capricious" palace facades.[32] Much like Giambullari, Vasari does not dwell on the position of the Duke or other seating arrangements, though he describes with detail all the paintings in the hall as well as the insignia and emblems. Given Vasari and Giambullari's descriptions, if the performance granted Cosimo political value, it was not because only he enjoyed the stage, but because he made possible a sumptuous event that everybody in the audience appreciated.

Autonomy

When it comes to the political gravity of artistic content, the difference between emission and reception, and between compliance and assent, are commonly overlooked. Let us take for instance a politically infused pictorial sign we have previously encountered, namely the Teatro all'antica's fresco depicting the Roman emperor Vespasian lowering a laurel wreath (figure 3.7). The message is plain enough, but its intention and the identity of the desired receivers of the message are uncertain. Spectators in the lower sections of the theatre had marginal visual access to this fresco, and even if they saw it, they were not required to earnestly approve its message. Many may not have known Emperor Vespasian's identity, much less the details of his civic architectural program.

And even if we were to imagine those viewers as passive receptors, the theatre remains an enclosed, private locale that limits spatial access: this is a small audience whose understanding of the power of their ruler was unlikely to depend on a painted wall. As Lex Hermans writes, despite the use of words such as "popolo" to describe spectators, "the audience of the courtly theatres usually consisted of the princely family and their relatives, courtiers, the local elite, and intellectuals."[33] The image of the Roman emperor probably functioned more as a pompous display for the Duke himself than as a rhetorical device to persuade the citizenry. Furthermore, the frescoes of the Teatro all'antica's back wall, including the painting of Vespasian, reiterated the tradition of depicting *viri illustres*. The presence of such illustrious men was recommended by Vasari not to glorify his contemporary rulers but "to turn the minds of their successors towards excellence and glory."[34]

The Renaissance state machinery had more direct and unambiguous means to convey political messages than the theatre. To make a stark contrast with theatrical performances, violent events such as executions strip the viewer of any choice of non-compliance, even if those occasions could adopt somewhat of a festive tone. It is in this sense that Machiavelli, in *The Prince*, praises Cesare Borgia for executing Remiro de Lorqua and displaying his body in two pieces in the piazza, as such a spectacle "left the people at once satisfied and stupefied."[35] Rituals of legitimization like executions are powerful because they negate the possibility of dialogue.[36]

I would reiterate, given the pervasive fusion of "theatre" and "spectacle," an essential difference: dramatic performances are not coercive. They do not attempt to keep the subject ignorant, and their messages are hardly subliminal. A performance in a courtly theatre is not the most efficient means to communicate a message to the population at large. In the case of the 1539 Medici wedding, the message of Cosimo's political prowess was likely directed towards leaders of other states, particularly the Emperor (who was not even in attendance).[37] Once we take the presence of the spectators into consideration, their valuations, judgments, and opinions cannot be ignored: "what an action means depends upon the moral stance from which it is observed."[38] In the moment that a theatrical performance occurs in the public arena, the possibility of discord and interpretation is created. As Saslow notes, "while Renaissance viewers may not have used the term in our modern pejorative mode, they could still resist propaganda not concordant with everyday reality as '*mere* rhetoric.'"[39]

Dissension about form and content is built into the performative. Certainly the value of *interpretatio* that existed in relation to poetry would have extended to drama, but not to public executions. Theatrical performances invite the viewers to a plural and contingent exegetical activity. Indeed, the production of lavish spectacles may end up creating opposition rather than acceptance. The diaries of the Florentine tailor Bastiano Arditi (1504–79) present us with an exceptional point of view from a non-privileged citizen who exhibited a critical consciousness despite his lack of formal education. Narrating the 1579 visit of Venetian ambassadors, Arditi complains that Duke Francesco I was indifferent to the famine suffered by the Tuscan citizens, meanwhile spending large amounts on entertaining the delegates with bullfighting and horseback games in the square of Santa Croce, and with tournaments in the Palazzo Pitti.[40] It is unlikely that Arditi was a lone dissenting voice. He simply had sufficient letters and resolution to record his thoughts.[41]

Courtly viewers were not necessarily convinced by rhetorical praises to the political leaders, though they may have acted as if they did. Castiglione's position on the subject in *The Courtier* is quite telling. The courtier's idolization of the prince seldom seems sincere. And even when the role of courtier goes beyond that of a "noble flatterer," it still remains shallow.[42] In contrast, the Argumento of Aretino's *La Cortigiana* emphasizes independence of thought when it states, "the fellow who wrote this story has a mind of his own."[43] The comedy, "falser than a chimera" but "truer than honesty," allows the viewers to "witness a small sampling of the courtly ways of men and women."[44] In *La Cortigiana*, which is a humorous response to Castiglione's *Courtier*, the main character Messer Marco is recommended, in order to become a courtier, to learn the arts of flattery and deception along with embracing other deviant and irreligious behaviours.[45] Flattery was, nonetheless, a serious problem throughout early modernity. In *The Prince*, Machiavelli recommends resisting self-deception and creating an environment in which advisors can freely speak their thoughts.[46] In *La Cortigiana*, Master Andrea concludes that, "whenever you hear someone saying anything good of the Roman court, tell him he's not telling the truth."[47] It is important, in any case, not to polarize the attitudes of playwrights and artists into a false dichotomy – either royal apologists or subversive critics.[48]

Cognitive autonomy is not merely an elevated philosophical stance. It is predicated on physiological decisions and even mundane choices. Acts of viewership are continuous acts of shifting attention. Audience members readjust their heads, their eyes, and their bodies. They make judgments, which sometimes become oral, engaging in conversations. The Prologo of Cecchi's *L'assiuolo* requests the audience to be so kind as to listen in silence until the performance is over.[49] Silence was not always granted, nor did it imply compliance or approval. The Prologo concludes that criticisms will not make the troupe angry nor will compliments make them arrogant: "Afterwards, everyone is free to censure or praise as he likes."[50] (And such engagements would only be intensified in public *commedia* performances, to the extent that actors had to compete for the audience's attention.)[51] Many viewers surely felt quite tired by the end of performances, as Giambullari's comment on *Il commodo* suggests: "the whole show being finished, and the fatigue of listening and watching having been chased away with very cool wines and sweetmeats."[52] Surely, many a spectator felt like Isabella d'Este, who found the 1502 performance of Plautus's *Bacchides* long and boring (*longa et fatidiosa*).[53]

Theatre theorists have stressed since the sixteenth century that viewing a play is not a passive activity. Serlio writes that viewing a stage design gives "great pleasure to the eye and satisfaction to the heart."[54] In modern times, authors like Rancière have stressed the notion of viewership as a performative act: "the spectator also acts ... observes, selects, compares, interprets."[55] Notably, there are significant etymological connections between theatre spectatorship and cognitive engagements. The word *theoria,* meaning "contemplation, speculation, a looking at, things looked at," derives from *theorein,* "to consider, speculate, look at," from *theoros,* "spectator."[56]

At a more general level, the issue of active viewership is far from foreign to aesthetic discourse and psychological studies.[57] As Rudolf Arnheim argued, visual perception is an intelligent action that involves simplification, analysis, synthesis, completion, and correction, among other activities. Arnheim's position explicitly harks back to the Renaissance, specifically to Leonardo's criticism of those "mathematicians who say that the eye has no spiritual power."[58] Michelangelo's poetry, in emphasizing the relationship between physical vision and the conceptualization of images within the heart or soul brings attention to human agency:

> The beauty that you see does come from her,
> But it grows when it rises to a better place,
> If through the mortal eyes it reaches the heart.[59]

Indeed, the active qualities of perception are emphasized by classical thinkers who were well-known in the Renaissance: Lucretius wrote on the viewer's capacity to actively direct attention; Cicero used *attentio* and *intentio* to signify mental direction; Augustine developed those concepts into a cognitive language.[60] And Plotinus stated that, "sense perceptions are not affections but activities and judgments concerned with affections."[61]

These theories defending the cognitive capacities of the viewer are at odds with traditional arguments used to defend the instructional value of theatrical performances. In early modern Italy, Horace's notion that poets should aim to profit and delight came to be aligned with Aristotle's *Poetics* in order to postulate theatre as a moral and didactic tool.[62] For example, as the Prologo of Cecchi's *Lo spirito* states, "He comes along to delight you and to be of use to you" (*per dileuttare, e per fare utile*).[63] Yet, as Gay McAuley points out, these didactic tropes are not straightforward: Aristotle's claims regarding the effects of tragedy are speculative, being more concerned with what it was hoped would happen than with what actually happened; and Horace's moral argument in defence of theatre was deployed by early modern authors not to reveal moral purposes but rather to protect theatre from its critics.[64] The need to defend theatrical performances would only intensify in post-Tridentine Italy, as is notably demonstrated in early seventeenth-century printed prefaces by authors like Flaminio Scala and Giovan Battista Andreini.[65] Konrad Eisenbichler discourages interpretations that assume the pedagogical goals of plays.[66] The less erudite viewers had "little opportunity to parse the actors' speeches in search of political theories, classical allusions, or learned borrowings."[67] Neither Giambullari's emphasis on the "fatigue of listening and watching," nor his clarification that wine helped with the weariness caused by the performance leads us to imagine that the spectators were carefully synthesizing scattered references.

Castelvetro in 1570 dispensed with ethical motivations to argue that the end of tragedy should be pleasure and not utility:

> Those who hold that poetry was invented chiefly for the sake of giving benefit, or to give benefit and delight together, should beware of opposing the authority of Aristotle, who here and elsewhere does not seem to assign any other end than delight.[68]

Castelvetro contended that a stage might be a dangerous locus for political expression. On the one hand, he writes, those who love liberty would not wish to see examples of individuals taking control over a government; on the other, kings and princes would not want to present ideas of political innovation and change in government. Moreover, because kings know that the lower classes enjoy observing the misfortunes of the elites, rulers should avoid producing tragedies in public. Comedies are better suited for republican states. Castelvetro's position thus dismisses political content precisely because the viewers are not passive entities; they may not parse the actors' speeches for subtleties, but they will interpret the plot of the play in relation to their own desires. In fact, the extrapolation of stage action to real life caused the need for explicit announcements. As Di Maria states, "it was not uncommon for spectators to receive assurances that they were watching atrocities perpetrated long ago and far away."[69]

Di Maria has shown the tenuousness, as he puts it, of two commonly accepted notions: that dramatists as courtiers were invested in the political system under which they wrote; and that princely commissions and dedications imply that authors reflected their patrons' ideology.[70] Even if the patrons may have requested a literary piece, their contribution was not ideological: "the poet determined the type of plot and how to dramatize it."[71] Artists themselves continuously defended their freedom and took pride in their genius.

The Wonders of Movement

Scenographic movement and mutability were means both to exhibit artistic innovation and to enable nobles to entertain large audiences with wonderful events. Despite the apparent stability that we may encounter in theatrical drawings, the actual performances of the sixteenth century experienced intermittent disruptions of action and space in the form of *intermedi.* These entertainments between the acts of a play began as music and dance and later evolved into a full play within a play.[72] Published Renaissance dramas seldom mention *intermedi,* but their popularity was undeniable. As Nino Pirrotta notes, "before long the spectators began to be more interested in the [*intermedi*] than in the plays they accompanied."[73] The program and scenography of the *intermedi* became increasingly convoluted throughout the sixteenth century, challenging the presumed primacy of Aristotelian unity and complicating the audience's understanding of performances. As the *intermedi* became increasingly popular, not only were they moved onstage, but designers also began creating separate scenographic apparatuses for these performances. As a result, the design of the set continuously changed its appearance throughout the evening.

Intermedi had been fashionable since the late fifteenth century when offstage musical intervals were featured during Leonardo's Milan performances. In the sixteenth century, the 1508 production of *La Cassaria* incorporated a *moresca* with performers acting as drunken cooks beating on cooking pots. And both the 1513 production of *La Calandria* and the 1515 Venetian production of Plautus's *Miles gloriosus* included songs, pantomimes, floats, and improvised dialogues between the acts.[74] In his *Secondo libro dell'architettura*, Serlio boasts of a theatre he constructed in Vicenza where multiple *intermedi* featured floats, elephants, and dances.[75] *Intermedi* with movable sets have a long history in Florentine performances. *Periaktoi* were prominently featured in Aristotile's design for the 1539 Medici wedding, and were re-introduced by Lanci in 1569. But the best-known examples of *intermedi* are Bernardo Buontalenti's scenographic works of 1586 and 1589.

The 1589 nuptials of Grand Duke Ferdinando I de' Medici to Christine de Lorraine was a portentous event in which the capacities of Florence's artists were put to the test to create a sumptuous spectacle, both public and private, that was meant to broadcast the political and cultural triumph of Florence and its new Medici ruler. Ferdinando ascended to the ducal seat in 1587 after the death of his brother Francesco I and quickly reversed the political positioning his sibling had established – realigning Tuscany away from a pro-Habsburg and pro-Spain position to a pro-Valois stand. This alignment manifested itself in Ferdinando's demands that Spanish governors be relieved of their posts in Tuscany and that debts owed to the Medici bank be paid promptly. Ferdinando rejected offers to marry an Austrian archduchess or a Braganza princess,[76] instead becoming betrothed to Christine de Lorraine, daughter of Charles III, Duke of Lorraine, and Claude de Valois, and granddaughter of Catherine de' Medici.

Ferdinando had always been interested in art and clearly understood the power of symbols. Given the pomp afforded to previous Medici weddings, it is no surprise that the new duke sought to create a lasting image of his political prowess and the power of the Medici lineage. The wedding celebrations included multiple events, many of which had clear political and martial connotations, such as Christine's triumphal entry and the staging of a naval battle in the courtyard of the Palazzo Pitti. As James Saslow's seminal study on the wedding has shown, the theatrical production sought to glorify the new couple and to demonstrate Ferdinando's aesthetic refinement, technological control, and acute awareness of the complexity of sociopolitical economy. [77]

The locale of the wedding's theatrical performances was the Medici Theatre, designed three years prior by Bernardo Buontalenti, who also renovated the space for the Medici nuptials. Buontalenti was responsible for the *intermedi* scenography as well as the coordination of the many artists and craftsmen involved in the project. The six *intermedi*, performed between acts, combined music, dance, costumes, and scenography and developed a program that glorified the ruling couple and the power of (musical) harmony – in turn reflecting a Neoplatonic vision of the ordered cosmos that conceptualized Medici rule as an origin of technological and social organization.[78] Lavish in ornamentation and detail, the *intermedi* incorporated complex sets and technical effects. Even a brief description of these *intermedi* attests to their programmatic complexity: a heavenly harmony of the spheres, surrounded by clouds; a contest between Muses and Pierides enclosed within a lush, courtly garden; Apollo descending to combat a fire-breathing dragon; Lucifer erupting from the flames of hell, expanding his bat-like wings amidst other infernal creatures; Amphitrite emerging from the waters on a decorated shell, singing amidst Tritons and nymphs; and to conclude, a heavenly apotheosis, radiant and vibrant, in which Apollo and Bacchus bequeath harmony and rhythm to humankind. The 1589 performance, Povoledo argues, materialized the threshold of Baroque scenography, as "the rational unity of the Renaissance was broken, the logical rules that defined space and unity of action were abandoned ... Imagination prevailed over logic."[79] But the Cinquecento stage was always concerned with experimentation and, as we have seen, unity and visual coherence were never truly regulatory values.

The disruptive qualities of the *intermedi* had been apparent since Leonardo's Milan performances, when the *intermedio* was confused with the main play,[80] but their popularity across the sixteenth century shows the welcomed dynamic instability of the period stage. Indeed, the tendency of *intermedi* to become increasingly complex did not aid clear communication: Giussepe Pavoni's account of the 1589 Medici wedding, for example, incorporates erroneous interpretations of the performed events and even critical remarks.[81] Politicized as Cinquecento theatrical performances were, cognitive autonomy was never seized from the viewer.

Utopian Tropes

It has become common practice to interpret early modern Italian theatrical spaces as a utopian locale where pictorial cityscapes, social conditioning, symbolic architecture, and urban plans converge in order to visually reinforce an authoritarian political apparatus. At a general level, the Italian Renaissance has been considered a fertile ground for utopian visions and ideal projects. Within the Cinquecento, the utopian comes to us as a literary genre as well as a pictorial and architectural mode. Examples of the former are not abundant: Anton Francesco Doni's *I mondi* (1552),

Francesco Patrizi's *Lacittà felice* (1553) and Lodovico Agostini's *La repubblica imaginaria* (written between 1585 and 1590, but not published until the twentieth century). This contrasts with what seems to be a very prolific visual mode of utopian and ideal representation – an abundance that is in turn possible through the scholarly act of affixing scenographic models, paintings, architectural treatises, and city plans (both real and imagined) under the binding mode of the "utopian-ideal." A recent iteration of this tendency to amalgamate ideal and utopian depictions is found in Rowe and Koetter, who argue that Castiglione's image of the courtier was not unlike the ideal city: allowing itself to be observed and enjoyed for its own sake, though, at the same time, producing real results.[82] In this explanation, the combination of utopian visions (from Filarete to Castiglione; from Machiavelli to Moore) come to be illustrated by Serlio's comic stage (figure 2.7), where the medieval world becomes rational, representing the modern project of urban planning. Though sometimes not overtly political, these visions articulate a decorous representation of the centralized state, linking them to Machiavelli (whose patent republican commitment, it should be noted, has vanished in this interpretation).[83] In the juxtaposition of scenographic streets in theatrical productions to urban planning, Serlio and Palladio come to be synthesized with the Rome of Sixtus V, a space where the straightened avenues are seen to move from means of communication to "instruments of urban control and regularization."[84] Using Serlio and the Teatro Olimpico as paradigms of linear perspective, Anthony Vidler states that, "thus the street, subject to perspective representation in the ideal theater, was transformed by this technique and shaped by it."[85] Vidler continues his analysis by arguing that the tragic scene became both an instrument of rational order and a theatre of utopia.[86]

In these interpretations, the theatrical is postulated as a rhetorical device dictating an ideal, utopian existence that correlates to an apparatus of political and social inscription. And this expression is apparently so natural and sincere that a hermeneutic synthesis of artworks as diverse as the Baltimore panel, the Teatro Olimpico, Serlio's urban stages, and imagined cities like Filarete's and constructed ones like Sabbioneta is incontrovertible. Yet in confronting the alluring idea of "utopia," one encounters a word "whose definitional capabilities have been completely devoured by its connotative properties."[87] As Françoise Choay elucidates, the passage of the word "utopia" into everyday language, along with its increased polysemy, makes impossible its adoption and usage in rigorous discourse. An ever-unfolding umbrella term, "utopia" refers to a multiplicity of notions: good government, idealizations of existing societies, designs of ideal cities, glorifications of a primitive golden age, secret societies, world empires/universal world peace, theocratic millennial kingdoms, and utopias proper (ideal imaginary societies described in their entirety as if currently functioning).[88] Moreover, utopias are not prescriptive. They require the active participation of the viewer or the reader – an exercise that itself destabilizes the meaning of a given utopian vision, as each observer valuates and interprets the imagined projects.[89]

Scholarship has found little space for Cornaro's theatre in these juxtapositions, though one could argue that the Bacino theatre was far more utopian than any stage design or painting: it was a conceptual exercise; it had denunciatory connotations; it brought forth a lost and idyllic classical age; it stressed the value of art and aesthetic pleasure; and it was actually an island (utopias are, after all, distant lands). Nonetheless, Cornaro's theatre lacks a crucial component in the scholarly narrative of utopian Renaissance theatres, for it is completely unconcerned with linear perspective and the scenographic representation of cities. The linear looms out and above this mode of explanation, at once empowering and criticizing linear perspective as a form that dictates a unified space, incising urban sites. Clearing the unknown, it cuts and hollows the medieval urban boscage to create wide-open, rational avenues. This development reveals a system of control and surveillance where "the tyranny of the geometrical does not allow for dirt, irregularity, or ultimately life."[90]

But one must be careful in ascribing ideal and utopian notions to linear perspective or seemingly representational depictions of the city. The introduction of pictorial tools to Italian Renaissance theatres brought with it visual and somatic tensions between the space of the viewers and that of the actors, in addition to tensions between the fictive space of the stage and the urban painted background. Fabio Finotti aptly describes the introduction of linear perspective into the Italian theatre as labyrinthine and anamorphic.[91] Studying the text of Ariosto's *La Cassaria*, perhaps the first comedy to incorporate linear perspective, Finotti brings attention to Volpino's monologue, which incorporates a series of enacted spatial events that are infused with a sense of anxiety:

> he [Erofilo], intent on watching out for the missing girl, goes here and there, all about the city ... I could probably defend myself from this incident, if only I had the space in which to reflect a little ... On the one hand, I suspect that the procurer may run off with the safe tonight, and

> on the other hand, I fear that the old master might suddenly appear and discover me, overwhelming me before I even have time to purchase a noose … But what lamp is this that goes in there?[92]

Finotti's interpretation brings attention to the last line, stressing the menacing image of the lamp's light approaching in the darkness as "a real and uncontrollable space opens up, looming behind them like an imminent threat."[93]

It is true: written sources from the fourteenth and fifteenth centuries correlate the transformation of urban spaces to moral and political organizational principles. Nicholas V, on his deathbed, stated that architecture reinforces faith and fosters piety.[94] And, as Tafuri posits, architecture was seen to have a political dimension: in Alberti, architecture has civilizing capacities, and writers like Francesco Patrizi argued that the form of the city (*forma urbis*) is the fruit of good government.[95] That there are correlations between those ideas and nineteenth-century urban theories and practices is undeniable, and there may be justification for the reverse projection of those modern theories into Renaissance urban projects.[96] In this interpretation, the utopian becomes possible because linear perspective has created a practice of emptying – a physical removal of the urban space by tearing out its emergent, spontaneous structure. Thus, the dark, medieval spaces are characterized as marginalized obscuring forces; they do not have a place in the utopian because the utopian compels a spatial discourse based on clarity.

And despite the common image of the medieval town as irregular and "spontaneous," hundreds of towns were built anew in the Middle Ages "according to a pre-conceived, well-ordered ground plan, which means that they do not have the narrow and twisting streets and the irregular labyrinthine ground plan."[97] We may consider Alberti's inclusion of both winding and straight streets in urban spaces, which has been described as a mingling of "medieval and renaissance ideas."[98] But when Alberti states that the curvature of the streets serves two purposes, creating more pleasing facades and increasing defensive advantages in street battles, he is not merely perpetuating an anachronistic notion, he is also emphasizing key values of Italian Renaissance urban architecture.[99] Later on, when Palladio's designs took into consideration the physical place, including the curvature of the streets in Vicenza and visual relations of the location where the buildings would be constructed, the importance of actual location versus imaginary and ideal places would continue to be fundamental to the architectural ideas of the Renaissance.[100]

The reason for curved streets is both aesthetic and pragmatic, and the curvature of streets need not be understood as the spirited resistance of medieval values. Orazio Scarabelli's engraving shows the only surviving view of Buontalenti's 1589 stage perspectives, which were used for *La pellegrina* and other plays (figure 4.3). The novelty of this design is the presence of three curved receding streets.[101] Buontalenti's impulse towards curvature is a movement towards the presentation of urban spaces as commonly experienced. It is significant that this novelty takes place within the context of the Medici wedding, one of those events where stage design and perfect alignment to the vanishing point seem so crucial. If strict linearity, geometric structure, opened avenues, control over the irregularities of nature, and the connection between prince and vanishing point were all so central, why are they abandoned here, at the climax of Italian Renaissance stage design and propaganda? It is true that the depiction of the urban space is carefully arranged, creating an ennobled and picturesque view. This is noticeable if one compares it with Serlio's comic stage (figure 2.7). Buontalenti's design has decisively left medieval architecture behind. The 1589 design incorporates round arches, windows with pediments, and classical sculpture. It is a comic view for a comedy, and it thus represents an urban space, but, like Riccio's design for *L'Ortensio*, it depicts buildings associated with higher classes.

Those noble viewers would have admired the curvature of Buontalenti's streets and certainly would not have thought of the design as having a medieval style. We can compare the design for *La pellegrina* with Taddeo Landini's fifth entry arch, created for the 1589 wedding celebrations, in this case the 30 April entry in to Florence (figure 4.4). In both cases, sculptures in niches frame a street that curves into the distance. It is the innovation of curvature and irregularity, not linear perspective, that created an imposing spectacle, in turn demonstrating the magnificence of the princely patron.

The assumption is that the constructions by Serlio and Palladio manifest a linear form of utopian mode that functions as an apparatus of constriction. This notion implies a specific position regarding the function of theatrical spaces as well as the function of line and the function of the utopian as genre. As previously mentioned, within the literary realm, the genre of utopia has its two main Cinquecento exponents in Anton Francesco Doni and Franciscus Patricius. Both authors invented distant and imaginary civilizations, but their worlds were conceived after the military invasions of the late fifteenth and sixteenth centuries, which left a heavy burden begetting neither optimism nor political

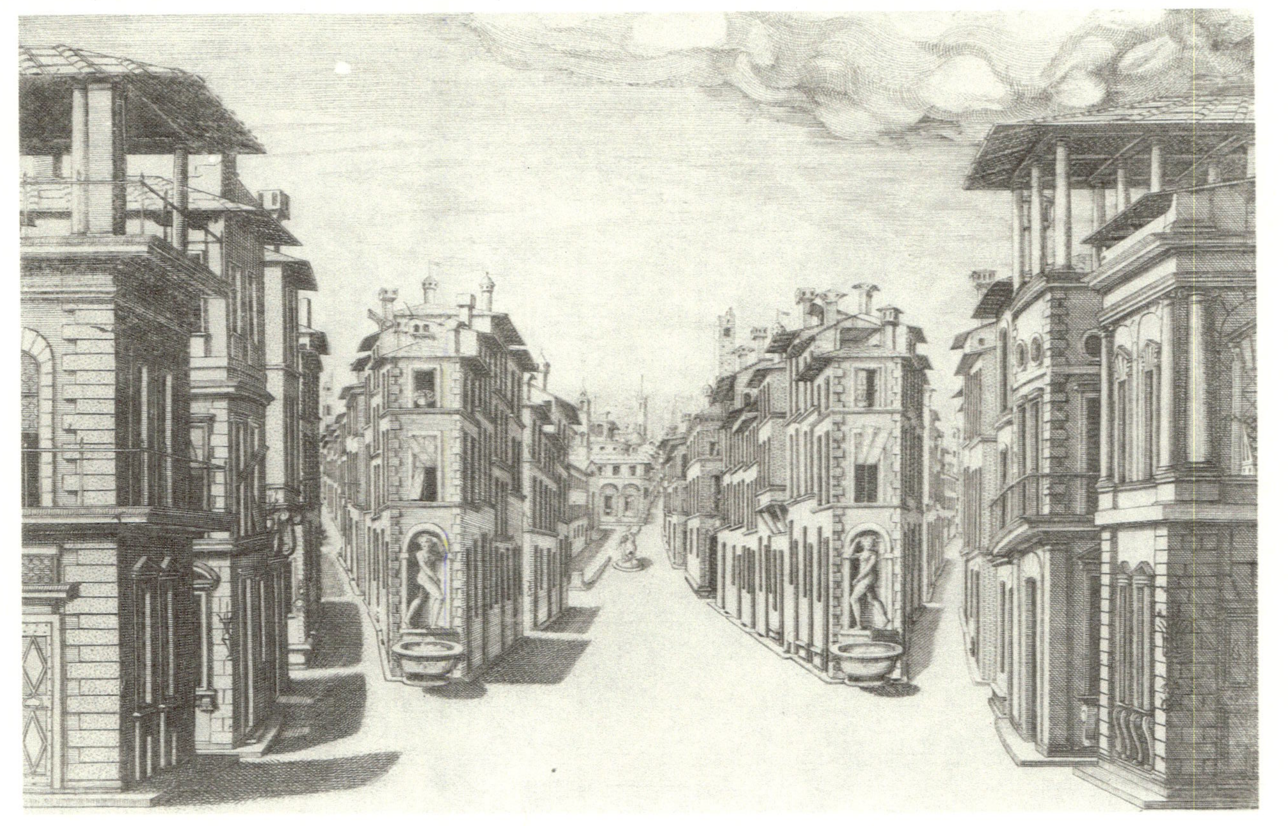

4.3 Orazio Scarabelli engraving of Buontalenti 1589 stage perspective for *La pellegrina*. New York, Metropolitan Museum of Art.

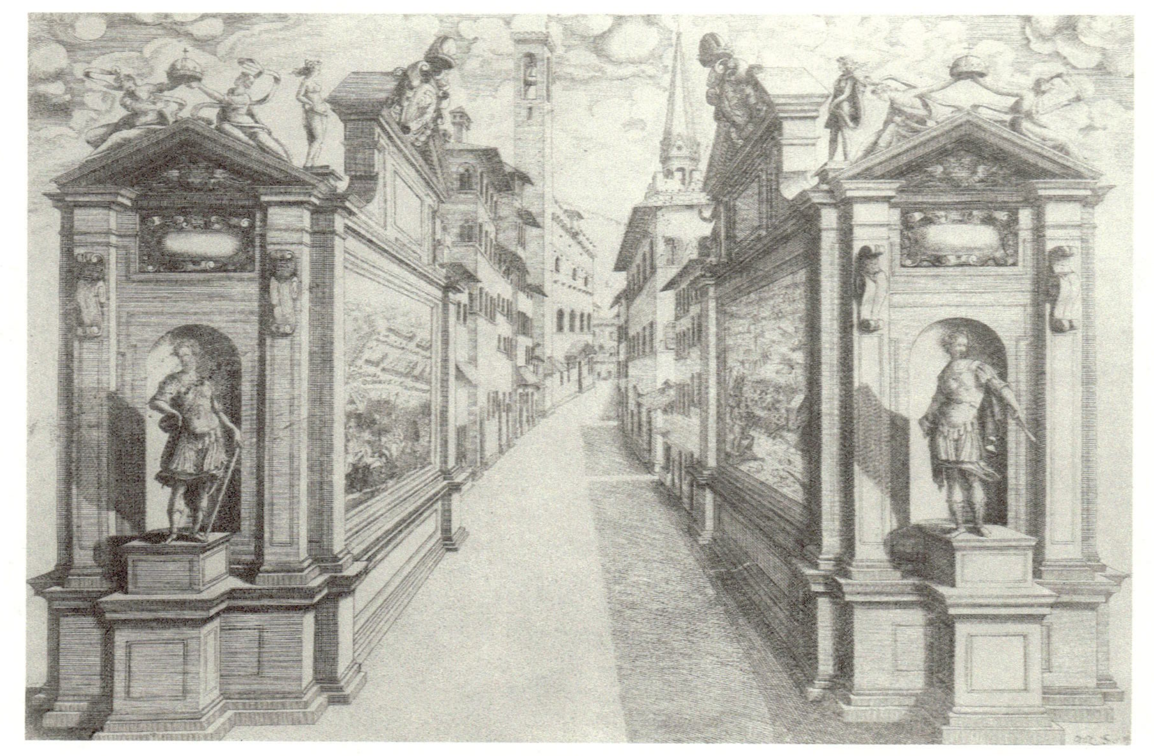

4.4 Orazio Scarabelli, engraving showing Taddeio Landini's fifth arch for the Medici entry of 1589. New York, Metropolitan Museum of Art.

liberty.[102] Patricius's *La città felice* (1553) introduces a rigid government where citizens are discouraged by the author from revolting against unjust rulers, while Doni's "New World" from the 1552 book *I mondi* (the plural in the title being quite relevant) incorporates a world full of disorientation, disillusionment, and pessimism.[103] These qualities, which set Cinquecento "utopias" apart from the narratives of untroubled regions where life is easy and cities embody structural clarity, are therefore divergent from the "good place" a utopia often is assumed to be.[104] Whenever the real entered the artistic imagination, issues of labour, war, internal rebellion, and slavery became pervasive in these so-called utopias.[105] As it has been pointed out, "the radial plan, with its regular geometry, a fantasy of humanistic cosmology, was transformed into a military machine."[106]

We do not encounter the memory of war, internal conflict, and siege in Cinquecento stage designs, but this presence often exists in the plays' texts. Many common theatrical plot devices in the sixteenth century, such as family members reuniting after many years, were explicitly predicated on wars, raids, and sacks.[107] This is the case of the prologue of Grazzini's *Il Frate*, which laconically states, "All you need to know is that the following story actually took place during the siege of Florence."[108]

The (c. 1530) play *The Moscheta*, written by Angelo Beolco (known as Ruzante), conveys a bleak world devastated by war, poverty, unjust laws, and social stagnation, where the hope for a parallel, utopian reality remains impossible.[109] And his *Parlamento* addresses the hardships alienation resulting and from the Wars of Cambrai. Ruzante's world was one of political tensions, intensified by Venice's conquest of the terra firma, including the submission of his native Padua. It has been argued that his political sympathies resonated with his Padovan country men, and that his plays were not performed in Venice after 1527 because Ruzante expressed anti-Venetian sentiments.[110]

The social environment in the Italy of the fifteenth and sixteenth centuries was not one of peace and tranquility – Leibniz's conceptualization of "the best of all possible worlds" is distant and foreign to the Renaissance. In his letter describing the first performance of *La Calandria*, Castiglione explicitly refers to the period's military turmoil: "the part about the wars was alas too true, to out sorrow."[111] "Ideal" means to do the best with imperfect circumstances. As Guicciardini's famous advice states, it is not the utopian or the ideal that is critical, but the capacity to face the realities of human existence:

> Good fortune is often the worst enemy of men, since it makes them wicked, irresponsible, and insolent; a man's superior quality is the capacity to resist good fortune rather than adversity.[112]

Machiavelli sent a song and four intermezzi to Guicciardini, then governor of Romagna, for a production of *The Mandrake* that was planned for Faenza in 1526. The *canzone* begins the play by introducing a core level of reality:

> Since life is brief,
> and many are the pains
> we all endure
> as we live and struggle,
> as we go along, pursuing our fancies,
> while the passing years are swallowed up –
> anyone who shuns pleasure,
> to live instead with pain and anguish,
> does not know the world's deceits,
> or the evils and the strange chances
> by which each mortal is all but overcome.[113]

The text itself of Machiavelli's *The Mandrake* has been understood to incorporate a critique of the Medici, who had ostracized him from political life. His prologue explicitly states that he wrote the play "to make his unhappy life more agreeable, because he has nowhere else to turn his face." Modern commentators have interpreted the play as a political allegory, seeing the character of Lucrezia, for example, as representing a young and barren Florence, and her impotent husband as Florence's ruler, Piero Soderini.[114] However plausible it is that Machiavelli had these parallels in mind, it is impossible to assess the extent to which audiences were attuned to such political resonances in sixteenth-century Italy. There is no documentary evidence of period political interpretations of the comedy; the play became an immediate success, with performances following in Venice and Rome, along with multiple editions in the sixteenth century.

Beyond artists' individual biographies, it is clear that violent events were certainly traumatic for the Italian consciousness, a trauma that was subsequently incorporated into plays. The memory of warfare coexists with a meta-theatrical analysis in Aretino, who re-worked *La Cortigiana* for the 1534 Venice edition, where Rome appeared in the aftermath of the 1527 Sack.[115] The Prologo of *The Horned Owl* explicitly highlights such upheavals: "And don't anyone think that this comedy originates from the Sack of Rome, or from the Siege of Florence, or because persons became displaced, or the families had to flee."[116] Referencing these events introduced a commentary on the frequent incorporation of tragic episodes in contemporary plays. The mention of the Florentine siege would have brought back many memories to the viewers, as the play was performed in Florence in late February or early March, during the 1550 carnival.[117] Of course, *The Horned Owl* was performed in the Florence of Cosimo I, and it was the siege of Florence that lead to the re-establishment of Medici rule in Florence. This may lead us to think that the staged city blazoned an idealized place where Medici rule made conflict obsolete. And yet the plays performed present not a utopian situation, but what has been called "a rather disquieting new order."[118]

Coda: The Line in Play

As the linear buttresses an apparatus of social inscription, the theatrical becomes a rhetorical sociopolitical expression: we have explored how these modes of explanation severely limit art-historical discourses. The question of homonymy arises. A city that appears in a painting is not the same as a city that appears in an architectural treatise. A city that appears in an urban proposal is not the same as a city that appears in a theatrical event. Even within those categories, we cannot assume a unified and codified value or meaning, much less one as inherently complex as the utopian.

Neither can it be assumed that seeming visual reiterations of urban spaces retain a given political or social signified, or that each reconceptualization of staged cities brought forth the values buttressing a previous performance. The natural art-historical tendency to understand each individual Renaissance artists in terms of their personal views, opinions, character, and interests dissipates when they enter the theatrical stage. Perhaps it is the old tension between art and design, or the impossibility of delimiting artistic intention in inherently plural theatrical productions – in either case, theatrical spaces occupy a liminal (and often uncomfortable) space between truth and fiction, intent and reception, theory and practice. Theatrical spaces resist reductive frameworks of interpretation.

The theatrical space is a constructed reality where materials and logistics establish their own potentialities and circumstances, and where a multiplicity of values come in contact, sometimes reinforcing each other, sometimes creating irreconcilable tensions. It has been argued that "the building of the streets inside the theater brought the space of the real into the domain of the ideal."[119] However, these positions remain possible only through the diverting use of metaphoric language that conceals more than it uncovers. A goal of the present study has been to set aside the multiple metaphorical, and at times anachronistic, reconceptualizations of the theatre in order to bring forth the memory of theatrical spaces as built environments that were, more often than not, ephemeral constructions made for audiences to enjoy in a dramatic, celebratory setting.

In *On Painting*, Alberti requested his readers to engage with the material as artists, not mathematicians. Given the amount of ink that has been expended on perspective and its potential meanings and significance, Alberti's treatise seems exceptionally terse and pragmatic. The difficulties of grappling with a stage design as a scenographic construction for a play quickly become academic impossibilities as theology, political representation, and the subjugation of the natural world in theoretical and concrete terms become inexorably affixed to perspectival constructions.

The line remains a threat that cuts open the natural sphere in order to create conditions favourable to the dream of the Enlightenment, a dream of spatial control. At the same time, a line is also a point of departure; a signifier of a change of direction that leads to heterogeneous spatialities. Let us reiterate de Certeau's observation: "the surface of this order is everywhere punched and torn open by ellipses, drifts, and leaks of meaning: it is a sieve-order."[120]

In these pages, I have proposed an alternative way to engage with the theatrical spaces of the sixteenth century, one in which we encounter the tendency to display the irregular, to expose it, rather than destroying it. Pondering the most profound, learned, and solemn meanings of theatrical spaces, whether it be on account of their artistic qualities or their political implications, we should keep in mind that there is something about theatre design that resists the severity of order: a playful experimentation that opens the possibility for acts of creation that never expected to be fully judged against sombre standards. In the intrinsic ephemerality of these theatrical productions, we encounter a positive value that made possible a polysemic reality where the intellectual met the superficial and the frivolous met the critical. As we contemplate, cherish, study, and wonder at the theatrical developments that took place in early modern Italy, we may remember that the prologue of

Aretino's *La Cortigiana* invites us to take our own judgments and verdicts with a grain of salt:

> HISTRION I: Okay, okay, so I made a mistake. No need to crucify me! It's only a play!
>
> HISTRION II: Yeah, you're right. It wouldn't be fair or proper to crucify a person over something as trivial as that.[121]

Notes

Introduction: Striking the Stage

1 "Istrione del prologo: *Sta molto ben, poich'io ho 'l torto. Oh corpo di me, part'egli onesto ch'a petizione d'una comedia io abbi ad essere crucifisso?* / Istrione dell'argomento: *Messer no che non mi pare né giusto né onesto; né si crucifiggono cosí per poco le persone.*" English translation in Aretino, *Cortigiana*, 51.

2 Benjamin, "Eduard Fuchs, Collector and Historian," 262. Rebecca Zorach's remarks also come to mind: "I work with constellations of related images, learned and popular, that 'think'… Sometimes this thinking can be documented in textual evidence, and sometimes it can't; images must then constitute their own form of evidence." *The Passionate Triangle*, 11.

3 This situation has not gone unnoticed, as shown in Di Maria, *The Italian Tragedy in the Renaissance*, 129.

4 This interpretative emphasis uses painting as a means to explain scenographic developments while also showing the various ways in which painters incorporated theatrical conventions such as Serlio's Vitruvian stages. Though interesting connections have been found, the connection scenography-painting neglects theatrical experiences as a whole, and, as a result, the visual experience (and artistic production) of theatres is reduced to "painting plus architecture." See Kernodle's *From Art to Theatre*; Kurt Badt, "Raphael's 'Incendio del Borgo'"; Rosand, "Theater and Structure in the Art of Paolo Veronese"; Howe, "Architecture in Vasari's 'Massacre of the Huguenots'"; Gould, "Sebastiano Serlio and Venetian Painting"; Gorse, "A Classical Stage for the Old Nobility: The Strada Nuova and Sixteenth-Century Genoa"; van Eck and Bussels, "The Visual Arts and the Theatre in Early Modern Europe."

5 That scenographic developments are noted in books exploring linear perspective shows the importance of theatrical productions for the development of the technique and its applicability beyond painting. Yet braketing out much of the theatrical experience (auditorium, audience, text), these interpretations often create an essentialist view where linear perspective is detached from how it was visually encountered in early modern theatres – a framework that in turn idealizes the goals and effects of linear perspective. See Kemp, *The Science of Art*; Damisch, *The Origin of Perspective*; Elkins, *The Poetics of Perspective*; Summers, *Real Spaces*; Belting, *Florence and Baghdad*.

6 Shearman, *Only Connect … Art and the Spectator in the Italian Renaissance*, 96–7.

7 Fried, *Absorption and Theatricality: Painting & Beholder in the Age of Diderot*. Fried's notion of theatricality, though rhetorically effective, further dissolves the already polysemic term "theatrical."

8 The notion that theatre and urban fabric become epistemologically unified – that the saying "the whole world's a stage" is not a rhetorical catchphrase but that it demonstrates a conceptual fusion in early modern consciousness – has been reiterated by the proposal that "'Stage' and 'street' are interchangeable ideas in the Renaissance"; Anne Marie Borys, "Through the Lens," 97–112. Certainly, the coalescing of "stage" and "street" was popular and effective; even today, the sentence "the whole world's a stage" invokes a metaphoric truth about the performative aspects involved in social exchange as well as about how the theatre explores life. Yet an effective metaphor (like any type of analogy) is successful precisely because one perceives the identity of the compared things as distinct.

9 McKinney and Butterworth, *The Cambridge Introduction to Scenography*, 3. These interpretations are nowadays common in performance studies – though perhaps they have not yet been fully integrated to early modern practices.

10 Howard, *What Is Scenography?*, xiii–xvi.

11 Povoledo, "Origins and Aspects of Italian Scenography," 311.

12 Sergardi, *Lingua scenica e terminologia teatrale nel Cinquecento*, 27; Ludovico Zorzi, Il teatro e la città, 95; Thomas A. Pallen, *Vasari on Theatre*, 3.

13 "Let me begin by turning to what is normally claimed to be the dominant, even totally hegemonic, visual mode of the modern era, that which we can identify with Renaissance notions of perspective in the visual arts and Cartesian ideas of subjective rationality in philosophy. For convenience, it can be called Cartesian perspectivalism"; Martin Jay, "Scopic Regimes of Modernity," 4. Jay's quotation here serves as an example of what is an

established synthesis of linear perspective and Cartesian philosophy in the scholarship, and which harkens back to Erwin Panofsky's interpretation of perspective in his seminal *Perspective and Symbolic Form*. On this topic see also the discussion in Elkins, *The Poetics of Perspective*, 23–4. Jay's emphasis on perspective as a "hegemonic visual mode" reiterates a political interpretation in which perspective emerges as a system of control. Merleau-Ponty, for example, wrote "Perspective is much more than a secret technique for imitating a reality ... It is the invention of a world dominated and possessed through and through." Maurice Merleau-Ponty, "Indirect Language and the Voices of Silence," 251. Merleau-Ponty's approach to perspective would remain palpable in postmodern discourses.

14 Tafuri, *Interpreting the Renaissance*, xxix.

15 Aronson, "Postmodern Design," especially 13.

16 Panofsky, *Perspective and Symbolic Form*, 28–9.

17 Elkins, *The Poetics of Perspective*, 22–6, 45–6.

18 Baxandall, *Painting and Experience in Fifteenth-Century Italy*, 124–8; John White, *The Birth and Rebirth of Pictorial Space*, 194.

19 Kernodle, *From Art to Theatre*, 176–8.

20 Nicoll, *The Development of the Theatre*, 72.

21 In recent years, Anne Marie Borys has restated this notion regarding Renaissance scenography: "The goal now was to make illusory space seem real. Perspective provided the primary means to do so": Borys, "Through the Lens," 100. See also, Foster, "Stagecraft as Statecraft."

22 Rosand, "Theater and Structure in the Art of Paolo Veronese," 220. See also Womack, "The Comical Scene."

23 Didi-Huberman, *Confronting Images*, 8. On this topic see also Nagel, *The Controversy of Renaissance Art*, 13–29

24 Finotti, "Perspective and Stage Design, Fiction and Reality in the Italian Renaissance Theater of the Fifteenth Century," 39.

25 Nagel, *The Controversy of Renaissance Art*, 17. A sophisticated awareness that, as Nagel notes, emerged "long before Bertold Brecht elaborated the logic of the *Verfremdungseffekt*."

26 Mitchell, *Iconology*, 39.

27 de Certeau, *The Practice of Everyday Life*, 107.

1 Magic and Mimesis: *La Calandria* and the Idea of Rome

1 "amendua sono oggi in Roma ed amendua or qui comparir li vedrete. Né crediate però che, per negromanzia, sí presto da Roma venghino qui; per ciò che la terra che vedete qui è Roma. La quale giá esser soleva sí ampia, sí spaziosa, sí grande che, trionfando, molte città e paesi e fiumi largamente

in se stessa riceveva; ed ora è sí piccola diventata che, come vedete, agiatamente cape nella città vostra." Argumento in Bernardo Dovizi da Bibbiena, *La Calandria*, author's translation. For an English translation of the play see Beecher, ed., *Renaissance Comedy*, 21–100. For the original Italian see "La Calandria" in Sanesi, ed., *Commedia del Cinquecento*, 9. See also Bibbiena, *La Calandria*, ed. Fossati, 22.

2 Aristotle, *Poetics*, 1450b27.

3 Horace, *Ars poetica*, 64, lines 189–90; Shironi, "The Reception of Ancient Drama in Renaissance Italy."

4 We will later address in depth the Teatro Olimpico, one of the best-studied Renaissance theatrical locales. On this theatre and its import see Magagnato, "The Genesis of the Teatro Olimpico" See also, Andreas Beyer, *Andrea Palladio: Triumpharchitektur für eine humanistische Gesellschaft*; Giangiorgio Zorzi, "Le prospettive del Teatro Olimpico di Vicenza nei disegni degli 'Uffizi' di Firenze e nei documenti dell'Ambrosiana' di Milano"; Oosting, "The Teatro Olimpico Design Sources." For Buontalenti see James Saslow, *The Medici Wedding of* 1589.

5 Peruzzi's prominent position in the history of theatrical design was established within the sixteenth century by Vasari, and the design for *La Calandria* was rather influential; nonetheless, it is important not to get carried away and ascribe determinist causality to artistic lineages, especially given the growing interest in the theatre as a medium within the sixteenth century and the many artists who participated in theatrical productions (all of whom brought with them the artistic values of the Italian Renaissance). Kernodle, *From Art to Theatre*, 177. See also Macgowan and Melnitz, *The Living Stage*, 79–80; Ludovico Zorzi, Il teatro e la città, 92–3; Tydeman, *The Theatre in the Middle Ages*; Pallen, *Vasari on Theatre*; Fleming, "Presenting the Spectators as the Show; Cairns, "Theatre as Festival."

6 Lodovico Castelvetro, *Poetica d'Aristotele vulgarizzata e sposta per L. C. riveduta et ammendata secondo l'originale, e la mente dell'autore* (Vienna: Gaspar Stainhofer, 1570; second edition Basel: Pietro de Sedabonis, 1576). Reprinted as *Poetica d'Aristotele vulgarizzata e sposta*, ed. Werther Romani (Bari: Laterza, 1978–9), 2 vols. For an abridged English translation see Lodovico Castelvetro, *On the Art of Poetry*. See also Weinberg, *A History of Literary Criticism in the Italian Renaissance*, vol. I, 366–563. Stephen Halliwell writes on Castelvetro's deviation from Aristotle: "… the all too familiar doctrine of the Three Unities, the classic case of a literary principle speciously foisted upon the *Poetics* (and therefore a pointed reminder of how little the treatise was actually read, as opposed to being simply

appealed to, even in the most self-consciously neo-classical circles)": *Aristotle's Poetics*, 287.

7 On the topic of the correspondence between drawing and built set see, e.g., Neiiendam, "'Il portico' and 'la bottega' on the Early Italian Perspective Stage," especially 38–40; Nicoll, *The Development of the Theatre*, 72; Evers, *Architekturmodelle der Renaissance*, 51. Though the drawing widely attributed to Peruzzi's project for La Calandria, scholars have raised question regarding its author (Hara, "Capturing eyes and moving souls") and the play for which it was made (Povoledo, "Origins and Aspects of Italian Scenography," 324–6). I here follow the common attribution, though ultimately the more significant elements of my interpretation reflect on Cinquecento stages as cultural phenomena and not on the often slippery particulars of attribution.

8 Blackburn, "Music and Festivities at the Court of Leo X"; Nagler, *A Source Book in Theatrical History*, 72; Andrews, *Scripts and Scenarios*, chapter 2.

9 Paola Poggi, "Architectonica perspectiva: la prospettiva solida de *Le Bacchidi* e la voluta ionica di Baldassarre Peruzzi," in *Baldassarre Peruzzi* 1481–1536, eds. Christoph L. Frommel, Arnauldo Bruschi, Howard Burns, Francesco Paolo Fiore, and Pier Nicola Pagliara (Venice: Marsilio, 2005), 443–55. See also Ault, "Peruzzi and the Perspective Stage."

10 For Genga's design see Pallen, *Vasari and Theatre*, 20–3 and 93–9. See also Pinelli and Rossi, *Genga Architetto*, 107–17; D'Amico, "Drama and the Court in 'La Calandria'"; Donald Beecher, "Introduction to The Calandria by Bernardo Dovizi da Bibbiena," in *Renaissance Comedy: The Italian Masters Volume II*, 23; Ruffini, *Commedia e festa nel Rinascimento. La "Calandria" alla corte di Urbino*; Attolini, *Teatro e spattacolo nel Rinascimento*, 113. For a study of the 1513 performance in relationship to the period's political circumstances see Martinez, "Etruria Triumphant in Rome."

11 Povoledo, "Origins and Aspects of Italian Scenography," 324–6. See also Pallen, *Vasari on Theatre*, 26; Brubaker, *Court and Commedia*, 41.

12 E.g., Badt, "Raphael's 'Incendio del Borgo'"; Rosand, "Theater and Structure in the Art of Paolo Veronese"; Howe, "Architecture in Vasari's 'Massacre of the Huguenots'"; Gould, "Sebastiano Serlio and Venetian Painting"; Gorse, "A Classical Stage for the Old Nobility"; Fleming, "Presenting the Spectators as the Show"; van Eck and Bussels, eds, *Theatricality in Early Modern Art and Architecture*; Johnson, "Jacopo Sansovino, Giacomo Torelli, and the Theatricality of the Piazzetta in Venice"; Ann Huppert, *Becoming an Architect in Renaissance Italy: Art, Science, and the Career of Baldassarre Peruzzi*, 85–109.

13 "Baldassarre fece al tempo di Leone X due scene che furono maravigliose, et apersono la via a coloro che ne hanno poi fatto a' tempi nostril": Vasari, *Le vite de' piu eccellenti pittori, scultori e architettori*, eds. Rosanne Bettarini and Paolo Barocchi, vol. 4, 323.

14 Ricci, "The Art of Scenography"; Neiiendam, "'Il portico' and 'la bottega' on the Early Italian Perspective Stage," 40. Burckhardt argued that the play was produced by Leo X in 1515 for the promotion of his brother Giuliano de' Medici to General of the Church. See Burckhardt, *The Architecture of the Italian Renaissance*, 271. Lotz writes that Peruzzi had previously taken a leading part in the construction of "the wooden 'theatre' on the Capitol in Rome which Leo X erected in 1513 on the occasion of the admission of his nephews Giuliano and Lorenzo de' Medici to the Roman patriciate": Lotz, *Architecture in Italy 1500–1600*, 46. Pallen and Cottino-Jones posit that the theatre was built by Rosselli. See Pallen, *Vasari on Theatre*, 36; and Marga Cottino-Jones, "Rome and the Theatre in the Renaissance," in *Rome in the Renaissance: The City and the Myth*, ed. P. A. Ramsey (Binghamton: State University of New York, 1982), 238.

15 See Pallen, *Vasari on Theatre*, 24. See also Povoledo, "Origins and Aspects of Italian Scenography," 324; Attolini, *Ṭeatro e spettacolo nel Rinascimiento*, 114–15.

16 Nicoll, *The Development of the Theatre*, 73. See also Tydeman, *The Theatre in the Middle Ages*, 238; Pallen, *Vasari on Theatre*, 26; Andrews, "The Renaissance stage," 35. See also Richter, "Recent Studies in Renaissance Scenography," *Renaissace News* 19, no. 4 (1966): 344–58, especially 347; Carlson, *Places of Performance*, 23; Biagi, "La prospettiva, la scenografia, lo spettacolo," 30; Povoledo, "Origins and Aspects of Italian Scenography," 324–6; Di Maria, *The Italian Tragedy in the Renaissance*; 134–6; Tafuri, "Il luogo teatrale dall'umanesimo a oggio," 28.

17 Burckhardt argues that the aim of scene-designers was in no instance "illusion in our present sense but an appearance of festive splendor." *The Architecture of the Italian Renaissance*, 272.

18 Hubert Damisch interprets the drawing as belonging to the genre of architectural *vedute*. See *The Origin of Perspective*, 203–6. Damisch's notion of "view" is linked to Brunelleschi's experiments, to architectural renderings, and to built architecture. Damisch's brief mention of contradiction and condensation remains linked to built architecture; indeed, despite his awareness of non-finite, not closed, and non-systematic systems, Damisch follows Kernodle in this differentiation of medieval and sixteenth-century stages, where the latter "become interested in integrating all the different elements of a single spectacle within a unified framework." Damisch, *A Theory of /Cloud/* (Stanford: Stanford University Press, 2002), 155.

19 Cairns, "Theatre as Festival," 108. See also Pallen, *Vasari on Theatre*, 26; Nicoll, *The Development of the Theatre*, 73.

20 The Tower of the Milizie was believed to be Torre di Nerone. Neiiendam, "'Il portico' and 'la bottega' on the Early Italian Perspective Stage," 40. See also Pallen, *Vasari on Theatre*, 26.

21 "The supremely capable Baldessare Peruzzi from Siena, was not he too a painter and very gifted at perspective?" Serlio, *Sebastiano Serlio on Architecture*, vol. 1, 37. "Il consumatissimo Baldessar Peruzzi senese fu ancor lui pittore, & nella prospettiva tato dotto." Sebastiano Serlio, *Libro primo [- quinto] d'architettura* (Venice: Melchiorre Sessa, 1551), 2:1r. Also in Vasari: "Attese anco alla prospettiva, e si fece in quella scienzia tale, che in essa pochi pari a lui abbiam veduti a'tempi nostri operare": G. Vasari, *Le vite*, ed. Milanesi, 6: 592. See also Jehane Kuhn, " 'La buona squola di Baldassarre': Vignola's Due regole as a Source for Peruzzi's Perspective Techniques" in *Baldassarre Peruzzi* 1482–1536, eds Christoph Frommel, Arnaldo Bruschi, Howard Burns, Francesco Paolo Fiore, and Pier Nicola Pagliara (Venice: Marsilio, 2005), 411–42; Kemp, *The Science of Art*, 70.

22 On the relationship between antiquarianism and narcissism see Kristeva, "Modern Theater Does Not Take (a) Place." For Peruzzi's surveillance and archaeological knowledge see Jacks, "The Simulachrum of Fabio Calvo." See also Ann Huppert, "Baldassarre Peruzzi as Archeologist in Terracina," in *Baldassarre Peruzzi 1482–1536*, ed. Christoph Frommel, Arnaldo Bruschi, Howard Burns, Francesco Paolo Fiore, and Pier Nicola Pagliara (Venice: Marsilio, 2005), 213–23; Ann Huppert, Becoming an Architect, 49–93; Pierre Gros, "Baldassarre Peruzzi, architetto e archeologo," in *Baldassarre Peruzzi 1482–1536*, 225–30; Gaston, "Merely Antiquarian"; Tafuri, *Interpreting the Renaissance*, 129.

23 Kernodle, *From Art to Theatre*, 174.

24 Elkins, *The Poetics of Perspective*. See also Elkins, "Renaissance Perspectives."

25 Baxandall, *Painting and Experience*, 127–8. See also John White, *Birth and Rebirth of Pictorial Space*, 194–201.

26 Luis Radford, "On the Epistemological Limits of Language: Mathematical Knowledge and Social Practice during the Renaissance," *Educational Studies in Mathematics* 52, no. 2 (2003): 123–50.

27 John White, *Birth and Rebirth of Pictorial Space*, 197. See also Florensky, "Reverse Perspective."

28 Bittner, "One Action."

29 Aronson, "Postmodern Design"; Di Maria, *The Italian Tragedy in the Renaissance*, 141.

30 Weinberg, *A History of Literary Criticism in the Italian Renaissance*, 349. Also, Halliwell, *Aristotle's Poetics*, 292. See also Javitch, "The Assimilation of Aristotle's Poetics in Sixteenth-Century Italy."
31 Di Maria, *The Italian Tragedy in the Renaissance*, 20
32 "Della favola, dice il vostro Aristotele che ella dee essere una e rappresentante una sola azzione d'un solo": Comanini, "Il Figino, ovvero del Fine della Pittura," 345 and 347. See English translation: Comanini, *The Figino, or On the Purpose of Painting*.
33 "Ma in ogni nostro favellare molto priego si consideri me non come matematico ma come pittore scrivere di queste cose": Alberti, "De pictura" in *Opere volgari, Vol.* 3, ed. Grayson.
34 The theoretical juxtaposition of urbanism and scenography has led Damisch and Krautheimer to argue that architecture and scenography are tantamount concepts, an argument in which the representation of urban spaces in theatres becomes an replication of the urban fabric, a mirror image. See: Damisch, *The Origin of Perspective*, 203; Krautheimer, "The Tragic and Comic Scenes of the Renaissance," especially 346.
35 Dawson, "Speaking Theatres"; Di Maria, *The Italian Tragedy in the Renaissance*, 129; McAuley, *Space in Performance*, 7.
36 Freud, *Civilization and Its Discontents*, 17.
37 Ibid.
38 "Di certa Iddea che mi viene nella mente": John Shearman, *Raphael in Early Modern Sources*, 1:735, doc. 1522/16. The phrase may have its origin in Castiglione.
39 Maier, "A 'True Likeness': The Renaissance City Portrait."
40 Aristotle, *Poetics*, 1450b37.
41 Tafuri, *Interpreting the Renaissance*, 129.
42 Carlson, *Places of Performance*, 23. See also Attolini, *Teatro e spettacolo nel Rinascimento*, 115.
43 I'm here borrowing a notion from Damisch, *Skyline*, 17.
44 Leonardo was quite aware of the shortcomings and problems of linear perspective, which he saw as a tool amongst others to reproduce inhabited space. See Leonardo, *On Painting*, 58–68.
45 Di Maria, *The Italian Tragedy in the Renaissance*, 132.
46 Peter Bondanella, "Giraldi Cinthio, Giambattista," 314–15. See also Morrison, *The Tragedies of G.-B. Giraldi Cinthio*, 12; Osborn, "G. B. Giraldi Cinthio's Dramatic Theory and Stage Practice."
47 "Perocché con l'apparato s'imita la vera azione, e si pone ella negli occhi degli spettatori manifestissima": Giraldi Cinthio, "Discorso intorno al comporre delle comedie e delle tragedie," 219. See also Osborn, "G. B.

Giraldi Cinthio's Dramatic Theory and Stage Practice," 42–3; Burckhardt, *The Architecture of the Italian Renaissance*, 271.

48 Testaverde, "Spectacle, Theatre, and Propaganda at the Court of the Medici," 129; Fiorani, *The Marvel of Maps*, 136 and 301 n. 62.

49 Kemp, *The Science of Art*, 176. The verisimilitude in the point of view has led the design to be described as presenting "una fedele riproduzione della Piazza della Signoria di Firenze." See Todarello, *Le arti della scena*, 353. Cairns argues for a polarized distinction between Lanci's "picture" and Peruzzi's "poem." See "Theatre as Festival," 110. Carlson has argued that Lanci's design follows "the Peruzzian-Serlian manner." See *Places of Performance*, 24.

50 Real space is a space in which to live, to be emplaced. On the philosophical notions of room and roominess as vital see, e.g., John Dewey, *Art as Experience*, 209. See also Morris, *The Sense of Space*, 1.

51 For a comparison between the buildings in Peruzzi and Vasari see Cairns, "Theatre as Festival," 115–16. See also Fenech Kroke, "Un théâtre pour *La Talanta*."

52 "*La Cortigiana*," in *Renaissance Commedy*, vol. 1, ed. Beecher, 111–204. The original Italian reads, "e mi vien da ridere perch'io penso che inanzi che questa tela si levassi dal volto di questa città, vi credevate che ci fussi sotto la torre de Babilonia, e sotto ci era Roma. Vedete Palazzo, San Pietro, La Piazza, La Guardia, l'Osteria de la Lepre, la Luna, la Fonte, Santa Caterina e ogni cosa. Ma adesso che ricognoscete che l'è Roma al Coliseo, a la Ritonda e alte cose."

53 Povoledo, "Origins and Aspects," 330.

54 Giraldi Cinthio, "Discorso intorno al comporre delle comedie e delle tragedie," 219–23. See also Osborn, "G. B. Giraldi Cinthio's Dramatic Theory and Stage Practice," 41–3.

55 Burckhardt, *The Architecture of the Italian Renaissance*, 272.

56 Di Maria, *The Italian Tragedy in the Ranaissance*, 131. See also Barthes, "Baudelaire's Theatre" in *Critical Essays*, 26.

57 Shearman, *Mannerism*, 112.

58 Gosebruch, "'Varietas' bei Alberti und der wissenschaftliche Renaissancebegriff."

59 Tafuri, *Interpreting the Renaissance*, 4–7.

60 Shearman, *Mannerism*, 137.

61 Pallen, *Vasari on Theatre*, 53. See also Orville K. Larson, "Vasari's Descriptions of Stage Machinery," *Educational Theatre Journal*, 9, no. 4 (1957): 287–99.

62 The divinity of artists has a long history, and one clearly present in Renaissance artistic discourses and biographies. See, e.g., Patricia Emison,

Creating the "Divine" Artist; and also Kris Kurz's excellent *Legend, Myth, and Magic in the Image of the Artist*, 61–90.

63 Pallen, *Vasari on Theatre*, 13.

64 Paola Ventrone, "La feste del 1471 e i caratteri della cerimonialità religiosa," 33; Povoledo, "Origins and Aspects," 285; Nerida Newbigin, *Feste d'Oltrarno: Plays in Churches in Fifteenth-Century Florence* (Florence: Olschki, 1996) and "The World Made Flesh: The 'Rappresentazioni' of Mysteries and Miacles in Fifteenth-Century Florence," in *Christianity and the Renaissance*, eds T. Verdon and J. Henderson (Syracuse, NY: Syracuse University Press, 1990).

65 Phillips-Court, *The Perfect Genre*, 6, 23–56.

66 Luigi Allegri, *Teatro e spettacolo nel medioevo*; translated in Pallen, *Vasari on Theatre*, 15.

67 Povoledo, "Origins and Aspects," 285.

68 Nagler, *A Source Book in Theatrical History*, 41–3. See also Ludovico Zorzi, *Il teatro e la città*, 69–75, figs. 31, 32; Pallen, *Vasari on Theatre*, 15–18, 60–1; Povoledo, "Origins and Aspects," 285; Belting, "Florence and Baghdad," 188–9; Eugenio Battisti, *Brunelleschi* (New York: Rizzoli, 1981), 300–7.

69 On Leonardo's theatrical works see Carlo Pedretti, "Dessins d'une scéne, exécutés par Léonard de Vinci pour Charle d'Amboise (1506-1507)" in *Le lieu théâtral à la Renaissance*, ed. J. Jacquot (Paris: Éditions du Centre National de la Recherche Scientifique, 1964), 25–34; Pedretti, Leonardo Architetto, 271–89; Kate Steinitz, "Le dessin de Léonard de Vinci pour la Représentation de la Danae de Baldassare Taccone," in *Le lieu théâtral à la Renaissance*, ed. J. Jacquot (Paris: Éditions du Centre National de la Recherche Scientifique, 1964), 35–40; Kate Steinitz "A Reconstruction of Leonardo da Vinci's Revolving Stage," *The Art Quarterly* XII, 4 (1949): 325–8; Kate Steinitz, "Leonardo architetto teatrale e organizzatore di feste," *Lettura Vinciana* 9 (Florence, 1970), 53–5. Supplementary, see also Martin Kemp, *Leonardo da Vinci: The Marvelous Works of Nature and Man* (London: Dent and Sons, 1981), 166–9; Povoledo, "Origins and Aspects," 290–8.

70 Kernodle, *From Art to Theatre*, 176.

71 Mellini, "Descrizione dell'apparato della commedia et intermedii d'essa recitata in Firenze" See also Pallen, *Vasari on Theatre*, 40; Povoledo, "Origins and Aspects," 297, with whom I here disagree on her notion that the surprise effect is subordinated to the demands of a unified location.

72 Povoledo, "Origins and Aspects," 295.

73 Leonardo's drawings exemplify this conflation: Ms. B, f. 52r and Ms. Ash II, 8a. See also Ackerman, *Origins, Imitation, Conventions* "Leonardo Da Vinci's Church Designs", 73; Leonardo, *The Notebooks of Leonardo da Vinci*, II: 56–7.

74 Tafuri, "Il luogo teatrale," 26.
75 On the Colosseum as sacred space see Di Macco, *Il Colosseo*, 30–4; Giambattista Capolari, *Architettvra: Con il suo comento et figvre Vetrvvio* (Perugia: Bigazzini, 1536). See also Ferruccio Marotti, *Storia documentaria del teatro italiano* (Milan: Feltrinelli, 1974), 122; Giuseppe Papagno and Amedeo Quondam, eds, *La Corte e lo spazio* (Rome: Bulzoni, 1982), 368; González Román, *Spectacula*, 23–4, 104.
76 Marotti, *Storia documentaria*, 111, 114–15. For Cesariano's edition see Vitruvius, *De architectura*. See also Manfredo Tafuri, "Cesare Cesariano e gli studi vitruviani del Quattrocento," A. Bruschi, C. Maltese, M. Tafuri, and R. Bonelli, eds, *Scritti rinascimentali d'architettura* (Milan: Il Polifilo, 1978), 387–467.
77 Allardyce Nicoll, *Masks, Mimes, and Miracles* (New York: Harcourt, Brace and Co. 1931), 200; Tydeman, *The Theatre in the Middle Ages*, 134.
78 Newbigin, "Secular and Religious Drama in the Middle Ages," 19.
79 "Delli discorsi vmani stoltissimo è da essere riputato quello, il qual s'astede alla credulità della negromatia, sorella della alchimia, partoritricie delle cose semplici a naturali; Ma è tanto più degnia di riprensione che l'alchimia, quato ella non partorisce alcuna cosa se no similie a se, cioè bugia; il che non interviene nella alchimia, la quale è ministratricie de'senplici prodotti della natura, il quale vfitio fatto esser no può da essa natura ..." For the complete passage and its English translation see Leonardo, *The Notebooks*, II, 304–5.
80 Barkan, *Unearthing the Past*, 60–1. See also Kris and Kurz, *Legend, Myth, and Magic in the Image of the Artist*, 71–84.
81 Benvenuto Cellini, *My Life*, 109 (§1.64).
82 For a recent analysis of the fantastic in relation to the miraculous see Kleinbub, *Vision and the Visionary in Raphael*, 102–19, 132–7. See also Wood, "Countermagical Combinations by Dosso Dossi."
83 Andrew Casper, "Display and Devotion: Exhibiting Icons and Their Copies," in *Religion and the Sense in Early Modern Europe*, ed. W. de Boer and C. Göttler, 43–62 (Leiden and Boston: Brill, 2013), 53.
84 Oldani and Yanitelli, "Jesuit Theater in Italy." See also Griffin, *Jesuit School Drama*.
85 Zampelli, "'Lascivi Spettacoli'," 550.
86 Oldani and Yanitelli, "Jesuit Theater in Italy," 22.
87 René Fülöp-Miller, *The Power and the Secret of the Jesuits*, 417. A point reiterated in Zampelli, "'Lascivi Spettacoli'," 552, 562–3.
88 See translation and bibliography listed at chapter 1, note 1.
89 Di Maria, *The Italian Tragedy in the Renaissance*, 132–3. See also Guidotti, *Scenografie di pensieri*, 175–85.

90 This function of the Prologo will be developed to great effect by Cinthio. See Osborn, "G. B. Giraldi Cinthio's Dramatic Theory and Stage Practice," 41–2, 54.

91 Alberti, *On Painting*, ed. Spencer, 78.

92 Tafuri, *Interpreting the Renaissance*, 129.

93 Martinez, "Etruria Triumphant," 69–70.

94 Ibid., 84.

95 Lucia Nuti, *Ritratti di città: Visione e memoria tra medioevo e settecento* (Venice: Marsilio, 1997), 43–67; Maier, "A 'True Likeness,'" 720.

96 Maier, "A 'True Likeness,'" 727. See also David Friedman, "'Fiorenza': Geography and Representation in a Fifteenth Century View," *Zeitschrift für Kunstgeschichte*, 64 (2001): 56–77. See also Frangenberg, "Chorographies of Florence," 75–87, 113–21; Giuseppina Carla Romby, *Descrizioni e rappresentazioni della città di Firenze nel XV secolo: Con la trascrizione inedita dei manoscritti di Benedetto Dei e un indice ragionato dei manoscritti utili per la storia della città* (Florence: Libreria Editrice Fiorentina: 1976); Enrico Guidoni, "La veduta di Firenze del lucchetto e della catena."

97 Maier, "Francesco Rosselli's Lost View of Rome."

98 Maier, "A 'True Likeness,'" 725.

99 Lotz emphasizes Peruzzi's interest in speculative experimentation as an architect. See *Architecture in Italy* 1500-1600, 48.

100 As Weinberg points out, for thirty years after the publication of the Aldus text in 1508, "there is practically no activity in the tradition of Aristotle's poetics." See *A History of Literary Criticism in the Italian Renaissance*, 367. See also Halliwell, *Aristotle's Poetics*, 291–4. Cf Badt, "Raphael's 'Incendio del Borgo,'" 49.

101 Giraldi Cinthio, *On Romances*, trans. and intro. Snuggs, xv. This interpretation is similar to that of Averroës, for whom poetry is a manifestation of truth in which the notion of "imitation" is lacking." See Weinberg, *A History of Literary Criticism in the Italian Renaissance*, 356.

102 Aristotle, *Poetics*, Book 9, 1451b. See also Halliwell, *Aristotle's Poetics*, 93 and 210.

103 Aristotle's notion of history and art relates to a Neoplatonic principle, namely that particular instantiations do not define the essence of a given entity: in both cases, the general and the conceptual operate as epistemological anchors. Peruzzi's irrational presentation, however, is at odds with Aristotle's emphasis on rationality, as the wonderful ought not to slip from explicable into inexplicable. See Halliwell *Aristotle's Poetics*, 75, n. 41. In any case, it is unlikely that Aristotle's notion of "the

wonderful" was translated into visual practices by Peruzzi, though it may have been a part of Cinthio's *maraviglie*, which correlates to scenographic and literary practices after 1550. See Shearman, *Mannerism*, 112–13, 144–51.

104 Halliwell, *Aristotle's Poetics*, 94.

105 Javitch, "The Assimilation of Aristotle's Poetics in Sixteenth-Century Italy," 54. See also Branca, *Poliziano e l'umanesimo della parola*, 3–36; Lacoue-Labarthe, "Stagings of Mimesis."

106 Woodruff, "Aristotle on Mimesis."

107 Mitchell, *Iconology*, 38.

108 Aristotle, *Physics*, 120–3, 173–5 (II. 194a, 199a).

109 Lacoue-Labarthe, *Typography*, 80, 255. See also Lacoue-Labarthe, "Stagings of Mimesis."

110 "Nin può dunque parte alcuna di poesia esser separata dal verisimile." Torquato Tasso, *Discorsi dell'arte poetica* (c. 1569), ed. A. Solerti (Torino: G.B. Paravia, 1901), 43–4.

111 "Omnia vero quae effingi licet, aut talia per apparentiam sunt, aut significatione et alegoriis talia, aut secondum opiniones hominum vel omnium, vel multorum, alia talia sunt secundum universale ipsum et ideam simpliciter pulchram, sed secundum singulare." Girolamo Fracastoro, *Navagero, della Poetica*, ed. Erico Peruzzi (Firenze: Alinea Editrice, 2005), 98. Originally printed as *Naugerius* (Venice, 1555). For the English translation of the text see Fracastoro, *Naugerius*, ed. Ruth Kelso (Urbana: University of Illinois Press, 1924).

112 "poeta vero illi [pictori] assimiletur qui nō hunc, non illum vult imitari, non uti forte sunt & defectus sustinent, sed universalem, & pulcherrimam ideā artificis sui cōtemplatus res facit, quales esse deceret ... poeta vero non hoc, sed simplicem ideam pulchritudinibus suis vestiam, quod universale Aristoteles vocat ... quare quae & pictores & poetae rebus addunt ad perfectione, non extra rem sunt." Fracastoro, *Naugerius*, ed. Kelso, 60; For the Latin text see ed. Peruzzi, 70–1. See also Pantin, "Poetic Fiction and Natural Philosophy in Humanist Italy"; Murray Bundy, "Fracastoro and the Imagination," in *Renaissance Studies in Honor of Hardin Craig*, ed. Baldwin Maxwell et al., 44–56 (Stanford: Stanford University Press, 1972).

113 Michael Davis, *The Poetry of Philosophy: On Aristotle's Poetics* (South Bend: St. Augustine's Press, 1999), 3.

114 Jacques Rancière, "Painting in the Text," 73.

115 Mitchell, *Iconology*, 31.

116 Belting, *Likeness and Presence*, 551.

117 Jacopo de'Barbari, 1502 letter to Elector Frederick the Wise of Saxony, in Luigi Servolini, *Jacopo de'Barbari* (Padua, 1944), 105–6: quoted in Belting, *Likeness and Presence*, 552. See also, Jay Levenson, *Jacopo de'Barbari and Northern Art of the Early Sixteenth Century* (PhD diss., New York University, 1978), 8ff and 342 ff.

118 Kemp, "From 'Mimesis' to 'Fantasia'."

119 Belting, *Likeness and Presence*, 551.

120 Ibid., 432.

121 Fredrika Jacobs, "Rethinking the Divide."

122 "La bona consuetudine adunque del parlare credo io che nasca dagli uomini che hanno ingegno e che con la dottrina ed esperienzia s'hanno guadagnato il bon giudicio e con quello concorrono e consentono ad accettar le parole che lor paion bone, le quali si conoscono per un certo giudicio naturale e non per arte o regula alcuna." Baldassare Castiglione, *Il libro del Cortegiano*, I: xxxv, ed. Nicola Longo (Milano: Garzanti, 2000), 78. My translation.

123 On the issue of collective response see Mukarovsky, *Aesthetic Function, Norm and Value as Social Facts*, 20. See also Moxey, *The Practice of Theory*, 36–9.

124 Jonas Barish, *The Antitheatrical Prejudice* (Berkeley: University of California Press, 1981), 2.

125 Lacoue-Labarthe, *Typography*, 260–1.

126 Neiiendam, "'Il portico' and 'la bottega.'"

127 Rosen, "Vasari and 'Vedute.'"

128 Elkins, *The Poetics of Perspective*, especially ch. 2.

129 Burckhardt, *The Architecture of the Italian Renaissance*, 272.

130 Gombrich, *Art and Illusion*, 60.

131 Ibid., 60.

132 Ibid., 60–1.

133 Translation in Pallen, *Vasari on Theatre*, 94. The complete text of the letter has been published in two books by Franco Ruffini, *Teatri prima del teatro: Visioni dell'edificio e della scena tra Umanismo e Rinascimento* (Rome: Bulzoni, 1983), 197–9; and *Commedia e festa nel Rinascimento: "La Calandria" alla corte di Urbino*, 307–10.

134 Translation in Pallen, *Vasari on Theatre*, 94

135 Povoledo, "Origins and Aspects," 320

136 Summers, *Real Spaces*, 431.

137 Ibid., 433.

138 Davis, *A General Theory of Visual Culture*, 124, also relevant 20–1.

139 Lacoue-Labarthe, *Typography*, 260–1.
140 Féral, "Theatricality."

2 The Artificial City on Stage

1 "e mi vien da ridere perch'io penso che inanzi che questa tela si levassi dal volto di questa città, vi credevate che ci fussi sotto la torre de Babilonia, e sotto ci era Roma. Vedete Palazzo, San Piero, La Piazza, La Guardia, l'Osteria de la Lepre, la Luna, la Fonte, Santa Caterina e ogni cosa. Ma adesso che ricognoscete che l'è Roma al Coliseo, a la Ritonda e alte cose." Aretino, *La Cortigiana*, ed. Angelo Romano (Milano: RCS, 1999). English text from Aretino, *Cortigiana*, trans. Campbell and Sbrocchi, 53.
2 Rowe and Koetter, *Collage City*, 14.
3 Rewa, "Introduction." In *Design and Scenography*, xi.
4 McKinney and Butterworth, *The Cambridge Introduction to Scenography*, 4.
5 Nicoll, *The Development of the Theatre*, 72.
6 On this drawing see Pope-Hennessy, "Some Aspects of the Cinquecento in Siena," especially 69–70; Donato Sanminiatelli, *Domenico Beccafumi* (Milan: Bramante, 1967), 153; Monbeig-Goguel, *Il manierismo fiorentino*, 82; Ludovico Zorzi, Il teatro e la città, 54 n. 72, 194 n. 99; Maccherini, "Domenico Beccafumi e 'L'Amore Costante' di Alessandro Piccolomini"; Phillip Rylands, *The Timeless Eye*, 62.
7 Pope-Hennessy, *"Some Aspects of the Cinquecento in Siena,"* 69
8 Though this naming – this "prescribed alliance," in Derrida's words – is the assigning of an essence that does not belong to the depicted space. Derrida, *On the Name*, 84–5.
9 Riposio, *Nova comedia v'appresento: Il prologo nella commedia del Cinquecento*. See also Osborn, "G. B. Giraldi Cinthio's Dramatic Theory and Stage Practice."
10 "La prima che crediate che que questi edifici, che voi vedete siano la città di Treviso, & se ben non gli assìmigliano in tutto: ingannarete voi stessi co'l darui a credere, che cosi era nel tempo ch'il caso che vi sarà per noi rappresentano interuenne." Gigio Artemio Giancarli, *Cingana* (Venice: Agostino Bindoni, 1550). Translation from Povoledo, "Origins and Aspects," 332.
11 Original text from Piccolomini, "L'amor costante." Translations mine.
12 Barthes, "Rhetoric of the Image," 39.
13 Derrida, *On the Name*, 85.
14 Rancière, *The Future of the Image*, 88.

15 Leonardo, *On Painting*, 28.
16 The term *puissance*, here with a Deleuzian emphasis, meaning "potential," "capacity for existence," and "capacity to affect and be affected." That is, in contrast with *pouvoir*, also found in Foucault, which denotes an instituted and reproduced system of power. See Deleuze and Guattari, *A Thousand Plateaus*, xvii.
17 Keir Elam, *The Semiotics of Theatre and Drama* (London: Routledge, 1980), 99.
18 Richard Schechner, *Performance Theory* (London: Routledge, 2003), 137.
19 Pope-Hennessy, "Some Aspects of the Cinquecento in Siena," 69. See also Monbeig-Goguel, *Il manierismo fiorentino*, 82.
20 What is more, "the notion of stage drama as the negation of the real fails to notice the extent to which the very reality of the stage can participate in the construction of the drama." Power, *Presence in Play*, 19.
21 As Matthew Potolosky outlines, "Audiences in ancient Greece, for example, hardly sat in rapt silence. Tragedies were performed during daylight in an enormous and often noisy amphitheatre. Elizabethan theatre audiences entirely surrounded the stage … In seventeenth-century France, it was common for members of the audience to sit on the stage, converse with actors during the performance, and request that they performed scenes more than once." *Mimesis* (New York and London: Routledge, 2006), 75. For a recent instantiation of the idea of absolute separation see, e.g., Féral, "Theatricality." For Diderot's position see, e.g., "On Dramatic Poetry" (1758).
22 This drawing is attributed to Antonio da Sangallo the Elder in the catalogue: Arthur Blumenthal, *Italian Renaissance Festival Design* (Madison: University of Wisconsin, 1973), 26–7. In subsequent studies the drawing is attributed to Aristotile. See Oenslarger, *Stage Design*, 12–13.
23 Vasari, *Le vite*, ed. Milanesi, 6:441.
24 "Anzi, come vogliono alcuni, gli fu posto qual sobrenombre, parendo che veramente nella prospettiva fusse quello che Aristotile nella filosofia." Ibid., 6:438.
25 Ludovico Zorzi, *Il teatro e la città*, 93; Pallen, *Vasari on Theatre*, 28–9.
26 Mamone, *Il teatro nella Firenze medicea*, 29. Ghisetti Giavarina, *Aristotile da Sangallo*, 38. Pallen, *Vasari on Theatre*, 27–33.
27 Alessandra Buccheri, *The Spectacle of Clouds: Italian Art and Theatre, 1439–1650* (Burlington: Ashgate, 2014), 74.
28 Il Riccio's design (E.191–1954) is housed in the Victoria and Albert Museum Department of Prints and Drawings. Another version of this drawing, albeit less detailed, exists in The Morgan Library and Museum

(1982.75:438). The woodcut can be found in the Library of Congress (FP - XVI - B687, no. 68). J. C. Walker's *Historical and Critical Essay on the Revival of the Drama in Italy* (Edinburgh: Mundell, 1805), 239 n. 7; Nicoll, *The Development of the Theatre*, 80–1; John Peacock, *The Stage Designs of Inigo Jones: The European Context*, 210; Miotto, "La scène de *L'Ortensio* de Bartolomeo Neroni dit Riccio, peintre et architecte."

29 Finotti, "Perspective and Stage Design," 29

30 Nevola, "Siena nel Rinascimiento: sistemi urbanistici e strutture istituzionali," especially 64; Attolini, *Teatro e spettacolo*, 137; Seragnoli, *Il teatro a Siena*, 14; Miotto, "La scène de *L'Ortensio*," 205–6. Susan Crabtree and Peter Beudert, *Scenic Art for the Theatre: History, Tools, and Techniques* (Boston: Focal Press, 2005), 375.

31 Vitruvius, *On Architecture*, 288–9.

32 Mario Carpo, *Architecture in the Age of Printing: Orality, Writing, Typography, and Printed Images in the History of Architectural Theory* (Cambridge: The MIT Press, 2001), 42–56.

33 Seragnoli, *Il teatro a Siena nel Cinquecento*, 147–8 and 152–4. Frank D'Accone argues it was performed during the second occasion. See D'Accone, *The Civic Muse*, 673–4. See also John Peacock, *The Stage Designs of Inigo Jones: The European Context* (Cambridge: Cambridge University Press, 1995), 210–12.

34 The Prologo of *L'Ortensio* states "Questa citta, che vedete, è Siena stessa perché dovendovisi condurre queste Donne, non hanno voluto dar loro disagio, pur di levarle da sedere. E se vi paresse più bella del solito, non ve ne maravigliate, perché gli Intronati l'hanno così fatta adornare, mossi dalla certa speranza, che tengono, che ella sotto così felice governo abbia ogni giorno a crescere in bellezza, e in dignita." A transcription of this, by Nerida Newbigin, can be found at http://www-personal.usyd.edu.au/~nnew4107/Texts/Sixteenth-century_Siena.html along with other transcriptions of the comedies of the Accademia degli Intronati.

35 "En effet, dans la perspective, on reconnaît, juste après les palais situés au premier plan sur le côtes de la scene, la via del Capitano – appelée alors via Larga –, identifiable grace à la façade du Dôme, avec ses hautes fleches, visible au fond à droite, meme si dans la réalité sa position est plus éloignée. On distingue aussi la piazza Postierla (oú debouche la rue du Capatiano) par la presence, sur la gauche, de la colonne qui soutenait – et soutient encore – l'un des emblems de la villa, la louve. Juste en face, on aperçoit la tour Forteguerri (encore existante) avec un petit arbre au sommet." Miotto, "La scène de *L'Ortensio*," 198–9.

36 Pope-Hennessy, "Some Aspects of the Cinquecento in Siena." See also, Pope-Hennessy, *Learning to Look*, 314.

37 Ludovico Zorzi, *Il teatro e la città*, 323 n. 22; George Kernodle, *The Theatre in History* (Fayetteville: University of Arkansas Press, 1989), 306; Tafuri, *Jacopo Sansovino e l' architettura del '500 a Venezia*, 46; Ferrari, *La scenografia*, 85.

38 Maria Ines Aliverti, *Una scena di città attribuita a Sebastiano Serlio* (Pisa: ETS, 2008).

39 D'Evelyn, *Venice and Vitruvius*, 268. D'Evelyn here follows Onians, *Bearers of Meaning*, 294–5.

40 Serlio, *Sebastiano Serlio on Architecture*, Vol. 1, 86. The original reads: "sopra tutte le altre cose si de' fare elettione delle case più piccole, & metterle davanti ... onde per tal supperiorità della casa più adietro, viene a rappresentar grandezza." Serlio, *Libro primo [- quinto] d'architettura*, "Della Scena Comica," 2:28r.

41 Donald Beecher, "Introduction to *The Pretenders* by Ludovico Ariosto," Donald Beecher, *Renaissance Comedy: The Italian Masters*, Vol. 1 (Toronto: University of Toronto Press, 2009), 44.

42 Sergio Costola, "Strategies of Subversion: The Power of Live Performance within the Walls of a Renaissance City," *International Journal of Arts and Technology* 2.3 (2009): 187–201.

43 McLuhan, *The Guttenberg Galaxy*, 19.

44 Tafuri, *Interpreting the Renaissance*, 8–9.

45 Vitruvius, *On Architecture*, 288–9.

46 Vitruvius, *Ten Books on Architecture: The Corsini Incunabulum*.

47 Scaglia, "A Vitruvianist's 'Thermae' Plan and the Vitruvianists in Rome and Siena."

48 Robert Tavernor, *On Alberti and the Art of Building* (New Haven and London: Yale University Press, 1998), 85–93; Battisti, "La visualizzazione della scena classica nella comedia umanistica."

49 González Román, *Spectacula*, 155–6. See also Bustamante, Garcia, and Franco *Dibujos de Arquitectura y Ornamentación de la Biblioteca Nacional, Siglos XVI y XVII*, 91.

50 Ercole Bottrigari, *La Maschera, overo della fabrica de'teatri et dello apparato delle scene tragisatiricomiche, Dialogo del M. Illustre S. Cavaliere Hercole Bottrigaro.* There are two surviving copies of this document, both in Bologna: one in the Biblioteca Universitaria and the other in the Museo internazionale a Biblioteca della musica di Bologna.

51 Giuliani, "'La Mascara' di Hercole Bottrigari."

52 González Román, *Spectacula*, 186. On the geometry of Viator see Andersen, *The Geometry of an Art*, 162–9.

53 Gonzalez Roman, *Spectacula*, 186. For Ferdinando Bibiena see Durand, "The Apogee of Perspective in the Theatre."
54 Womack, "The Comical Scene," 41.
55 Serlio has been criticized for being pragmatic, though such criticisms fail to understand a most essential aspect of what a theatrical design is. See Kemp, *The Science of Art*, 66. See also Nicoll, *The Development of the Theater*, 75; Sabine Frommel, *Sebastiano Serlio Architect*, 9; Gassner and Allen, *Theatre and Drama in the Making*, 237–8; Wittkower, *Architectural Principles in the Age of Humanism*, 18.
56 Ackerman, *Distance Points*, 376.
57 Derrida, *The Truth in Painting*, 37–147.
58 Quintilian, *The Orator's Education*, VIII §61. Baxandall, *Painting and Experience in Fifteenth-Century Italy*, 131.
59 Baxandall, *Painting and Experience in Fifteenth-Century Italy*, 133.
60 Wohl, *The Aesthetics of Italian Renaissance Art: A Reconsideration of Style*, 9.
61 Foster, "Stagecraft as Statecraft," 78.
62 Trans. in Pallen, *Vasari on Theatre*, 94.
63 "Nè si può immaginare, como egli in tanta stettezza di sito accomodarsse tante strade, tanti palazzi, e tante bizzarrie di tempi di loggie ... Ordinò egli similmente le lumiere, i lumi di dentro che servono all prospettiva." Vasari, *Le vite*, ed. Milanesi, 4:600.
64 Serlio, *Sebastiano Serlio on Architecture*, Vol. 1, 83. The original reads: "superbi palazzi, amplissimi Tempii, diversi casamenti ... spaziose piazze ornate di varii edifici, drittisime e lunghe strade incrociate da altre vie, archi trionfali, altissime colonne, piramide, obelischi e mille altre cose belle, ornate d'infiniti lumi, grandi, mezzani e piccoli, secondo che l'arte lo comporta, li quail sono cosi artificiosamente ordinati che rappresentano tante gioie lucidissime, come saria diamanti, rubini, zaffiri, smeraldi e cosa simili." Serlio, *Libro primo [- quinto] d'architettura*, 2:27r.
65 Peacock, *The Stage Designs of Inigo Jones*, 99–101.
66 Magagnato, *Teatri italiani del Cinquecento*, 46. Cf. Povoledo, "Origins and Aspects," 343 n. 18.
67 Another design by the same hand, also housed in the British Museum, attests to the aesthetic emphasis on effusively ornate proscenium arches framing an eerily symmetrical urban space.
68 Grosz, "Architectures of Excess," 261, 265.
69 Shearman, *Mannerism*, 153.
70 Venturi, *Complexity and Contradiction in Architecture*, 41.
71 Tafuri, *Interpreting the Renaissance*, 19.

72 Shearman, *Mannerism*, 151.
73 Ibid., 158–61. See also, Phillips-Court, *The Perfect Genre*, 157.
74 Alberti, *On Painting*, trans. Spencer, 55; Alberti, "De pictura" in *Opere volgari, Vol.* 3, ed. Grayson. In "De pictura," the passage reads, "comparationibus haec omnia discuntur. Inest enim in comparandis rebus vis, ut quid plus, quid minus, quidve aequale adsit, intelligamus."
75 Harries, *Infinity and Perspective*, 64–77, 184–99.
76 Arnheim, *Visual Thinking*, 39. In this sense, Arnold Aronson writing about stage design states, "we are spatial creatures; we respond intuitively to space … it is the apprehension of space that may be the most profound and powerful experience of live theatre." *Looking into the Abyss*, 1.
77 On the 1574 and 1628 productions of Tasso's *Aminta* see Maria Galli Stampino, *Staging the Pastoral, Tasso's "Aminta" and the Emergence of Modern Western Theatre* (Tempe: Arizona Center for Medieval and Renaissance Studies, 2005). On the French court's interest for Italian theatre see John Powell, *Music and Theatre in France 1600–1680* (Oxford: Oxford University Press, 2000), especially ch. 9.
78 Much has been written on *Il teatro delle Favole Rappresentative*. I here recommend Richard Andrews's recent scholarship, especially his edition *The Commedia dell'arte of Flaminio Scala: A Translation and Analysis of 30 Scenarios* (Lanham, Toronto, and Plymouth: The Scarecrow Press, 2008); and "How – and Why – Does One Print Scenarios? Flaminio Scala, 1611," *Italian Studies* 61, no. 1 (2006): 36–49. For the original text see Flaminio Scala, *Il teatro delle Favole Rappresentative*, ed. F. Marotti (Milan: Il Polifilo, 1976).
79 Andrews, *The Commedia dell'arte of Flaminio Scala*, xiv, 1.
80 In her various publications, M.A. Katritzky has explored the visual world of the early commedia to great lengths in "Italian Comedians in Renaissance Prints," *Print Quarterly* 4, no. 3 (1987): 236–54; *A Study in the Commedia dell'arte 1560–1620 with Special Reference to the Vissual Records* (New York and Amsterdam: Rodopi, 2006), esp. 177–86; and "The Commedia dell'arte: New Perspective and New Documents," *Early Theatre* 11, no. 2 (2008): 141–54.
81 Katritzky, *A Study in the Commedia*, 184
82 See n. 40 above.
83 Bettella, *The Ugly Woman*, 70–5.
84 "Serlio was not a perspectivist of notable mathematical competence … It is a wonder that his perspectival drawings of actual buildings work as well as they do." Kemp, *The Science of Art*, 66.
85 Carpo, *Alberti, Raffaello, Serlio e Camillo*, 113.

86 Ludovico Zorzi, *Il teatro e lacittà*, 28–9, 56 n. 23. Povoledo, "Origins and Aspects," 317–18.

87 Zaccarini, "Una scena cinquecentesca con la piazza di Ferrara." See also Adriano Franceschini, "Nota sopra un bolleto scenografico ferrarese del sec. XVI," in Antonio Samaritini and Ranieri Varese, eds, *L'Aquila Bianca: Studi di storia Estense per Luciano Chiappini* (Ferrara: Corbo, 2000), 391–410.

88 Baldassarre Peruzzi, *Progetto di scenografia*. Biblioteca Reale, Turin, inv.nr. 15728. On this image see, e.g., Neiiendam, "'Il portico' and 'la bottega,'" 37–8.

89 Serlio, "On Tragic Stage Scenery," *Sebastiano Serlio on Architecture*, Vol. 1, 88. "In queste scene benché alcuni hanno dipinto qualche personagi che rappresentano il vivo, come saria una femina ad un balcone, o dentro d'una porta, etiamdio qualche animale: queste cose non consiglio che si faccino, perché non hanno il moto, & pure rappresentano il vivo, ma qualche persona che dorma a bon proposito: overo qualche cane, o altro animale che dorma, perche non hanno il moto." Serlio, "Della scena tragica," *Libro primo [- quinto] d'architettura*, 2:29r.

90 Rajchman, *Constructions*.

91 Merleau-Ponty, "Eye and Mind," *The Primacy of Perception and Other Essays* (Evanston, IL: Northwestern University Press, 1964), 165.

3 Palladio, Scamozzi, and the Built Theatre as Enclosure

1 Grazzini, *Frate Alberigo*, 300.

2 Zanre, *Cultural Non-conformity in Early Modern Florence*, 144.

3 Cremante, *Teatro del Cinquecento: La tragedia*, 745; Di Maria, *The Italian Tragedy in the Renaissance*, 213 n. 19.

4 Christoph Frommel, "Scenografia teatrale"; Jones and Penny, *Raphael*, 210; Fabrizio Cruciani, *Teatro nel Rinascimento: Roma 1450–1550* (Rome: Bulzoni, 1983), 459–66.

5 Foster, "Stagecraft as Statecraft," 66.

6 Venturi, *Complexity and Contradiction in Architecture*, 44. Venturi here reflects on James Ackerman, *The Architecture of Michelangelo*. (London: Zwemmer, 1961), 139.

7 E. H. Gombrich, "The Style all'antica: Imitation and Assimilation," in *Gombrich on the Renaissance, Vol. 1: Norm and Form*, 122–8 (New York: Phaidon, 1985).

8 Tafuri, *Interpreting the Renaissance*, 11.

9 Quoted in Pevsner, *A History of Building Types*, 63. See Filarete, *Treatise on Architecture*, I:159.

10 Valentini and Zucchetti, *Codice topografico*, 238. See also P. Fidenzoni, *Il teatro di Marcello.*

11 Peter Fane-Saunders, *Pliny the Elder and the Emergence of Renaissance Architecture* (Cambridge: Cambridge University Press, 2016), 48–9.

12 Roberto Valentini and Giuseppe Zucchetti, *Codice topografico della città di Roma* (Rome: 1940), 447.

13 Rucellai, *Il Giubileo dell'anno 1450 secondo una relazione di Giovanni Rucellai*, 577. His son encountered the same problem; see Bernardo Rucellai (1448–1514), *De urbe Roma.*

14 Pliny the Elder, *Natural History*, XXXVI: XXIV, 89.

15 Ibid.

16 Fane-Saunders, *Pliny the Elder and the Emergence of Renaissance Architecture.*

17 Tydeman, *The Theatre in the Middle Ages*, 46.

18 "Il Teatro era proprio come una casa di Venere piena di lascivia." Ligorio, *Circhi, teatri e anfiteatri*, 28 (my translation). See also Coffin, *Pirro Ligorio.* Sherer, "Error or Invention?"

19 Holt Parker, "The Observed of All Observers: Spectacle, Applause, and Cultural Poetics in the Roman Theatre Audience," in *The Art of Ancient Spectacle*, ed., B. Bergmann and C. Kondoleon (New Haven and London: Yale University Press, 1999), 163–79; William J. Bouwsma, *The Waning of the Renaissance* (New Haven and London: Yale University Press), 140–1; Potolsky, *Mimesis*, 72.

20 Alberti, *On the Art of Building*, Book VIII, ch. 7.

21 Finotti adds, "in the classical scene the periacti were rotating structures, placed on the sides of the scene, dominated by a fixed backdrop. The rotation of the machinery changed the sides of the stage settings, but it didn't open its backdrop to a vanishing point." "Perspective and Stage Design," 24.

22 di Giorgio Martini, *Trattati di architettura, ingegnieria e arte militare*, 54–5. Pevsner notes that while Francesco di Giorgio writes that the auditorium should be semi-circular (*emicirco*), his elevations present circular buildings. Pevsner, *A History of Building Types*, 63.

23 On this references see, e.g., Stinger, *The Renaissance in Rome*, 77; Pierre de la Ruffinière du Prey, *The Villas of Pliny from Antiquity to Posteriority* (Chicago: The University of Chicago Press, 1994), 68–73. For information and bibliography on the villa at a more general level see Christoph Frommel, Stefano Ray, and Manfredo Tafuri, eds, *Raffaello architetto*, 343–56.

24 Eiche, "A New Look at Three Drawings for Villa Madama and Some Related Images." See also Coffin "The Plans of the Villa Madama."

25 Frommel, *Architecture of the Italian Renaissance*, 27–34.

26 Tafuri, "Il luogo teatrale dall'Umanesimo a oggi," 27–8.

27 Pallen, *Vasari on Theatre*, 49.
28 "That neither the Villa Madama nor the theater at Piacenza was ever built matters little in the long-term history of the theater." Foster, "Stagecraft as Statecraft," 66.
29 Strong, *Art and Power*, 34. See also Hermans, "The Performing Venue."
30 Eco, "Semiotics of Theatrical Performance."
31 Buccheri, *The Spectacle of Clouds*, 74.
32 Kemp, *"From 'Mimesis' to 'Fantasia,'"* 350.
33 Friedrich Nietzsche, "On the Uses and Disadvantages of History for Life," *Untimely Meditations*, 75.
34 Donald Beecher, "Introduction to *The Pretenders* by Ludovico Ariosto," in Donald Beecher, *Renaissance Comedy: The Italian Masters*, Vol. 1 (Toronto: University of Toronto Press, 2009), 41.
35 "Nelle altre cose ha seguitato l'uso degli Antichi; e se vi parrà che in qualche parte l'abbia alterato, considerate che sono alterati ancora e i tempi e i costumi, i qualison qualli che fanno variar le operazioni e le leggi dell'operare." Translation from Annibal Caro, *The Ragged Brothers*, in *Renaissance Comedy*, vol. I, trans. Massimo Ciaovolella and Donald Beecher (Toronto: University of Toronto Press, 2008), 218. For the Italian text see *Commedia degli straccioni*, ed. Marziano Guglielminetti (Turin: Eiunaudi, 1967).
36 "Questo argomento, cosi interzato, moverà forse troppo la colera a questi stilichi; perchè scempio o doppio solamente è stato usato dagli Antichi nelle lor Comedie. Avvertite che, sebben non si trova anco dicieto che non si possa fare; e anco s'è mosso a farlo con qualche ragione ... Ma la legge della Comedia non si trova in tutto stabilita; l'esempio è molto vario; ognuno ha il suo capo; ogni capo le sue openioni; e ogni openion le sue ragioni." Ibid.
37 Grotowski, *Towards a Poor Theatre*, 32–3. See also McAuley, *Space in Performance:* 2 and 7; Rancière, *The Emancipated Spectator*, 7.
38 van Eck and Bussels, "The Visual Arts and the Theatre in Early Modern Europe," 12. See also Pérez-Gómez and Pelletier, *Achitectural Representation and the Perspective Hinge*, 337.
39 D'Evelyn, *Venice and Vitruvius*, 270. *Vitruvius, De architectura*, V.III, f. LXXVr: 13–20. See also Manfredo Tafuri, "Cesare Cesariano e gli studi vitruviani del Quattrocento," in A. Bruschi, C. Maltese, M. Tafuri, and R. Bonelli, eds, *Scritti rinascimentali d'architettura* (Milan: Il Polifilo, 1978), 387–467.
40 For the editions of Terence see especially T.E. Lawrenson and Helen Purkis, "Les éditions illustrées de Térence dans l'historie du théâtre," in *Le lieu théâtral à la Renaissance*, 1–23 and 8 plates (Paris: Centre National de

la Recherche Scientifique, 1964). See also Friedrich Lippmann, The art of Wood-Engraving in Italy in the Fifteenth Century (London: B. Quaritch, 1888), 92–4; Kernodle, From Art to Theatre, 160–4; Ludovico Zorzi, *Il teatro e lacittà*, 40 n. 22.; Damisch, *The Origin of Perspective*, 222; Povoledo, "Origins and Aspects," 299–300; West, "The Idea of a Theater."

41 "The work of the painter attempts to be pleasing to the multitude; therefore do not disdain the judgments and views of the multitude when it is possible to satisfy their opinions." Alberti, *On Painting*, 97.

42 Serlio, "On Tragic Stage Scenery," *Sebastiano Serlio on Architecture*, Vol. 1, 88. "lontani che i spettatori non le possino vedere per fianco." Serlio, "Della Scena Tragica," *Libro primo [- quinto] d'architettura*, 2:29r.

43 A. Ademollo, "Introno al teatro drammatico italiano dal 1550 in poi," Nuova antologia di scienze, lettere ed arti, 2nd ser. (1881), XXVI, 53. Cited and translated in Foster, "Stagecraft as Statecraft," 76. Foster, in any case, argues that this explanation belies an essential concern with political hierarchy.

44 Zorach, *The Passionate Triangle*, 23. Her emphasis.

45 Andreas Beyer, *Andrea Palladio*, 45–6. Palladio's oeuvre consciously incorporates theatrical resonances. It has been argued that Villa Rotonda embodies the aesthetic qualities of Vitruvius's satiric stage. Palladio himself addressed the performative qualities of his famous villa in his *Four Books on Architecture*, describing the building as "surrounded by other pleasant hills which resemble a vast theatre": Palladio, *The Four Books on Architecture*, 94. For the original text see Palladio, *I quattro libri dell'architettura*. See also Burns, Fairburn, and Boucher, *Andrea Palladio, 1508–1580:* 110–11; Azzi Visentini, "The Gardens of Villas in the Veneto from the Fifteenth to the Eighteenth Centuries"; Winton, "The Satyric Scene."

46 Oosting, "The Teatro Olimpico Design Sources," 260

47 Giangiorgio Zorzi, "Le prospettive del Teatro Olimpico di Vicenza nei disegni degli 'Uffizi' di Firenze e nei documenti dell' 'Ambrosiana' di Milano."

48 Donald James Gordon, *The Renaissance Imagination* (Berkeley and Los Angeles: University of California Press, 1975), 247–65.

49 Damisch argues that the Olimpico is exclusively the triumph of the antiquarian interest in reconstructing ancient models. Damisch, *The Origin of Perspective*, 224–5.

50 "The solution represented by the Teatro Olimpico was unique in its perfection." Povoledo, "Origins and Aspects," 329.

51 Benjamin, "The Work of Art in the Age of Its Technological Reproducibility." Benjamin argues that the "aura" of an artwork is absent in its reproduction. Baudrillard adds, "there is, to use Walter Benjamin's

expression, an aura of the simulacrum just as he described an aura of the original": *The Conspiracy of Art*, 117

52 Bryson, *Vision and Painting*, 94.
53 Rosand, "Theater and Structure in the Art of Paolo Veronese," 222.
54 Ibid.
55 Gordon, *The Renaissance Imagination*, 263.
56 "La prospettiva di dentro é parimenti ammirabile, e benissimo intesa ..." Filippo Pigafetta in *Due lettere descrittive l'una dell'ingresso a Vicenza della Imperatrice Maria d'Austria nell'anno MDLXXXI l'altra della recita nel Teatro Olimpico dell'Edippo di Sofocle nel MDLXXXV* (Valentino Crescini: Padua, 1830), 26. Translated in Nagler, *A Source Book in Theatrical History*, 84.
57 Greenwood, *Shifting Perspectives and the Stylish Style*, 192.
58 For the Teatro all'antica see: Forster, "Stagecraft as Statecraft." See also *Il teatro all'antica di Sabbioneta*, Mauro Bini, ed. (Modena: Il Bulino, 1991); Hermans, "The Performing Venue"; Stefano Mazzoni, "Vincenzo Scamozzi Architetto-Scenografo," in *Vincenzo Scamozzi 1548–1616*. (Venice: Marsilio, 2003), 71–86; Borys, "Through the Lens."
59 Borys, "Through the Lens," 105.
60 Phillips-Court, *The Perfect Genre*, 201.
61 Rancière, *The Politics of Aesthetics*, 18.
62 Damisch, *The Origin of Perspective*, 399. For Leonardo's problematization of linear perspective see Leonardo, *On Painting*, ed. Kemp, 58–68.
63 Foster, "Stagecraft as Statecraft."
64 Maaike Bleeker, *Visuality in the Theatre: The Locus of Looking*, 42, 205 n. 5. See also Hans-Thies Lehmann, *Postdramatisches Theater* (Frankfurt am Main: Verlag der Autoren, 1999), 288; Szondi, *Theorie des Modernen Dramas*, 16.
65 Pallen, *Vasari on Theatre*, 35.
66 "quantunque la prima volta per la gran moltitudine fosse turbato il rappresentarla, la seconda fu confermato il giudizio primiero." Di Maria, *The Italian Tragedy in the Renaissance*, 213 n. 23. See also Cremante, *Teatro del Cinquecento*, 745.
67 "cusi li Atheniensi prima, tal aggreste principio revolgendo in spectaculo urbano, lo chiamoreno theatro, cioé visorio, nel quale, stando grandissima turba, dalla longa ancora senza impedimento alcuno vedesse et potesse anche essere visto." Prisciani, *Spectacula*, 37. See also G. Ferrari, "Il manoscritto *Spectacula* di Pellegrino Prisciani"; Povoledo, "La sala teatrale a Ferrara"; Ludovico Zorzi *Il teatro e la città*, 76–8.
68 Foster, "Stagecraft as Statecraft," 69.
69 "Whatever the painted persons do among themselves or with the beholder, all is pointed towards ornamenting or teaching the *istoria*." Alberti, *On Painting*, trans. Spencer, 78. For Alberti, these figures create a sense of

unity; however, in the Teatro all'antica, they fragment they unity because of the many focal points throughout the walls.

70 On the history of this maxim see Brian Curran, "Teaching (and Thinking About) the High Renaissance," 37.

71 Burroughs, "Michelangelo at the Campidoglio."

72 Foster, "Stagecraft as Statecraft."

73 Cf writing about modern theatre, Lyotard states that there are two barriers or limits. One divides the exterior (reality) from interior; the other one differentiates between what is to be perceived from what remains unseen (underneath, lights, wings): Lyotard, "The Tooth, the Palm."

74 Fleming, "Presenting the Spectators as the Show."

75 González Román, *Spectacula*, 88. For the comparison to the Colosseum, Di Macco, *Il Colosseo*, 47.

76 This performance is mentioned in the introduction to the Sulpitius edition of Vitruvius, *Lucii Vitruvii Pollionis ad Caesarem Augustum de architectura liber primus -decimus*, ed. Joannes Sulpitius (Sulpizio da Veroli) (Rome: Eucharius Silber, 1486). See also Grund, ed., *Humanist Comedies*, xiv–xvi; Fabricio Cruciani, *Teatro nel Rinascimento*, 224–5; Hartmut Beyer, "Carlo and Marcellino Verardi's *Fernandus servatus* and the Poem *Supra casum Hispani regis* by Petrus Martyr"; Povoledo, "Origins and Aspects," 299; Campbell, *Scenes and Machines*, 11; Campbell, "The First Edition of Vitruvius."

77 Fiocco, "La Casa di Alvise Cornaro." *Bolletino del Museo Civico di Padova* LVII (1968): 7–16. See also Fiocco, "Alvise Cornaro e il teatro."

78 Lucchesini, *I teatri di Firenze*, 53.

79 Mamone, *Il teatro nella Firenze medicea*, 17–19. See also Pallen, *Vasari on Theatre*, 10–11, n. 126.

80 Povoledo, "Origins and Aspects," 286.

81 Damisch, *The Origin of Perspective*, 222–3.

82 Three classical plays were performed in this occasion: *Penulo*, *Ippolito*, and *Adelphi*. Povoledo, "Origins and Aspects," 314.

83 Trans. in Pallen, *Vasari on Theatre*, 94

84 Fortini-Brown, *Private Lives in Renaissance Venice*, 123.

85 Marin Sanudo, *I diarii*, ed. Rinaldo Fulin, Federico Stefani, Nicolò Barozzi, Guglielmo Berchet, and Marco Allegri (Venice: F. Visentini, 1879–1903), 19:443; quoted in Fortini-Brown, *Private Lives in Renaissance Venice*, 123.

86 D'Evelyn, *Venice and Vitruvius*, 272.

87 Johnson, "The Short, Lascivious Lives of Two Venetian Theaters, 1580–85."

88 Ibid.

89 "multa verba et actus turpia lascivia et inhonestissima." Quoted in Johnson, "The Short, Lascivious Lives of Two Venetian Theaters," 939 n. 15.
90 Aureli, *The Possibility of an Absolute Architecture*, 69.
91 Hermans, "The Performing Venue," 93.
92 Tafuri, *Venice and the Renaissance*, 148.
93 Huse and Wolters, *The Art of Renaissance Venice*, 48.
94 Tafuri, *Venice and the Renaissance*, 148.

4 The Medici Theatres, Political Aspirations, and Cognitive Autonomy

1 "di poi abbia ciascuno licenzia di biasimare o di lodare, secondochè gli detta la natura; perchè nè i biasimi gli faranno montare in collera, nè le lodi in superbia." Cecchi, *L'assiuolo*, 80. Translation from Eisenbichler (*The Horned Owl*), 235.
2 Celenza, *The Lost Italian Renaissance*, 87.
3 Phillips-Court, *The Perfect Genre*, 14 n. 2.
4 Battisti, *Rinascimento e barocco*; Bryson, *Vision and Painting*; Damisch, *The Origin of Perspective*; Edgerton, *The Heritage of Giotto's Geometry*, 89–91; Grafton, *Leon Battista Alberti*, 93. Gombrich, *Art and Illusion*, 250; Goodman, *Languages of Art*; Harries, *Infinity and Perspective*, 16–17, 64–103; Jay, "Scopic Regimes of Modernity," 56–7; Kemp, *The Science of Art*; Moffit, *Painterly Perspective and Piety*; Saint-Martin, *Semiotics of Visual Language*, 109–44; John White, *The Birth and Rebirth of Pictorial Space*, 192–7.
5 Baxandall, *Painting and Experience in Fifteenth-Century Italy*, 124–7.
6 "si vide à poco à poco surgere un Sole nel Cielo della Prospettiva." P.F. Giambullari, *Apparato et feste nelle nozze dello Illustrissimo Signor Duca di Firenze e della Duchessa sua Consorte* (Florence: Benedetto Giunta, 1589) cited in Sara Mamone, *Il teatro nella Firenze medicea*, 96.
7 González Román, *Spectacula*, 139–40. The Fabio Calvo translation was not published until the twentieth century: Vicenzo Fontana and Paolo Marachiello, *Vitruvio e Raffaello. Il "De Architectura" de Vitruvio nella traduzione inedita di Fabio Calvo Ravennate* (Rome: Officina Edizioni, 1975); Ciapponi, "Fra Giocondo da Verona and His Edition of Vitruvius"; Carol Herselle Krinsky, "Cesare Cesariano and the Como Vitruvius Edition of 1521," PhD diss (New York University: 1965).
8 Orrell, *The Theatres of Inigo Jones and John Webb*, 218–19.
9 Damisch, *The Origin of Perspective*, 399.
10 Ibid., 398.

11 Peter Brand, "Ariosto and Ferrara," in *A History of Italian Theatre*, ed. Joseph Farrell and Paolo Puppa, 44–50 (Cambridge: Cambridge University Press, 2006), 19.
12 Costola, "The Politics of a Theatrical Event." See also Costola, "La prima rappresentazione dei Suppositi di Ariosto nel 1509."
13 Costola, "The Politics of a Theatrical Event."
14 Chastel, "Cortile et théatre," 43–4. See also Heydenreich, *Architecture in Italy 1400–1500*, 145; Biermann, "Das Palastmodell Giuliano da Sangallos für Ferdinard I. König von Neapel"; *Wiener Jahrbuch für Kunstgeschichte* xxiii (1970): 154–95; Worgul, "Das Palastmodell Giuliano da Sangallos für Ferdinard I. König von Neapel. Versuch einer Rekontruktion"; Jurén, "Le project de Giuliano da Sangallo pour le palais du roi de Naples"; Hersey, *Alfonso II and the Artistic Renewal of Naples 1585–1495*.
15 T. V. Strozzi, "Aeolostichon," IV in *Strozzi Poetae Pater et Filius* (Venice, 1513), c. 125v. See also Zambotti, "Diario ferrarese dall'anno 1476 sino al 1504" and "*Diario ferrarese* (1409–1502)."
16 Povoledo, "Origins and Aspects," 302–3.
17 Fabrizio Cruciani, *Il teatro del Campidoglio e le feste romane del* 1513. See also Cruciani, *Teatro nel Rinascimento*, 406–34; Arnaldo Bruschi, "Il teatro Capitolino del 1513"; Pevsner, *A History of Building Types*, 65; Damisch, *The Origin of Perspective*, 221–2; Cottino-Jones, "Rome and the Theatre in the Renaissance," 237–47; Stinger, *The Renaissance in Rome*, 257; Povoledo, "Origins and Aspects," 315 n. 8, 324.
18 Cottino-Jones, "Rome and the Theatre in the Renaissance," 238; Arnaldo Bruschi, "Riconstruzione e nota critica nell'architettura del teatro capitolino" in Cruciani, *Il teatro*, 139–62.
19 Cruciani, *Il teatro*, 21–67.
20 Povoledo, "Origins and Aspects," 313.
21 "[R]epresentavano alla mente un edificio eterno et antique pieno de delectation." Cantelmo's letter has been reprinted in Giuseppe Campori, *Lettere artistiche inedite* (Modena: Soliani, 1866), 3–5; and Alessandro D'Ancona, *Origini del teatro Italiano* (Turin: Loescher, 1891), 381–3. For an interpretation of the performance's description in the letter see Povoledo, "Origins and Aspects," 313–14 n. 6.
22 "[R]epresentavano alla mente un edificio eterno et antique pieno de delectation."
23 Povoledo, "Origins and Aspects," 314–15.
24 Saslow, *The Medici Wedding of* 1589, 81.

25 Vasari, *Le vite*, ed. Milanesi, 6:439–41; Attolini, *Teatro e spettacolo nel Rinascimiento*, 120; Mamone, *Il teatro nella Firenze medicea*, 29; Pallen, *Vasari on Theatre*, 29; Gareffi, *La scrittura e la festa*, 220–30.

26 *Per molti, donna, anzi per mille amanti / creata fusti, e d'angelica forma; / or par che 'n ciel si dorma, / s'un sol s'appropia quell ch'è dato a tanti. / Ritorna a' nostri pianti / il sol degli occhi tuo, che par che schivi / chi del suo dono in tal miseria è nato* (For many, even a thousand lovers, Lady / were you created, with angelic form; / now heaven must be sleeping, / if one can take for himself what was given to many. / Give back to our weeping eyes / the sun of your eyes, which seems to be avoiding / those born in such misery without its gifts.) Saslow, *The Poetry of Michelangelo*, 423.

27 Watt, "*Veni, sponsa*," 22. See also Sang Woo Kim, "Historiography of Duke Cosimo I de' Medici's Cultural Politics and Theories of Cultural Hegemony and Opposition," *Michigan Journal of History* (Winter 2006): 1–70.

28 For the original text see M.P.F. Giambullari, *Copia d'una lettera di M. Pier Francesco Giambullari*. For the translation see Minor and Mitchell, *A Renaissance Entertainment*, 97–217.

29 In Minor and Mitchell, *A Renaissance Entertainment*. For the original text see M.P.F. Giambullari, *Copia d'una lettera di M. Pier Francesco Giambullari*, 22–64.

30 Ibid., 135.

31 Ibid., 224.

32 "Nelle nozze, che si fecero a dì 27 di giugno l'anno 1539 fece Aristotile nel cortile grande del palazzo de' Medici, dove è la fonte un'altra scena, che rappresentò Pisa, nella quale vinse se stesso, sempre migliorando, e variando, onde non è possibile mettere insieme mai nè la più variata sorte di finestre e porte, nè facciate di palazzi più bizzarre, e capricciose, nè strade o lontani, che meglio sfuggano, e facciano tutto quello, che l'ordine vuole della prospettiva. Vi fece oltra di questo, il campanile torto del Duomo, la cupola ed il tempio tondo di San Giovanni, con altre cose di quella città." Vasari-Milanesi, ed., *Le vite*, ed. Milanesi, 6:441–2.

33 Hermans "The Performing Venue," 95.

34 "Che per accendere gl'animi di coloro che venivano, alla virtù et alla gloria." Vasari, *Le vite*, ed. Milanesi, 3:169. For this translation and the connection to the Teatro all'antica, see Hermans, "The Performing Venue," 95.

35 Machiavelli, *The Prince*, 30. On this section of *The Prince* see Erica Benner, *Machiavelli's Prince*, 101–4; Mousley, "*The Prince* and Textual Politics."

36 Dovey, *Framing Places*, 15.

37 Watt, "*Veni, sponsa*," 33–4.

38 Edelman, *Constructing the Political Spectacle*, 124.
39 Saslow, "La place du prince."
40 Arditi writes about "Il gioco con gianetti e ammazzorno alquianti tori" on 4 October, and of "uno combattimento d'una sbarra con dimolti altri passatempi di trionfi e altri tratenimenti" on the night of 14 October. He adds, "Mi occorre narrare una cosa degna di grande ammirazione e degna di grande considerazione: che al duca Francesco Maria, figliolo del duca Cosimo d'etá d'anni 40, gli fussi capace vedere morire di fame il contado e la città con tutti e' poveri sua suditi ed essere capace di spendere e trattenere gli'imbasciadori veniziani colla nobilità che'era venuta in loro compagnia." Arditi, *Diario di Firenze e di altre parti della cristianità (1574–1579)*, 216–18.
41 Grendler, *Critics of the Italian World*, ch. 3.
42 Castiglione, *Il Libro del Cortegiano*, 2:18.
43 Aretino, *Cortigiana*, trans. Campbell and Sbrocchi, 58.
44 Ibid., 57–8.
45 Aretino, *Cortigiana*, act I, scene xxiv. See also: Burke, *The Fortunes of the Courtier*, 106–7; Larivaille, *Pietro Aretino fra Rinascimento e Manierismo*, 212; Andrews, *Scripts and Scenarios*, 74–5. Aretino showed a more relaxed attitude towards flattery in his *Il marescalto*, where his circle of friends and patrons is praised.
46 Niccolò Machiavelli, *The Prince*, 93–5.
47 Aretino, *Cortigiana*, act I, scene xxiv.
48 Costola, "The Politics of a Theatrical Event," 196.
49 "Solo di tanto pregano ciascuno che si degni ascoltare loro Assiuolo con silenzio fino che finito sia." Cecchi, *L'assiuolo*, 80. Trans. Eisenbichler.
50 "di poi abbia ciascuno licenzia di biasimare o di lodare, secondochè gli detta la natura; perchè nè i biasimi gli faranno montare in collera, nè le lodi in superbia." Ibid.
51 Francesco Andreini, for example, despairingly addresses public performances in his *Bravure del Capitano Spavento*, 88:

> CAPITANO: [...] la povera commedia e la misera tragedia, le quali vergognosamente se ne vanno per le pubbliche piazze, e sopra i pubblici banchi dei ciarlatani, tutte stracciate, che a fatica si riconoscono.
>
> TRAPPOLA. È vero padrone, e me ne creppa il cuore, avend'io una certa inclinazione alla drammatica poesia; ma questa è colpa di quelli che governano le cittadi, e ciò sia detto con pace loro, i quali a modo niuno non dovrebbero permettere che una commedia e una tragedia fusse rappresentata così vilmente sopra dei banchi, ma sibbene in luogo privato, con quell'onore e con quella magnificenza che se le conviene.

52 Minor and Mitchell, *A Renaissance Entertainment*, 353.

53 Andrews, *Scripts and Scenarios*, 33. For the actual letters of Isabella and other courtiers, see Irineo Sanesi, *Storia dei generi letterari italiani*, vol. I, 188.

54 Serlio, *Sebastiano Serlio on Architecture*, vol. 1, 83. "[G]rand contentezza d'occhio e satisfazzioni d'animo." Serlio, *Libro primo [- quinto] d'architettura*, 2:27r.

55 Rancière, *The Emancipated Spectator*, 13.

56 Rausch, *Theoria*. See also van Eck and Bussels, "The Visual Arts and the Theatre in Early Modern Europe," 12; Heidegger, "Science and Reflection," 163.

57 Merleau-Ponty, *Phenomenology of Perception*, 33–5; Richard Wright, ed., *Visual Attention* (Oxford: Oxford University Press, 1998); Hoffman, *Visual Intelligence*; Findlay and Gilchrist, *Active Vision*; Changizi, *The Vision Revolution*.

58 Arnheim, *Visual Thinking*, 13, 20. See also Crary, *Techniques of the Observer*, 98–100.

59 "La beltà che tu vedi è ben da quella / ma cresce poi c'a miglior loco sale / se per glio occhi mortali all'alma corre." *The Poetry of Michelangelo*, trans. James Saslow (New Haven and London: Yale University Press), 122, poem 42 ("Dimmi di grazia"). See also 118, poem 38 ("Quanta dolcezza al cor per gli occhi porta").

60 Neumann, "Aufmerksamkeit." For a summary of Neumann and further analysis see Hartfield, "Attention in Early Scientific Psychology", especially 8–11. For the primary sources see: Lucretius, *On the Nature of Things*, IV.811–13; Cicero, *De oratore (On the Orator)* III. 192; Augustine, *Confessions*, III.11.19, X.40.65 X.25.56, and *De musica* VI.5.9.

61 Plotinus, *Enneads*, III.6.1. For Plotinus, the conceptual process is not unitary, but is composed "of the perceived object, desire, and memory." See Hendrix, "Perception as a Function of Desire in the Renaissance," 99.

62 *"Aut prodesse uolunt aut delectare poetae / aut simul et iucunda et idonea dicere uitae."* Horace, *On the Art of Poetry*, 333–4.

63 Giovan Maria Cecchi, *Lo spirito*, quoted in Konrad Eisenbichler, "How Bartolomeo Saw a Play," in *The Renaissance in the Streets, Schools, and Studies*, 259–78 (Toronto: Toronto University Press, 2008), 259.

64 McAuley, *Space in Performance*, 237–8.

65 Giovan Battista Andreini's 1612 *Prologo in Dialogo fra Momo e la Verità* exemplifies these defences, explicitly addressing the issue of morality and theatre within their contemporary climate: "Benché sia superfluo che i comici de' moderni tempi s'affatichino in dimostrare la nobiltà e concessione di quest'arte comica, tratta dall'onesto e virtuoso loro operare, nondimeno per far chiaro a quelli che vessati sono da' malevoli

che lecitissima e di profitto è questa virtuosa professione, mosso mi sono per ora a stampare questo Prologo in Dialogo ed altre più gravi ragioni. Benché bastare dovrebbe che la comedia di ch'io parlo è moderna, nel cui tempo tutte le cose sono modernate in guisa che d'altra riforma nel bel culto cristiano non v'è bisogno. Non più, non più s'ascoltano in queste nostre comedie le detrazzioni del prossimo, le derisioni de' fatti cristiani, gl'incanti e quegli atti così sfacciati, onde quasi gloriose d'infamia le scene prime si gloriavano; non più dalle città discacciate sono, ma da quelle e da quelle di santa Chiesa chiamate; non più i Sacri Canoni negano a' comici le confessioni e comunioni." Giovan Battista Andreini, *Prologo in Dialogo fra Momo e la Verità* (Ferrara: Baldini, 1612). Reprinted in *La commedia dell'arte e la società barocca. La professione del teatro*, eds F. Marotti and G. Romei (Rome, Bulzoni: 1991), 473–88; also cited and studied in Florinda Nardi, "Scrivere la Commedia dell'arte. Testi, pretesti e contesti," in *Miti antichi e moderni. Studi in onore di Edo Bellingeri*, eds. D. Gavrilovich et al, 167–75 (Rome: Universitalia, 2013), 169 n. 3. See also Robert Henke, *Peformance and Literature in the Commedia dell'arte* (Cambridge: Cambridge University Press, 2002), 185–96.

66 Eisenbichler, "How Bartolomeo Saw a Play," 262.

67 Ibid.

68 Castelvetro, *On the Art of Poetry*. Quoted in Daniel Gerould, ed., *Theatre, Theory, Theatre*, 116.

69 Di Maria, *The Italian Tragedy in the Renaissance*, 97.

70 Ibid., 22–3, 98.

71 Ibid., 23.

72 For a historical survey of the *intermedi* see Povoledo, "Origins and Aspects," 335–83.

73 Nino Pirrotta, "Studies in the Music of Renaissance Theatre," in *Music and Theatre from Poliziano to Monteverdi* (Cambridge: Cambridge University Press, 1975), 47.

74 Povoledo, "Origins and Aspects," 336–9.

75 Serlio, *Sebastiano Serlio on Architecture*, vol. 1, 83. Serlio, *Libro primo [- quinto] d'architettura*, 2:27r.

76 Roy Strong studies the political significance of the marriage and the various performances in *Art and Power: Renaissance Festivals, 1450–1650* (Berkeley and Los Angeles: University of California Press, 1984), 126–52.

77 Saslow, *The Medici Wedding of* 1589. The wedding celebrations are described in *Diario descritto da Giuseppe Pavoni delle feste celebrate nelle solennissime nozze delli Serenissimi Sposi, il Signor don Ferdinando Medici e la Signora Donna Cristina di Lorena Grand Duchi di Toscana, nel quale con*

brevita si esplica il Torneo, la Battaglia Navale, la comedia con gli intermedi, et alter feste occorse di giorno, in giornio per tutto il dí 15 Maggio MDLXXXXIX (Bologna, 1589).

78 Saslow, *The Medici Wedding of 1589*, 1, 20.

79 Povoledo, "Origins and Aspects," 383.

80 Ibid., 291, 336. See also Pirrotta, "Studies in the Music of Renaissance Theatre," 47–8.

81 Saslow, *The Medici Wedding of 1589*, 149.

82 Rowe and Koetter, *Collage City*, 14.

83 Ibid., 14. For Machiavelli's republicanism see, e.g., Mansfield and Tarcov, "Introduction," in Machiavelli, *Discourses on Livy*, xvii–xliv.

84 Vidler, *The Scenes of the Street and Other Essays*, 18–19.

85 Ibid.

86 Ibid., 21.

87 Rancière, *The Politics of Aesthetics*, 40.

88 Eliav-Feldon, *Realistic Utopias*, 3–4.

89 "The very attempt to determine the meaning of the concept 'utopia' shows to what extent every definition in historical thinking depends necessarily upon one's perspective." Mannheim, *Ideology and Utopia*, 166–7.

90 Schich, "Complexity and Convention," 33.

91 Finotti, "Perspective and Stage Design," 28.

92 Quoted and translated in ibid., 28.

93 Ibid.

94 "At vero quam illa vulgaris opinio doctorum hominum relationibus fundata, magnis aedificiis perpetuius quadmmodo monumentis, ac testimonies paene sempiternis, quai a deo fabricates, in dies usuque adeo corroboratur et confirmatur, ut in vivos posterosque illarum adminirabilium constructionum conspectore continue traducatur; ac per hunc modum conservatur et augetur, atque sic conservata et facta, admirabili quadam dovotione conditur, et capitur." Giannozzo Maneti, "Vita Nicolai V Summi Pontificis," 3:2, in *Rerum Italicarum scriptores*, ed. Maratori (Milan: Societatis Palatinae, 1731), 949–50. Also quoted in Tafuri, *Interpreting the Renaissance*, 290 n.9.

95 Tafuri, *Interpreting the Renaissance*, 46–7.

96 Ibid., 23.

97 Wim Boerefijn, "Designing the Medieval New Town," 52.

98 Eaton, *Ideal Cities*, 49.

99 Kruft, *A History of Architectural Theory from Vitruvius to the Present*, 109.

100 Aureli, *The Possibility of an Absolute Architecture*, 47–83.

101 Saslow, *The Medici Wedding of 1589*, 82–3, 243–4.
102 Santosuosso, "A Society in Disarray: Satirical Poets and Mannerist Painters in the Age of the Italian Wars."
103 Grendler, "Utopia in Renaissance Italy: Doni's 'New World'," Grendler, *Critics of the Italian World: 1530–1560: Anton Francesco Doni, Nicolò Franco & Ortensio Lando*; Eliav-Feldon, *Realistic Utopias*, 19–21. For the original texts see Doni, *I mondi e gli inferni*; Patricius's *La città felice.*
104 This notion parallels other recent historical reconsiderations of utopian discourse. See e.g., Leslie, *Renaissance Utopias and the Problem of History*, 1–24.
105 Manuel and Manuel, *Utopian Thought in the Western World*, 170; Rosen, "Pietro Tacca's *Quattro Mori* and the Conditions of Slavery in Early Seicento Tuscany." As Rosen notes, Vasari the Younger's *La città ideale* reads "Si trovano molti Principi grandi ... havere un' luogo grande p. tenere schiavi mentre che I loro legni sono in porto, quale luogo si chiama comunemente Bagno."
106 Adams and Nussdorfer, "The Italian City, 1400–1600," 228. See also Kruft, *A History of Architectural Theory from Vitruvius to the Present*, 114.
107 This issue has been emphasized by Konrad Eisenbichler in his translation and notes of *The Horned Owl*. See Cecchi, *The Horned Owl*, (Waterloo: Wilfried Laurier University press, 1981), 75 n. 2. See also, Cecchi, *The Horned Owl* in Donald Beecher, ed., *Renaissance Comedy: The Italian Masters* (Toronto: University of Toronto Press, 2009), II: 285 n.2.
108 Cecchi, *The Horned Owl* in *Renaissance Comedy*, ed. Beecher, II: 301.
109 Antonio Franceschetti and Kenneth Barlett, "Introduction to *The Moscheta*" in Donald Beecher, *Renaissance Comedy: The Italian Masters* (Toronto: University of Toronto Press, 2009), II: 175.
110 Nancy Dersofi, "Introduction," in Ruzante, *L'Anconitana / The Woman from Ancona* (Berkeley and Los Angeles: University of California Press, 1994), 9–10.
111 Translated in Martinez, "Etruria Triumphant," 87 n. 3.
112 *"La buona fortuna degli uomini è spesso el maggiore inimico che abbino, perché gli fa diventare spesso cattivi, leggieri, insolenti; però è maggiore paragone di uno uomo el resistere a questa che alle avversitá."* Guicciardini, *Riccordi*, §164 (author's translation.)
113 Niccolò Machiavelli, *The Mandragola*. Trans. Leonard Sbrocchi and J. Douglas Campbell, in *Renaissance Comedy*, ed. Donald Beecher, II: 115–62. (Toronto: University of Toronto Press, 2009), 115. The original text reads: "Perchè la vita è breve / E molte son le pene / Che vivendo e stentando ognun sostiene; / Dietro alle nostre voglie / Andiam

passando e consumando gli anni: / Chè chi 'l piacer si toglie / Per viver con angoscie e con affani, / Non conosce gli'iganni / Del mondo, o da quai mali, / E da ache strani casi, / Oppresi quasi – sian tutti i mortali". Machiavelli, "Canzone," *La Mandragora.*

114 See, e.g., Theodore A. Sumberg, "*La Mandragola*: An Interpretation," *Journal of Politics* 23 (1961): 320–40; Alessandro Parronchi, "La prima reppresentazione della 'Mandragola.' Il modello dele' aparato. L'allegoria," *La Bibliofilia* 64 (1962): 37–86; Carnes Lord, "On Machiavelli's 'Mandragola,' *The Journal of Politics* 41, no. 3 (1979): 806–27; Susan Behuniak-Long, "The Significance of Lucrezia in *La Mandragola*" *The Review of Politics* 51, no. 2 (1989): 264–80.

115 Larivaille, *Pietro Aretino fra Rinascimento e manierismo,* 123–37. See also Larivaille, "Vers un théâtre à une seule voix: Les prologues de l'Arétin au 'Marescalco' et à 'La Cortigiana' du 1534," in *L'écrivain face a son public à la Renaissance* (Paris: Vrin, 1989); Andrews, *Scripts and Scenarios,* 67–74.

116 *"Nè sia chi creda, che questa Commedia si cominci o dal Sacco di Roma, o dall'Assedio di Firenze, o da spandimenti di persone, o da sbaragliamento di famiglie."* Cecchi, *L'assiuolo,* 7. Trans. Konrad Eisenbichler, in Cecchi, *The Horned Owl,* 3–4.

117 Cecchi, Eisenbichler's "Introduction to *The Horned Owl,*" 223, 231 n.1.

118 Ibid., 228.

119 Vidler, *The Scenes of the Street,* 18.

120 de Certeau, *The Practice of Everyday Life,* 107.

121 See Introduction, note 1.

Bibliography

Ackerman, James. *The Architecture of Michelangelo.* London: Zwemmer, 1961.

–. *Distance Points: Essays in Theory and Renaissance Art and Architecture.* Cambridge: The MIT Press, 1994.

–. "Leonardo da Vinci's Church Designs." In *Origins, Imitation, Conventions: Representation in the Visual Arts*, 67–94. Cambridge, MA: The MIT Press, 2002.

–. "On the Origins of Architectural Photography" in *Origins, Imitation, Conventions: Representation in the Visual Arts*, 95–124. Cambridge: The MIT Press, 2001.

–. *Origins, Imitation, Conventions: Representation in the Visual Arts.* Cambridge, MA: The MIT Press, 2002.

Adams, Nicholas and Laurie Nussdorfer. "The Italian City, 1400-1600." In *The Renaissance from Brunelleschi to Michelangelo: The Representation of Architecture*, 205–31. New York: Rizzoli, 1997.

–. *Delineation of the City of Rome.* Ed. by Mario Carpo and Francesco Furlan. Tempe: ACMRS, 2007.

Aliverti, Maria Ines. *Una scena di città attribuita a Sebastiano Serlio.* Pisa: ETS, 2008.

–. *On the Art of Building in Ten Books.* Trans. Robert Tavernor and Neil Leach Joseph Rykwert. Cambridge: The MIT Press, 1991.

Alberti, Leon Battista. *On Painting.* Trans. John R. Spencer. New Haven and London: Yale University Press, 1966.

–. *On Painting and On Sculpture: The Latin Texts of "De Pictura" and "De statua"*, ed. with translations by Grayson. London: Phaidon, 1972.

–. *Opere volgari Vol.* 3. Ed. Cecil Grayson. Bari: G. Laterza e Figli, 1973.

Allegri, Luigi. *Teatro e spettacolo nel medioevo.* Bari: Laterza, 1990.

Andersen, Kirsti. *The Geometry of an Art: The History of the Mathematical Theory of Perspective from Alberti to Monge.* New York: Springer, 2007.

Andreini, Francesco. *Bravure del Capitano Spavento*, ed. R. Tessari. Giardini: Pisa 1987.

Andreini, Giovan Battista. *Prologo in Dialogo fra Momo e la Verità*. Ferrara: Baldini, 1612.

Andrews, Richard. *The Commedia dell'arte of Flaminio Scala: A Translation and Analysis of 30 Scenarios*. Lanham, Toronto, and Plymouth: The Scarecrow Press, 2008.

–. "How – and Why – Does One Print Scenarios? Flaminio Scala, 1611." *Italian Studies* 61, no. 1 (2006): 36–49.

–. "The Renaissance stage." In *A History of Italian Theatre*, 31–8. Cambridge: Cambridge University Press, 2006.

–. *Scripts and Scenarios: The Performance of Comedy in Renaissance Italy*. Cambridge: Cambridge University Press, 1993.

Arditi, Bastiano. *Diario di Firenze e di altre parti della cristianità* (1574–1579), ed. Roberto Cantagalli. Florence: Instituto Nazionale di Studi sul Rinascimento, 1970.

Aretino, Pietro. *La Cortigiana*. Ed. by Angelo Romano. Milano: RCS, 1999.

–. *Cortigiana*. Trans. J. Douglas Campbell and Leonard G. Sbrocchi. Ottawa: Dovehouse Editions, 2003. Reprinted in *Renaissance Comedy, Vol. I*, ed. Donald Beecher. Toronto: University of Toronto Press, 2008.

Aristotle. *Physics*. Vol. I: Books 1–4. Trans. P.H. Wicksteed and F.M. Cornford. Cambridge, MA: Harvard University Press – Loeb Classical Library, 1929.

–. *Poetics*. Trans. George Whalley. Montreal and Kingston: McGill-Queen's University Press, 1997.

Arnheim, Rudolf. *Visual Thinking*. Berkeley and Los Angeles: University of California Press, 1969.

Aronson, Arnold. *Looking into the Abyss*. Ann Arbor: University of Michigan Press, 2005.

–. "Postmodern Design." *Theatre Journal* 43, no. 1 (Mar. 1991): 1–13.

Attolini, Giovanni. *Teatro e spattacolo nel Rinascimento*. Bari: Editori Laterza, 1988.

Augustine, *Confessions*. Vol. 1. Trans. Carolyn Hammond. Cambridge, MA: Harvard University Press – Loeb Classical Library, 2014.

–. *De musica*. Berlin: Walter de Gruyter, 2017.

Ault, Thomas. "Peruzzi and the Perspective Stage." *Theatre Design & Technology* 43, no. 3 (Summer 2007): 33–50.

Aureli, Pier Vittorio. *The Possibility of an Absolute Architecture*. Cambridge: The MIT Press, 2011.

Azzi Visentini, Margherita. "The Gardens of Villas in the Veneto from the Fifteenth to the Eighteenth Centuries." In *The Italian Garden: Art, Design and Culture*, ed. John Dixon Hunt, 93–126. Cambridge: Cambridge University Press, 1996.

Badt, Kurt. "Raphael's 'Incendio del Borgo'," *Journal of the Warburg and Courtauld Institutes* 22, no. 1/2 (Jan–Jun 1959): 35–59.

Barish, Jonas. *The Antitheatrical Prejudice*. Berkeley: University of California Press, 1981.

–. "The Problem of Closet Drama in the Italian Renaissance." *Italica* 71, no. 1 (Spring 1994): 4–30.

Barkan, Leonard. *Unearthing the Past: Archeology and Aesthetics in the Making of Renaissance Culture*. New Haven, CT: Yale University Press, 1999.

Barolsky, Paul. *Infinite Jest: Wit and Humor in Italian Renaissance Art*. Columbia: University of Missouri Press, 1978.

Barth, Fritz. *Martial Signifiers: Fortress Complexes by Francesco di Giorgio*. Stuttgart and London: Axel Menges, 2011.

Barthes, Roland. *Critical Essays*. Evanston, IL: Northwestern University Press, 2000.

–. "Rhetoric of the Image." In *Image, Music, Text*, 32–51. New York: Hill and Wang, 1977.

–. *Critical Essays*. Evanston: Northwestern University Press, 2000.

Battisti, Eugenio. *Brunelleschi*. New York: Rizzoli, 1981.

–. *Rinascimiento e Barroco*. Turin: Einaudi, 1960.

–. "La visualizzazione della scena classica nella comedia umanistica." In *Rinascimiento e Barocco*, 96–111. Turin: Giulio Einudi, 1960.

Batty, Michael. *Cities and Complexity*. Cambridge, MA and London: The MIT Press, 2005.

Baudrillard, Jean. *The Conspiracy of Art*. Los Angeles: Semiotext(e), 2005.

Baxandall, Michael. *Painting and Experience in Fifteenth-Century Italy*. Oxford: Oxford University Press, 1988.

Beecher, Donald, ed. *Renaissance Comedy: The Italian Masters. Vol. I.* Toronto: University of Toronto Press, 2008.

–. *Renaissance Comedy: The Italian Masters. Vol. II.* Toronto: University of Toronto Press, 2009.

Behuniak-Long, Susan. "The Significance of Lucrezia in *La Mandragola*." *The Review of Politics* 51, no. 2 (1989): 264–80.

–. *Florence and Baghdag: Renaissance Art and Arab Science*. Cambridge and London: The Belknap Press of Harvard University Press, 2011.

Belting, Hans. *Likeness and Presence: A History of the Image Before the Era of Art*. Chicago: The University of Chicago Press, 1994.

Benjamin, Walter. "Eduard Fuchs, Collector and Historian," in *Selected Writings*, 260–302. Cambridge and London: Harvard University Press, 2002.

–. "The Work of Art in the Age of Its Technological Reproducibility," in *The Work of Art in the Age of Its Technological Reproducibility and Other Writings on Media*, 19–55. Cambridge: Harvard University Press, 2008.

Benner, Erica. *Machiavelli's Prince: A New Reading*. Oxford: Oxford University Press, 2013.

Beresford, Maurice. *New Towns of the Middle Ages: Town Plantation in England, Wales, and Gascony*. New York: Praeger, 1967.

Bettella, Patrizia. *The Ugly Woman: Transgressive Aesthetic Models in Italian Poetry from the Middle Ages to the Baroque*. Toronto: University of Toronto Press, 2005.

Beyer, Andreas. *Andrea Palladio: Triumpharchitektur für eine humanistische Gesellschaft*. Frankfurt am Main: Fischer, 1987.

Beyer, Hartmut. "Carlo and Marcellino Verardi's *Fernandus servatus* and the Poem *Supra casum Hispani regis* by Petrus Martyr: Drama and Diplomacy in Papal Rome under Alexander VI." In *Drama, Performance and Debate: Theatre and Public Opinion in the Early Modern Period*, ed. Jan Bloemendal, Peter Eversmann, and Elsa Strietman, 35–56. Leiden: Brill, 2012.

Biagi, Alessandro. "La prospettiva, la scenografia, lo spettacolo." In *Baldassarre Peruzzi, Architetto: 20 luglio–20 agosto Ancaiano-Sovicille, commemorazione V centenario della nascita*. Siena: Periccioli, 1981.

Bibbiena, Bernardo Dovizi da. "The Calandria." In *Renaissance Comedy: The Italian Masters, Vol. II*, ed. by Donald Beecher, trans. Leonardo Sbrocchi and J. Douglas Campbell, 21–100. Toronto: University of Toronto Press, 2009.

–. *La Calandria*. Ed. Paolo Fossati. Turin: Guilio Einaudi, 1967.

Biermann, Hartmut. "Das Palastmodell Giuliano da Sangallos für Ferdinard I. König von Neapel," *Wiener Jahrbuch für Kunstgeschichte* xxiii (1970): 154–95.

Bingaman, Amy, Lise Sanders, and Rebecca Zorach. *Embodied Utopias: Gender, Social Change, and the Modern Metropolis*. London and New York: Routledge, 2002.

Bittner, Rüdiger. "One Action." In *Essays on Aristotle's Poetics*, ed. Amelie Oksenber Rorty, 97–110. Princeton, NJ: Princeton University Press, 1992.

Biow, Douglas. *In Your Face: Profession Improprieties and the Art of Being Conspicuous in Sixteenth-Century Italy*. Stanford: Stanford University Press, 2010.

Blackburn, Bonnie J. "Music and Festivities at the Court of Leo X." *Early Music History* 11 (1992): 1–37.

Bleeker, Maaike. *Visuality in the Theatre: The Locus of Looking*. New York: Palgrave Macmillan, 2011.

Blum, Gerd. "Palladio's Villa Rotonda und die Tradition des 'idealen Ortes': Literarische Topoi und die landschaftliche Topographie von Villen der italienischen Renaissance." *Zeitschrift für Kunstgeschichte* 70 (2007): 169–71.

Blumenthal, Arthur. *Italian Renaissance Festival Design*. Madison: University of Wisconsin Press, 1973.

Boerefijn, Wim. "Designing the Medieval New Town." *Urban Morphology* 4, no. 2 (2000): 49–62.

Bondanella, Peter. "Giraldi Cinthio, Giambattista." In Stanley Hochman, *McGraw-Hill Encyclopedia of World Drama*, vol. 1, 314–15. New York: McGraw-Hill, 1984.

Borys, Ann Marie. "Through the Lens: Image and Illusion at Play in the Ideal City." In *Architecture as a Performing Art*, ed. M. Feuerstein and G. Read. Burlington: Ashgate, 2014, 97–112.

Bottrigari, Ercole. *La Maschera, overo della fabrica de'teatri et dello apparato delle scene tragisatiricomiche, Dialogo del M. Illustre S. Cavaliere Hercole Bottrigaro, ms., Civico Museo Bibliografico Musicale di Bologna. Cod 47 B 45.*

Bourne, Molly. "Francesco II Gonzaga and Maps as Palace Decoration in Renaissance Mantua." *Imago Mundi* 51 (1999): 51–82.

Bouwsma, William J. *The Waning of the Renaissance, 1550–1640*. New Haven, CT and London: Yale University Press, 2002.

Branca, Vittore. *Poliziano e l'umanesimo della parola*. Torino: Giulio Einaudi, 1983.

Brand, Peter. "Ariosto and Ferrara." In *A History of Italian Theatre*, ed. Joseph Farrell and Paolo Puppa, 44–50. Cambridge: Cambridge University Press, 2006.

Brubaker, David. *Court and Commedia: The Italian Renaissance Stage*. New York: Richard Rosen Press, 1975.

Bruschi, Arnaldo. "Riconstruzione e nota critica nell'architettura del teatro capitolino." In *Il teatro del Campidoglio e le feste romane del 1513*, ed. Fabrizio Cruciani, 139–62. Milan: Polifilo, 1968.

–. "Il teatro Capitolino del 1513." *Bollettino del Centro Internazionale di Studi di Architettura Andrea Palladio* 16 (1974): 189–218.

Bryson, Norman. *Vision and Painting: The Logic of the Gaze*. New Haven, CT: Yale University Press, 1983.

Buccheri, Alessandra. *The Spectacle of Clouds: Italian Art and Theatre, 1439–1650*. Burlington, VT: Ashgate, 2014.

Bundy, Murray. "Fracastoro and the Imagination." In *Renaissance Studies in Honor of Hardin Craig*, ed. Baldwin Maxwell, W.D. Briggs, Francis R. Johnson, and E.N.S. Thompson, 44–56. Stanford, CA: Stanford University Press, 1972.

Burckhardt, Jacob. *The Architecture of the Italian Renaissance*. London: Secker and Warburg, 1985.

Burke, Peter. *The Fortunes of the Courtier*. University Park: The Pennsylvania State University, 1995.

Burns, Alfred. "Hippodamus and the Planned City." *Historia: Zeitschrift für Alte Geschichte*, no. Bd. 25, H. 4 (4th Qtr 1976): 414–28.

Burns, Howard, Linda Fairbairn, and Bruce Boucher. *Andrea Palladio, 1508–1580: The Portico and the Farmyard*. Exhibition catalogue. London: Council of Great Britain, 1975.

Burroughs. *From Signs to Design: Environmental Process and Reform in Early Renaissance Rome*. Cambridge, MA: The MIT Press, 1990.

–. "Michelangelo at the Campidoglio: Artistic Identity, Patronage, and Manufacture." *Artibus et Historiae* 14, no. 28 (1993): 85–111.

Bustamante García, Agustín, and Fernando Marías Franco. *Dibujos de Arquitectura y Ornamentación de la Biblioteca Nacional, Siglos XVI y XVII*. Madrid: Ministerio de Cultura, 1991.

Cairns, Christopher. "Theatre as Festival: The Staging of Arentino's *Talanta* (1542) and the Influence of Vasari." In *Italian Renaissance Festivals and the European Influence*, ed. J. R. Mulryne and Margaret Shewring, 105–17. Lewiston, Queenston, Lampeter: The Edwin Mellen Press, 1992.

–., ed. *The Commedia dell'arte: from the Renaissance to Dario Flo*. Lewinston, NY: The Edwin Mellen Press, 1988.

Campbell, Lily. "The First Edition of Vitruvius." *Modern Philology* 29 no. 1 (1931): 107–10.

–. *Scenes and Machines on the English Stage during the Renaissance*. Cambridge: Cambridge University Press, 1923.

Campori, Giuseppe. *Lettere artistiche inedite*. Modena: Soliani, 1866.

Capolari, Giambattista. *Architettvra: Con il suo comento et figvre Vetrvvio*. Perugia: Bigazzini, 1536.

Carlson, Marvin. *Places of Performance: The Semiotics of Theatre Architecture*. Ithaca, NY: Cornell University Press, 1993.

Caro, Anibale. "Gli straccioni." In *Commedie del Cinquecento*, Vol. 2, ed. Nino Borsellino, 193–279. Milan: Feltrinelli, 1967.

Carpo, Mario. *Alberti, Raffaello, Serlio e Camillo*. Geneva: Librairie Droz, 1993.

–. *Architecture in the Age of Printing: Orality, Writing, Typography, and Printed Images in the History of Architectural Theory*. Cambridge, MA: The MIT Press, 2001.

Casey, Edward S. *Getting Back into Place: Toward a Renewed Understanding of the Place-World*. Bloomington and Indianapolis: Indiana University Press, 1993.

Casper, Andrew. "Display and Devotion: Exhibiting Icons and Their Copies." In *Religion and the Sense in Early Modern Europe*, ed. W. de Boer and C. Göttler, 43–62. Leiden and Boston: Brill, 2013.

Castelvetro, Ludovico. *On the Art of Poetry*. Trans. Andrew Bongiorno. Binghamton, NY: Medieval and Renaissance Texts and Studies, 1984.

–. *Poetica d'Aristotele vulgarizzata e sposta per L.C. riveduta et ammendata secondo l'originale, e la mente dell'autore*. Vienna: Gaspar Stainhofer, 1570; second edition Basel: Pietro de Sedabonis, 1576. Reprinted as *Poetica d'Aristotele vulgarizzata e sposta*, ed. Werther Romani, 2 vols. Bari: Laterza, 1978–9.

Castiglione, Baldassare. *Il libro del Cortegiano*. Ed. Nicola Longo. Milan: Garzanti, 2000.

Cecchi, Giovan Maria. *L'assiuolo: Commedia e saggio di proverbi*. Milan: Daelli, 1863.

–. *The Horned Owl*. Ed. Konrad Eisenbichler. Waterloo: Wilfrid Laurier University Press, 1981.

Celenza, Christopher. *The Lost Italian Renaissance: Humanists, Historians, and the Latin's Legacy*. Baltimore, MD: Johns Hopkins University Press, 2005.

Cellini, Benvenuto. *My Life*. Trans. Julia Bondanella and Peter Bondanella. Oxford: Oxford University Press, 2002.

Chambers, David, and Brian Pullan, *Venice: A Documentary History, 1450–1630*. Toronto: University of Toronto Press, 2001.

Changizi, Mark. *The Vision Revolution: How the Latest Research Overturns Everything We Thought We Knew about Human Vision*. Dallas, TX: Ben Bella, 2009.

Chastel, André. "Cortile et théâtre." In *Le lieu théâtral à la Renaissance*, ed. Jean Jacquot, 41–7. Paris: Éditions du Centre National de la Recherche Scientifique, 1964.

Choay, Françoise. *The Rule and the Model: On the Theory of Architecture and Urbanism*. Cambridge, MA and London: The MIT Press, 1997.

Ciapponi, Lucia. "Fra Giocondo da Verona and His Edition of Vitruvius," *Journal of the Warburg and Courtauld Institutes* 47 (1984): 72–90.

Cicero, Marcus Tullius. *On the Orator*. Cambridge, MA: Harvard University Press – Loeb Classical Library, 1942.

Clarke, John R. *Art in the Lives of Ordinary Romans: Visual Presentation and Non-Elite Viewers in Italy,* 100 *B.C.-A.D.* 315. Berkeley and Los Angeles: University of California Press, 2003.

–. *Pirro Ligorio. The Renaissance Artist, Architect, and Antiquarian*. University Park: Pennsylvania University Press, 2003.

Coffin, David. "The Plans of the Villa Madama," *The Art Bulletin* 49, no. 2 (1967): 111–22.

Comanini, Gregorio. "Il Figino, ovvero del Fine della Pittura." In *Trattati d'arte del Cinquecento*, vol. III, ed. Paola Barocchi. Bari: Laterza, 1962.

–. *The Figino, or On the Purpose of Painting: Art Theory in the Late Renaissance*, ed. Ann Doyle-Anderson and Giancarlo Maiorino. Toronto: University of Toronto Press, 2001.

Cooper, Frederick A. "Jacopo Pontormo and Influences from the Renaissance Theater." *The Art Bulletin* 55, no. 3 (1973): 380–92.

–. "The Politics of a Theatrical Event: The 1509 Performance of Ariosto's I suppositi," *Mediaevalia* 33 (2012): 195–228.

–. "Strategies of Subversion: The Power of Live Performance within the Walls of a Renaissance City." *International Journal of Arts and Technology* 2.3 (2009): 187–201.

Cottino-Jones, Marga. "Rome and the Theatre in the Renaissance." In *Rome in the Renaissance: The City and the Myth*, ed. P.A. Ramsey, 237–47. Binghampton: Center for Medieval and Renaissance Studies, State University of New York, 1982.

Crabtree, Susan, and Peter Beudert, *Scenic Art for the Theatre: History, Tools, and Techniques*. Boston: Focal Press, 2005.

Costola, Sergio. "La prima rappresentazione dei Suppositi di Ariosto nel 1509." In *Lucrezia tra Letteratura e Storia*, ed. Michele Bordin and Paolo Trovato, 75–96. Florence: L.S. Olschki, 2006.

Crary, Jonathan. *Techniques of the Observer: On Vision and Modernity in the Nineteenth Century*. Cambridge, MA and London: MIT Press, 1992.

Cremante, Renzo. *Teatro del Cinquecento: La tragedia*. Milan and Naples: Ricciardi, 1988.

Cruciani, Fabricio. *Il teatro del Campidoglio e le feste romane del* 1513. Milan: Polifilo, 1968.

Curran, Brian. "Teaching (and Thinking About) the High Renaissance: With Some Observations on its Relationship to Classical Antiquity." In *Rethinking the High Renaissance*, ed. Jill Burke, 27–56. Burlington, VT: Ashgate, 2012.

D'Accone, Frank. *The Civic Muse: Music and Musicians in Siena during the Middle Ages and the Renaissance*. Chicago: The University of Chicago Press, 1997.

D'Amico, Jack. "Drama and the Court in 'La Calandria'." *Theatre Journal* 43 (1991): 93–106.

Damisch, Hubert. *The Origin of Perspective*. Cambridge, MA: The MIT Press, 1994.

–. *Skyline*. Trans. John Goodman. Stanford: Stanford University Press, 2001.

–. *A Theory of /Cloud/*. Stanford, CA: Stanford University Press, 2002.

D'Ancona, Alessandro. *Origini del teatro Italiano*. Turin: Loescher, 1891.

Davis, Michael. *The Poetry of Philosophy: On Aristotle's Poetics*. South Bend, IN: St Augustine's Press, 1999.

Davis, Robert. *The War of the Fists: Popular Culture and Public Violence in Late Renaissance Venice.* New York and Oxford: Oxford University Press, 1994.

Dawson, Olivia. "Speaking Theatres: The 'Olimpico' Theatres of Vicenza and Sabbioneta and Camillo's Theatre of Memory." In *The Renaissance Theatre: Texts, Performance, Design. Vol.* 2, ed. Christopher Cairns, 85–92. Aldershot: Ashgate, 1991.

de Certeau, Michel. *The Practice of Everyday Life.* Berkeley: University of California Press, 1984.

Deleuze, Gilles, and Felix Guattari. *A Thousand Plateaus.* Minneapolis: University of Minnesota Press, 1987.

–. *On the Name.* Stanford: Stanford University Press, 1995.

Derrida, Jacques. *The Truth in Painting.* Chicago: University of Chicago Press, 1987.

De Tolnay, Charles. "Michelangelo Studies." *The Art Bulletin* 22, no. 3 (1940): 127–37.

D' Evelyn, Margaret Muther. *Venice & Vitruvius.* New Haven, CT and London: Yale University Press, 2012.

Deleuze, Gilles and Felix Guattari. *A Thousand Plateaus.* Minneapolis: University of Minnesota Press, 1987.

Dewey, John. *Art as Experience.* New York: Perigree, 1980.

Diamond, Elin. "*Gestus*, Signature, Body in the Theater of Aphra Behn." In *Unmasking Mimesis. Essays on Feminism and Theater.* London: Routledge, 1997.

Diderot, Denis. "On Dramatic Poetry" (1758). In *European Theories of the Drama,* Barrett H. Clark, ed., 286–99. New York: Crown, 1947.

Didi-Huberman, Georges. *Confronting Images.* University Park: The Pennsylvania State University Press, 2005.

di Giorgio Martini, Francesco. *Trattati di architettura, ingegnieria e arte militare.* Ed. Conrado Maltese. Milano: Polifilo, 1967.

Di Macco, Michela. *Il Colosseo: Funzione simbolica, storica, urbana.* Rome: Bulzoni, 1971.

Di Maria, Salvatore. *The Italian Tragedy in the Renaissance: Cultural Realities and Theatrical Innovations.* Lewisburg, PA: Bucknell University Press, 2002.

Doni, Anton Francesco. *I mondi e gli inferni.* Ed. Patrizia Pellizzari. Turin: Giulio Einaudi, 1994.

Dovey, Kim. *Framing Places: Mediating Power in Built Form.* London and New York: Routledge, 1999.

du Prey, Pierre de la Ruffinière. *The Villas of Pliny from Antiquity to Posterity.* Chicago: University of Chicago Press, 1994.

Durand, Carroll. "The Apogee of Perspective in the Theatre: Ferdinando Bibiena's *Scena per angolo.*" *Theatre Research International* 13, no. 1 (1988): 21–9.

Eaton, Ruth. *Ideal Cities: Utopianism and the (Un)Built Environment.* London: Thames and Hudson, 2002.

Eco, Umberto. *Art and Beauty in the Middle Ages.* Trans. Hugh Bredin. New Haven and London: Yale University Press, 1986.

–. "Semiotics of Theatrical Performance." *The Drama Review* 21, no. 1 (1977): 107–17.

Edgerton, Samuel. *The Heritage of Giotto's Geometry: Art and Science on the Eve of the Scientific Revolution.* Ithaca, NY: Cornell University Presss, 1991.

Eiche, Sabine. "A New Look at Three Drawings for Villa Madama and Some Related Images, " *Mitteilungen des Kunsthistorischen Institutes in Florenz* 36. Bd., H. 3 (1992): 275–86.

Eisenbichler, Konrad. "How Bartolomeo Saw a Play." In *The Renaissance in the Streets, Schools, and Studies,* ed. Konrad Eisenbichler and Nicholas Terpstra, 259–78. Toronto: Toronto University Press, 2008.

Eisenbichler, Konrad, and Nicholas Terpstra, eds. *The Renaissance in the Streets, Schools, and Studies.* Toronto: Toronto University Press, 2008.

Elam, Keir. *The Semiotics of Theatre and Drama.* London: Routledge, 1980.

Eliav-Feldon, Miriam. *Realistic Utopias: The Ideal Imaginary Societies of the Renaissance 1516–1630.* Oxford: Claredon Press, 1982.

–. *The Poetics of Perspective.* Ithaca and London: Cornell University Press, 1994.

Elkins, James. "Renaissance Perspectives." *Journal of the History of Ideas* 53, no. 2 (1992): 209–30.

Elkins, James, and Robert Williams, eds. *Renaissance Theory.* New York and London: Routledge, 2008.

Emison, Patricia. *Creating the "Divine" Artist: From Dante to Michelangelo.* Boston: Brill, 2004.

Evers, Bernd. *Architekturmodelle der Renaissance, Die Harmonie des Bauens von Alberti bis Michelangelo.* Munich: Prestel, 1995.

Fanelli, Giovanni. *Firenze.* Rome: Laterza, 1980.

Fane-Saunders, Peter. *Pliny the Elder and the Emergence of Renaissance Architecture.* Cambridge: Cambridge University Press, 2016.

Fenech Kroke, Antonella. "Un théâtre pour *La Talanta*: Giorgio Vasari, Pietro Aretino et l'apparato de 1542." *Revue de l'Art* 168 (2010): 53–64.

Féral, Josette. "Theatricality: The Specificity of Theatrical Language." *SubStance,* no. 31 (2002): 94–108.

Ferrari, G. "Il manoscritto Spectacula di Pellegrino Prisciani." In *La corte e lo spazio: Ferrara Estense*, ed. G. Papagno and A.Quondam, 431–49. Rome: Bulzoni, 1982.

Ferrati, Giulio. *La scenografia*. Milan: Umberto Allegretti, 1902.

Feuerstein, Günter. *Urban Fiction: Strolling through Ideal Cities from Antiquity to the Present Day*. Stuttgard and London: Axel Menges, 2008.

Fidenzoni, P.. *Il teatro di Marcello*. Rome: Liber, 1970.

Filarete, Antonio Avelino. *Treatise on Architecture*, ed. J. R. Spencer. New Haven: Yale University Press, 1965.

Findlay, John and Iain Gilchrist, *Active Vision: The Psychology of Looking and Seeing*. Oxford: Oxford University Press, 2003.

Finotti, Fabio. "Perspective and Stage Design, Fiction and Reality in the Italian Renaissance Theater of the Fifteenth Century." *Renaissance Drama, New Series* 36/37 (2010): 21–42.

Fiocco, Giuseppe. "Alvise Cornaro e il teatro." in *Essays Presented to Rudolf Wittkower on His Sixty-fifth Birthday*, ed. D. Fraser and H. Hibbard, 34–9. London: Phaidon, 1967.

–. "La casa di Alvise Cornaro." *Bolletino del Museo Civico di Padova* LVII (1968): 7–16.

Fiorani, Francesca. *The Marvel of Maps*. New Haven, CT: Yale University Press, 2005.

Fleming, Alison. "Presenting the Spectators as the Show: The Piazza degli Uffizi as Theater and Stage." *The Sixteenth Century Journal* XXXVII, no. 3 (2006): 701–20.

Florensky, Pavel. "Reverse Perspective." In *Beyond Vision: Essays on the Perception of Art*, trans. by Wendy Salmond, 201–72. London: Reaktion, 2002.

Fontana, Vicenzo, and Paolo Marachiello. *Vitruvio e Raffaello. Il "De Architectura" de Vitruvio nella traduzione inedita di Fabio Calvo Ravennate*. Rome: Officina Edizioni, 1975.

Fortini Brown, Patricia. "The Antiquarianism of Jacopo Bellini." *Artibus et Historiae* 13, no. 26 (1992): 64–84.

–. *Private Lives in Renaissance Venice: Art, Architecture, and the Family*. New Haven, CT and London: Yale University Press, 2005.

–. *Venice and Antiquity: The Venetian Sense of the Past*. New Haven, CT: Yale University Press, 1996.

Forster, Kurt. "Stagecraft and Statecraft: The Architectural Integration of Public Life and Theatrical Spectacle in Scamozzi's Theater at Sabbioneta," *Oppositions* 9 (1977): 63–87.

Fracastoro, Girolamo. *Naugerius* (Venice, 1555). Reprinted as *Navagero, della Poetica*, ed. Enrico Peruzzi. Florence: Alinea Editrice, 2005.

–. *Naugerius*. Ed. Ruth Kelso. Urbana: University of Illinois Press, 1924.
Franceschetti, Antonio, and Kenneth Bartlett. "Introduction to *The Moscheta*." In *Renaissance Comedy: The Italian Masters, Vol. II*, ed. Donald Beecher, 175. Toronto: University of Toronto Press, 2009.
Franceschini, Adriano. "Nota sopra un bolleto scenografico ferrarese del sec. XVI." In Antonio Samaritini and Ranieri Varese, eds, *L'Aquila Bianca: Studi di storia Estense per Luciano Chiappini*, 391–410. Ferrara: Corbo, 2000.
Foucault, Michel. *Discipline and Punish: The Birth of the Prison*. London: Penguin, 1977.
–. "Of Other Spaces." *Diacritics* 16, no. 1 (Spring 1986): 22–7.
–. *The Order of Things*. New York: Random House, 1994.
Frangenberg, Thomas. "Choreographies of Florence. The Use of City Views and City Plans in the Sixteenth Century." *Imago Mundi* 46 (1994): 41–64.
Freud, Sigmund. *Civilization and Its Discontents*. Trans. James Strachey. New York and London: W. W. Norton, 1961.
Fried, Michael. *Absorption and Theatricality:Painting and Beholder in the Age of Diderot*. Berkeley: University of California Press, 1980.
Friedman, David. "'Fiorenza': Geography and Representation in a Fifteenth Century View." *Zeitschrift für Kunstgeschichte*, 64 (2001): 56–77.
Frommel, Christoph. *Architecture of the Italian Renaissance*. London: Thames and Hudson, 2007.
–. "Scenografia teatrale." In *Raffaello architetto*, ed. Christoph Frommel, Stefano Ray, and Manfredo Tafuri, 225–8. Milan: Electra, 1984.
Frommel, Christoph, Arnaldo Bruschi, Howard Burns, Francesco Paolo Fiore, and Pier Nicola Pagliara. *Baldassarre Peruzzi, 1482–1536*. Venice: Marsilio, 2005.
Frommel, Christoph, Stefano Ray, and Manfredo Tafuri, eds. *Raffaello architetto*. Milan: Electra, 1984.
Frommel, Sabine. *Sebastiano Serlio Architect*. Trans. by Peter Spring. Milan: Electra, 2003.
Frye, Northrop. "Varieties of Literary Utopas." *Daedalus* 94, no. 2 (1965): 323–47.
Fülöp-Miller, René. *The Power and the Secret of the Jesuits*. New York: Viking, 1930.
Gareffi, Andrea. *La scrittura e la festa: Teatro, festa e letteratura nella Firenze del Rinascimiento*. Bologna: Il Mulino, 1991.
Gassner, John, and Ralph G. Allen. *Theatre and Drama in the Making*. New York: Applause Theatre Books, 1992.

Gaston, Robert W. "Merely Antiquarian: Pirro Ligorio and the Critical Tradition of Antiquarian Scholarship." In *The Italian Renaissance in the Twentieth Century*, ed. Allen J. Grieco, 355–73. Florence: Leo S. Olschki, 2002.

Gerould, Daniel, ed. *Theatre, Theory, Theatre: The Major Critical Texts from Aristotle and Zeami to Soyinka and Havel*. New York: Applause, 2000.

Geuss, Raymond. *Public Goods, Private Goods*. Princeton, NJ: Princeton University Press, 2001.

Ghirardo, Diane Yvonne. "Festival Bridal Entries in Renaissance Ferrara." In *Festival Architecture*, ed. by Sarah Bonnemaison and Christine Macy, 43–73. London and New York: Routledge, 2008.

Ghisetti Giavarina, Adriano. *Aristotile da Sangallo: Architettura, scenografia e pittura tra Roma e Firenze nella prima metà del Cinquecento*. Rome: Multigrafica, 1990.

Giambullari, M.P.F. *Copia d'una lettera di M. Pier Francesco Giambullari, al molto Magnifico M. Giovanni Bandini Oratore dello Illustrissimo Signor Duca di Firenze appresso la Maestà Cesarea*. In A. Landi, *Il commodo: Commedia col apparato et feste nelle nozze dello Illustrissimo Signor Duca di Firenze et della Duchessa sua consorte, con le sue stanze, madriali, comedia & intermedij, in quelle recitate*, con una lettera di *M.P.F. Giambullari*. Florence: Giunta, 1539.

Giancarli, Gigio Artemio. *Cingana*. Venice: Agostino Bindoni, 1550.

Gilbert, Creighton. "A New Sight in 1500: The Colossal." In *'All the World's a Stage ...' Art and Pageantry in the Renaissance and Baroque*, ed. Barbara Wisch and Susan Scott Munshower, 396–415. University Park: Pennsylvania State University Press, 1990.

Gillespie, Stuart. "Gl'Ingannati." In *Shakespeare's Books: A Dictionary of Shakespeare Sources*, 192–6. London and New York: Continuum.

Giraldi Cinthio, Giovambattista. *De' romanzi, delle comedie e delle tragedie*. Milan: Daelli, 1864.

–. "Discorso intorno al comporre delle comedie e delle tragedie." In *Scritti Critici*, ed. Camillo Guerrieri Crocetti, 171–224. Milan: Marzorati, 1973.

–. *On Romances*. Translated by Introduction bu Henry L. Snuggs. Lexington: University of Kentucky Press, 1968.

Giuliani, Maria Carla. "*La Mascara* di Hercole Bottrigari." *Bolletino del Centro internazionale di studi di architettura Andrea Palladio* 1982: 85–102.

Gombrich, E. H. *Art and Illusion*. Princeton, NJ: Princeton University Press, 1960.

–. *Gombrich on the Renaissance*. New York: Phaidon, 1985.

–. "Review of John Shearman, *Only Connect...*," *New York Review of Books*, March (1993): 19–21.

González Román, Carmen. *Spectacula*. Málaga: Universidad de Málaga, 2001.

Goodman, Nelson. *Languages of Art: An Approach to a Theory of Symbols.* Indianapolis: Bobbs-Merrill, 1968.

Gordon, Donald James. *The Renaissance Imagination.* Berkeley and Los Angeles: University of California Press, 1975.

Gordon, Scott. *Controlling the State.* Cambridge: Harvard University Press, 2002.

Gorse, George L. "A Classical Stage for the Old Nobility: The Strada Nuova and Sixteenth-Century Genoa," *The Art Bulletin* 79, no. 2 (1997): 301–27.

Gosebruch, Martin. "'Varietas' bei Alberti und der wissenschaftliche Renaissancebegriff," *Zeitschrift für Kunstgeschichte* XX (1957): 229–38.

Gould, Cecil. "Sebastiano Serlio and Venetian Painting," *Journal of the Warburg and Courtauld Institutes* 25, no. 1/2 (1962): 56–64.

Goulthorpe, Mark. "From Autoplastic to Alloplastic Tendency." In *Anymore,* ed. by Cynthia Davidson, 206–15. Cambridge, MA and London: The MIT Press, 2000.

Grafton,Anthony. *Leon Battista Alberti: Master Builder of the Italian Renaissance.* Cambridge, MA: Harvard University Press, 2000.

Grazzini, Anton Francesco. *Frate Alberigo.* In *Renaissance Comedy, Vol. II,* ed. Donald Beecher, trans. Bruno Ferraro, 300–21. Toronto: University of Toronto Press, 2009.

Greenwood, John Philip Peter. *Shifting Perspectives and the Stylish Style: Mannerism in Shakespeare and his Jacobean Contemporaries.* Toronto: Toronto University Press, 1988.

–. *Critics of the Italian World, 1530–1560: Anton Francesco Doni, Nicolò Franco and Ortensio Lando.* Madison and London: University of Winsconsin Press, 1969.

Grendler, Paul. "Utopia in Renaissance Italy: Doni's 'New World'." *Journal of the History of Ideas* 26, no. 4 (1965): 479–94.

Griffin, Nigel. *Jesuit School Drama: A Checklist of Critical Literature.* London: Grant and Cutler, 1976.

Gros, Pierre. "Baldassarre Peruzzi, architetto e archeologo." In *Baldassarre Peruzzi 1482–1536,* ed. Christoph Frommel, Arnaldo Bruschi, Howard Burns, Francesco Paolo Fiore, and Pier Nicola Pagliara, 225–30. Venice: Marsilio, 2005.

Grosz, Elizabeth. "Architectures of Excess," In *Anymore,* ed. Cynthia Davidson, 260–6. Cambridge, MA, and London: The MIT Press, 2000.

Grund, Gary., ed. *Humanist Comedies.* Cambridge and London: Harbard University Press - The I Tatti Renaissance Library, 2005.

Grotowski, Jerzy. *Towards a Poor Theatre.* London: Methuen, 1969.

Guicciardini, Francesco, *The History of Italy.* Trans. by Sydney Alexander. Princeton: Princeton University Press, 1984.

–. *Ricordi*. Ed. Raffaele Spongano. Florence: Sansoni, 1951.

Guidoni, Enrico. *Storia dell'urbanistica. Il Duecento*. Rome: Laterza, 1992.

Guidotti, Angela. *Scenografie di pensieri*. Lucca: Maria Pacini Fazzi Editore, 2002.

Halliwell, Stephen. *Aristotle's Poetics*. Chicago: University of Chicago Press, 1998.

Hara, Mari Yoko. "Capturing Eyes and Moving Souls: Peruzzi's Perspective Set for *La Calandria* and the Performative Agency of Architectural Bodies." *Renaissance Studies* 31, no. 4 (2016): 586–607.

Harries, Karsten. *Infinity and Perspective*. Cambridge, MA: The MIT Press, 2001.

Harry, Drew, Dietmar Offernhuber, and Judith Donath. "The Social Role of Virtual Architecture." In *Space between People*, ed. Stephan Doesinger, 64–70. Munich, London, and New York: Prestel, 2008.

Hartfield, Gary. "Attention in Early Scientific Psychology." In *Visual Attention*, ed. R. D. Wright, 3–25. New York: Oxford University Press, 1998.

Heidegger, Martin. "Science and Reflection." In *The Question Concerning Technology and Other Essays*, trans. William Lovitt. New York: Harper and Row, 1977.

Hendrix, John. "Perception as a Function of Desire in the Renaissance." In *Renaissance Theories of Vision*, ed. John Hendrix and Charles Carman, 99–115. Burlington, VT: Ashgate, 2010.

Henke, Robert. *Performance and Literature in the Commedia dell'arte*. Cambridge: Cambridge University Press, 2002.

Hermans, Lex. "The Performing Venue: The Visual Play of Italian Courtly Theatres in the Sixteenth Century." In *Theatricality in Early Modern Art and Architecture*, eds Caroline van Eck and Stijn Bussels, 93–103. London: Blackwell, 2011.

Herrick, Marvin T. *Italian Comedy in the Renaissance*. Urbana and London: University of Illinois Press, 1966.

Hersey, George. *Alfonso II and the Artistic Renewal of Naples 1585–1495*. New Haven: Yale University Press, 1969.

Hewitt, Barnard. *The Renaissance Stage: Documents on Serlio, Sabbattini, and Furttenbach*. Coral Gables, FL: University of Miami Press, 1958.

Hewlett, Mary. "Fortune's Fool: The Influence of Humanism on Francesco Burlamacchi, 'Hero' of Lucc." In *The Renaissance in the Streets, Schools, and Studies*, ed. Konrad Eisenbichler and Nicholas Terpstra, 125–56. Toronto: Toronto University Press, 2008.

Heydenreich, Ludwig. *Architecture in Italy, 1400–1500*. New Haven and London: Yale University Press, 1996.

Hoffman, Donald D. *Visual Intelligence: How We Create What We See*. New York: W.W. Norton and Company, 1998.
Hollier, Denis. *Against Architecture: The Writings of George Bataille*. Cambridge, MA: The MIT Press, 1989.
Horace. *Ars poetica*. In *Epistles: Book II and Epistle to the Pisones ('Ars Poetica')*, ed. Niall Rudd, 58–74. Cambridge: Cambridge University Press, 1989.
Howard, Deborah. *The Architectural History of Venice*. New Haven, CT: Yale University Press, 2002.
Howard, Pamela. *What Is Scenography?* London and New York: Routledge, 2001.
Howe, Eunice. "Architecture in Vasari's 'Massacre of the Huguenots'," *Journal of the Warburg and Courtlauld Institutes* 39 (1976): 258–61.
Huppert, Ann. "Baldassarre Peruzzi as Archeologist in Terracina." In *Baldassarre Peruzzi 1482–1536*, ed. Christoph Frommel, Arnaldo Bruschi, Howard Burns, Francesco Paolo Fiore, and Pier Nicola Pagliara, 213–23. Venice: Marsilio, 2005.
–. *Becoming an Architect in Renaissance Italy: Art, Science, and the Career of Baldassarre Peruzzi*. New Haven, CT: Yale University Press, 2015.
Huse, Norbert, and Wolfgang Wolters. *The Art of Renaissance Venice: Architecture, Sculpture, and Painting*, 1460–1590. Chicago: University of Chicago Press, 1990.
Hyatt, Mayor. *Selected Writings*. New York: Metropolitan Museum of Art, 1983.
Jacks, Phillip J. "The Simulachrum of Fabio Calvo: A View of Roman Architecture all'antica in 1527." *The Art Bulletin* 72, no. 3 (1990): 453–81.
Jacobs, Fredrika. "Rethinking the Divide: Cult Images and the Cult of Images." In *Renaissance Theory*, ed. James Elkins and Robert Williams, 95–114. New York: Routledge, 2008.
Jacquot, Jean, ed. *Le lieu thèâtral à la Renaissance*. Paris: Éditions du Centre National de la Recherche Scientifique, 1964.
Jameson, Fredric. "Of Islands and Trenches: Neutralization and the Production of Utopian Discourses." In *The Ideologies of Theory: Essays, 1971–86*, 75–103. Minneapolis: University Of Minnesota Press, 1988.
Javitch, Daniel. "The Assimilation of Aristotle's *Poetics* in Sixteenth-Century Italy." In *The Cambridge History of Literary Criticism Vol. 3: The Renaissance*, ed. Glyn P. Norton, 53–65. Cambridge: Cambridge University Press, 1999.
Jay, Martin. "Scopic Regimes of Modernity." In *Vision and Visuality*, ed. Hal Foster, 3–23. Seattle: Bay Press, 1988.
Jeanneret, Michel. *Perpetual Motion*. Baltimore, MD: The John Hopkins University Press, 2001.

Johnson, Eugene J. "Jacopo Sansovino, Giacomo Torelli, and the Theatricality of the Piazzetta in Venice." *The Journal of the Society of Architectural Historians* 59, no. 4 (2000): 436–53.

–. "The Short, Lascivious Lives of Two Venetian Theaters, 1580-85," *Renaissance Quarterly* 55, no. 3 (2002): 936–68.

Jones, P. J. "Communes and Despots: The City State in Late-Medieval Italy." *Transactions of the Royal Historical Society, 5th series* 15: 71–96.

Jones, Roger, and Nicholas Penny, *Raphael.* New Haven, CT: Yale University Press, 1983.

Jurén, Vladimir. "Le projet de Giuliano da Sangallo pour le palais du roi de Naples," *Revenue de l'art* 25 (1974): 66–70.

Katritzky, M.A. "The Mountback: A Case Study in Early Modern Theater Iconography," in *Evidence and Inference in History and Law: Interdisciplinary Dialogues,* 231–86. Evanston: Northwestern University Press, 2003.

–. "The Commedia dell'arte: New Perspective and New Documents." *Early Theatre* 11, no. 2 (2008): 141–54.

–. "Italian Comedians in Renaissance Prints." *Print Quarterly* 4, no. 3 (1987): 236–54.

–. "The Mountebank: A Case Study in Early Modern Theater Iconography." In *Evidence and Inference in History and Law: Interdisciplinary Dialogues,* ed. William Twining and Iain Hampsher-Monk, 231–86. Evanston, IL: Northwestern University Press, 2003.

–. *A Study in the Commedia dell'arte 1560–1620 with Special Reference to the Visual Records.* New York and Amsterdam: Rodopi, 2006.

Kemp, Martin. "From 'Mimesis' to 'Fantasia": The Quattocento Vocabulary of Creation, Inspiration, and Genius in the Visual Arts." *Viator* 8 (1977): 347–98.

–. *Leonardo da Vinci: The Marvellous Works of Nature and Man.* London: Dent and Sons, 1981.

–. *The Science of Art: Optical Themes in Western Art from Brunelleschi to Seurat.* New Haven: Yale University Press, 1990.

Kendrick, Christopher. *Utopia, Carnival, and Commonwealth in Renaissance England.* Toronto: University of Toronto Press, 2004.

Kernodle, George R. *From Art to Theatre: Form and Convention in the Renaissance.* Chicago: University of Chicago Press, 1965.

–. *The Theatre in History.* Fayetteville: University of Arkansas Press, 1989.

Kettering, Emil. *Nähe: Das Denken Martin Heideggers.* Pfüllingen: Neske, 1987. Kieckhefer, Richard. *Forbidden Rites: A Necromancer's Manual of the Fifteenth Century.* University Park: Pennsylvania University Press, 1998.

Kieckhefer, Richard. *Forbidden Rites: A Necromancer's Manual of the Fifteenth Century.* University Park: Pennsylvania University Press, 1998.

Kim, Sang Woo. "Historiography of Duke Cosimo I de' Medici's Cultural Politics and Theories of Cultural Hegemony and Opposition," *Michigan Journal of History* (Winter 2006): 1–70.

Klein, Norman. *The Vatican to Vegas.* New York and London: The New Press, 2004.

Klein, Robert, and Henri Zerner. "Vitruve et le théâtre de la renaissance italienne." In *Le lieu théâtral à la Renaissance*, ed. J. Jacquot, 49–60. Paris: Centre National de la Recherche Scientifique, 1964.

Kleinbub, Christian. *Vision and the Visionary in Raphael.* University Park: Pennsylvania State University Press.

Korsch, Evelyn. "Diplomatic Gifts on Heri III's Visit to Venice in 1574," *Studies in the Decorative Arts*, no. 15 (2007): 83–113.

Krass, Leon R. *The Beginning of Wisdom: Reading Genesis.* Chicago: University of Chicago Press, 2003.

Krauss, Rosalind. *The Originality of the Avant-Garde and Other Modern Myths.* Cambridge, MA: The MIT Press, 1985.

Krautheimer, Richard. "The Panels in Urbino, Baltimore and Berlin Reconsidered." In *The Renaissance from Brunelleschi to Michelangelo: The Representation of Architecture*, 233–57. New York: Rizzoli, 1997.

–. "The Tragic and Comic Scenes of the Renaissance. The Baltimore and Urbino Panels." In *Studies in Early Christian, Medieval, and Renaissance Art*, 345–59. New York: New York University Press, 1969.

Krinsky, Carol Herselle. "Cesare Cesariano and the Como Vitruvius Edition of 1521." PhD diss., New York University, 1965.

Kris, Ernst, and Otto Kurz. *Legeend, Myth, and Magic in the Image of the Artist: A Historical Experiment.* New Haven and London: Yale University Press, 1979.

Kristeva, Julia. "Modern Theater Does Not Take (a) Place." In *Mimesis, Masochism, and Mime*, ed. Timothy Murray, 277–81. Ann Arbor: University of Michigan Press, 1997.

Kruft, Hanno-Walter. *A History of Architectural Theory from Vitruvius to the Present.* New York: Princeton Architectural Press, 1994.

Kuhn, Jehane. "'La buona squola di Baldassarre': Vignola's *Due regole* as a Source for Peruzzi's Perspective Techniques." In *Baldassarre Peruzzi 1482–1536*, ed. Christoph Frommel, Arnaldo Bruschi, Howard Burns, Francesco Paolo Fiore, and Pier Nicola Pagliara, 411–42. Venice: Marsilio, 2005.

Lacan, Jacques. "Of the Gaze as *Objet Petit a.*" In *The Four Fundamental Concepts of Psychoanalysis*, trans. Alan Sheridan. New York: W.W. Norton, 1998.

Lacoue-Labarthe, Philippe. "Stagings of Mimesis." *Angelaki* 8, no. 2 (2003): 55–72.

–. *Typography: Mimesis, Philosophy, Politics.* Stanford, CA: Stanford University Press, 1989.

Láng, Benedek. *Unlocked Books.* University Park: Pennsylvania State University, 2008.

Larivaille, Paul. *Pietro Aretino fra Rinascimento e Manierismo.* Rome: Bulzoni, 1980.

–. "Vers un théâtre à une seule voix: Les prologues de l'Arétin au 'Marescalco' et à 'La Cortigiana' du 1534." In *L'écrivain face a son public à la Renaissance,* ed. Adelin-Charles Fiorato and Jean-Claude Margolin, 217–34. Paris: Vrin, 1989.

Larson, Orville K. "Vasari's Descriptions of Stage Machinery." *Educational Theatre Journal,* 9, no. 4 (1957): 287–99.

Laver, James. *Drama: Its Costume and Decor.* London: The Studio Publications, 1951.

Lawrenson, T.E., and Helen Purkis. "Les éditions illustrées de Térence dans l'histoire du théâtre." In *Le lieu théâtral à la Renaissance,* ed. J. Jacquot, 1–23 and 8 plates. Paris: Centre National de la Recherche Scientifique, 1964.

Lefebvre, Henry. *The Production of Space.* Oxford and Cambridge: Blackwell, 1991.

Lehmann, Hans-Thies. *Postdramatisches Theater.* Frankfurt am Main: Verlag der Autoren, 1999.

Leonardo da Vinci. *Libro di pittura: Codice Urbinate lat. 1270 nella Biblioteca apostolica vaticana.* 2 vols. Ed. Carlo Pedretti and Carlo Vecce. Florence: Giunti, 1995.

–. *The Notebooks.* Ed. Jean Paul Richter. Vol. II. New York: Dover, 1970.

–. *On Painting.* Ed. Martin Kemp. New Haven and London: Yale University Press, 1989.

Leslie, Marina. *Renaissance Utopias and the Problem of History.* Ithaca and London: Cornell University Press, 1998.

Levenson, Jay. "Jacopo de'Barbari and Northern Art of the Early Sixteenth Century." PhD diss., New York University, 1978.

Ligorio, Pirro. *Circhi, teatri e anfiteatri. Glie edifici di Roma antica nelle piante del Cinquecento.* Ed. Sissi Aslam. Rome: Edizioni della Citta, 1994.

Lippmann, Friedrich. *The Art of Wood-Engraving in Italy in the Fifteenth Century.* London: B. Quaritch, 1888.

Lord, Carnes. "On Machiavelli's 'Mandragola.'" *The Journal of Politics* 41, no. 3 (1979): 806–27.

Lotz, Wolfgang. *Architecture in Italy 1500–1600.* New Haven and London: Yale University Press, 1995.

Lucchesini, Paolo. *I teatri di Firenze.* Rome: Newton-Compton, 1991.

Lucretius Carus, Titus. *On the Nature of Things*, Vol 1. Cambridge, MA: Harvard University Press – Loeb Classical Library, 1992.
Lynch, Kevin. *The Image of the City*. Cambridge and London: MIT Press, 1960.
Lyotard, Jean-François. "The Tooth, the Palm." In *Mimesis, Masochism, and Mime: The Politics of Theatricality in Contemporary French Thought*, ed. Timothy Murray, 282–8. Ann Arbor: University of Michigan Press, 1997.
Maccherini, Michele. "Domenico Beccafumi e 'L'Amore Costante' di Alessandro Piccolomini." *Prospettiva*, January 1992: 63–5.
Di Macco, Michela. *Il Coloseo: Funzione simbolica, storica, urbana*. Roma: Bulzoni, 1971.
Machiavelli, Niccolò. *The Mandragola*. Trans. Leonard Sbrocchi and J. Douglas Campbell. In *Renaissance Comedy, Vol. II*, ed. Donald Beecher, 115–62. Toronto: University of Toronto Press, 2009.
–. *The Prince*. Trans. Harvey Mansfield. Chicago: University of Chicago Press, 1998.
–. *Tutte le opere*. Ed. Mario Martelli. Florence: Sansoni, 1971.
Macgowan, Kenneth, and William Melnitz. *The Living Stage*. Englewood Cliffs, NJ: Prentice- Hall, 1955.
Magagnato, Licisco. "The Genesis of the Teatro Olimpico." *Journal of the Warburg and Courtauld Institutes* 14, no. 3/4 (1951): 209–20.
–. *Teatri italiani del Cinquecento*. Venice: Neri Pozza, 1954.
Maier, Jessica. "Francesco Rosselli's Lost View of Rome: An Urban Icon and Its Progeny." *Art Bulletin* XCIV, no. 3 (2012): 395–411.
–. "A 'True Likeness': The Renaissance City Portrait," *Renaissance Quarterly* 65, no. 3 (2012): 711–52.
Mamone, Sara. *Il teatro nella Firenze medicea*. Milan: Mursia, 1981.
Manetti, Giannozzo. "Vita Nicolai V Summi Pontificis." In *Rerum Italicarum scriptores*, ed. Muratori. Milan: Societatis Palatinae, 1731.
Mannheim, Karl. *Ideology and Utopia: An Introduction to the Sociology of Knowledge*. New York: Harcourt Brace Jovanovich, 1936.
Mansfield, Harvey and Nathan Tarcov. "Introduction." In Machiavelli, *Discourses on Livy*, xvii–xliv. Chicago: Chicago University Press, 1996.
Manuel, Frank, and Fritzie Manuel. *Utopian Though in the Western World*. Cambridge, MA: Harvard University Press, 1979.
Marciak, Dorothée. *La place du prince: perspective et pouvoir dans le théâtre de cour des Médicis, Florence*, 1539–1600. Paris: Honoré Champion, 2005.
Marcigliano, Alessandro. *Chivalric Festivals at the Ferrarese Court of Alphonso II d'Este*. Bern: Peter Lang, 2003.
Martinez, Ronald L. "Etruria Triumphant in Rome: Fables of Medici Rule and Bibbiena's *Calandra*." *Renaissance Drama, New Series*, 36/27 (2010): 69–98.

Marotti, Ferruccio. *Storia documentaria del teatro italiano.* Milan: Feltrinelli, 1974.

Marotti, Ferruccio, Giovanna Romei, and Ferdinando Taviani, eds. *La commedia dell'arte e la società barocca. La professione del teatro.* Rome: Bulzoni, 1991.

McAuley, Gay. *Space in Performance: Making Meaning in the Theatre.* Ann Arbor: University of Michigan Press, 1999.

McKinney, Joslin, and Philip Butterworth, *The Cambridge Introduction to Scenography.* Cambridge: Cambridge University Press, 2009.

McLuhan, Marshall. *The Gutenberg Galaxy.* Toronto: University of Toronto Press, 1962.

Mellini, Domenico. "Descrizione dell'apparato della commedia et intermedii d'essa recitata in Firenze il giorno di S. Stefano l'anno 1565 nella gran sala del palazzo di sue Ecc. Illust. nelle Reali Nozze dell'Illust. et Eccell. S. il S. Don Francesco Medici Principe di Fiorenza e di Siena e della Regina Giovanna d'Austria sua consorte." In *Il teatro nella Firenze medicea,* by Sara Mamone, 97–102. Milan: Gruppo Ugo Mursia Editore, 1981.

Merleau-Ponty, Maurice. "Eye and Mind." In *The Primacy of Perception and Other Essays.* Evanston, IL: Northwestern University Press, 1964.

–. "Indirect Language and the Voices of Silence." In *The Merleau-Ponty Reader,* ed. Ted Toadvine and Leonard Lawlor, 241–82. Evanston, IL: Northwestern University Press, 2007.

–. *Phenomenology of Perception.* Trans. Colin Smith. London and New York: Routledge, 2002.

Minor, Andrew, and Bonner Mitchell, *A Renaissance Entertainment: Festivities for the Marriage of Cosimo I, Duke of Florence, in 1539. An Edition of the Music, Poetry, Comedy, and Descriptive Account, with Commentary.* Columbia, MO: University of Missouri Press, 1968.

Miotto, Luciana. "La scène de *L'Ortensio* de Bartolomeo Neroni dit Riccio, peintre et architecte." In *Alessandro Piccolomini (1508–1579): Un siennois à la croisée des genres et des savoirs,* ed. Marie-Françoise Piéjus, Michel Plaisance, and Matteo Residori, 189–213. Paris: Centre Interuniversitaire de Recherche sur la Renaissance Italienne, Université Sorbonne Nouvelle, 2011.

Mitchell, W. J. T. *Iconology: Image, Text, Ideology.* Chicago: Chicago University Press, 1986.

Moffit, John. *Painterly Perspective and Piety: Religious Uses of the Vanishing Point, from the 15th Century to the 18th Century.* Jefferson, VA: McFarland and Co, 2008.

Monbeig-Goguel, Catherine. *Il manierismo fiorentino.* Milan: Fabbri, 1971.

Momo, Arnaldo. *La crisi del modello teatrale del Rinascimento.* Venice: Marsilio, 1981.

Monbeig-Goguel, Catherine. *Il manierismo fiorentino.* Milan: Fabbri, 1971.

Moore, Kenneth. *Plato, Politics, and a Practical Utopia.* London and New York: Continuum, 2012.

Morris, David. *The Sense of Space.* Albany: State University of New York Press, 2004.

Morrison, Mary. *The Tragedies of G.-B. Giraldi Cinthio.* Lewiston, NY: The Edwin Mellen Press, 1997.

Mousley, Andrew. "*The Prince* and Textual Politics." In *Niccolò Machiavelli's* The Prince: *New Interdisciplinary Essays*, ed. Martin Coyle, 167–9. Manchester: Manchester University Press, 1995.

Moxey, Keith. *The Practice of Theory: Poststructuralism, Cultural Politics, and Art History.* Ithaca and London: Cornell University Press, 1994.

Mukarovsky, Jan. *Aesthetic Function, Norm and Value as Social Facts.* Ann Arbor: University of Michigan, 1979.

–. "Art as Semiotic Fact." In *Semiotics of Art*, ed. Ladislav Matejka and Irwin Titunik, *3–10*. Cambridge, MA, and London: The MIT Press, 1976.

Murray, Peter. *The Architecture of the Italian Renaissance.* New York: Schocken Books, 1986.

Nagel, Alexander. *The Controversy of Renaissance Art.* Chicago: University of Chicago Press, 2011.

Nagler, Alois Maria. *A Source Book in Theatrical History.* New York: Dover, 1952.

Nardi, Florinda. "Scrivere la Commedia dell'arte. Testi, pretesti e contesti." In *Miti antichi e moderni. Studi in onore di Edo Bellingeri*, ed. Donatella Gavrilovich, Carmelo Occhipinti, Donatella Orecchia, and Pamela Parenti, 167–75. Rome: UniversItalia, 2013.

Neiiendam, Klaus. "'Il portico' and 'la bottega' on the Early Italian Perspective Stage: A Comparative Study in Theatre Iconography." In *The Renaissance Theatre: Texts, Performance, Design. Vol. 2*, ed. Christopher Cairns, 29–40. Aldershot: Ashgate, 1991.

Neumann, Odmar. "Aufmerksamkeit." In *Historisches Worterbuch der Philosophie*, ed. Joachim Ritter, 635–46. Basel: Schwabe, 1971.

Nevola, Fabrizio. "Siena nel Rinascimiento: Sistemi urbanistici e strutture istituzionali" (c. 1400–1520), *Bullettino Senese di Storia Patria* CVI, (1999): 44–67.

Newbigin, Nerida. *Feste d'Oltrarno: Plays in Churches in Fifteenth-Century Florence.* Florence: Olschki, 1996.

–. "Secular and Religious Drama in the Middle Ages." In *A History of Italian Theatre*, ed. Joseph Farrell and Paolo Puppa, 9–27. Cambridge: Cambridge University Press, 2006.

–. "The Word Made Flesh: The Rappresentazioni of Mysteries and Miracles in Fifteenth-Century Florence." In *Christianity and the Renaissance: Image and Religious Imagination in the Quattrocento*, ed. T. Verdon and J. Henderson, 361–75. Syracuse, NY: Syracuse University Press, 1990.

Newton, Stella Mary. "Renaissance Theatre." *Early Music* 6, no. 2 (Apr. 1978): 310.

–. "Stage Design for Renaissance Theatre." *Early Music* 5, no. 1 (Jan. 1977): 12–18.

Nicoll, Allardyce. *The Development of the Theatre*. New York: Harcourt, Brace and World, 1966.

–. *Masks, Mimes, and Miracles*. New York: Harcourt, Brace and Co., 1931.

Nietzsche, Friedrich. "On the Uses and Disadvantages of History for Life." *Untimely Meditations*. Cambridge: Cambridge University Press, 1997.

Nuti, Lucia. *Ritratti di città: Visione e memoria tra medioevo e settecento*. Venice: Marsilio, 1997.

Oenslarger, Donald. *Stage Design: Four Centuries of Scenic Invention*. New York: International Exhibitions Foundations, 1974.

Oldani, Louis J., and Victor R. Yanitelli, "Jesuit Theater in Italy: Its Entrances and Exits." *Italica* 76, no. 1 (1999): 18–32.

Onians, John. *Bearers of Meaning: The Classical Orders in Antiquity, the Middle Ages, and the Renaissance*. Princeton, NJ: Princeton University Press, 1988.

Oosting, Thomas. "The Teatro Olimpico Design Sources." *Educational Theatre Journal* 22, no. 3 (1970): 256–67.

Orgel, Stephen. *The Illusion of Power*. Berkeley: University of California Press, 1975.

Orrell, John. *The Human Stage*. Cambridge: Cambridge University Press, 1988.

–. *The Theatres of Inigo Jones and John Webb*. Cambridge: Cambridge University Press, 1985.

Osborn, Peggy. "G. B. Giraldi Cinthio's Dramatic Theory and Stage Practice: A Creative Interaction." In *Scenery, Set and Staging in the Italian Renaissance*, ed. Christopher Cairns, 39–58. Lewiston, Queenston, and Lampeter: Edwin Mellen Press, 1996.

Palladio, Andrea. *The Four Books on Architecture*. Trans. Robert Tavernor and Richard Schofield. Cambridge, MA: The MIT Press, 1997.

–. *I quattro libri dell'architettura*, Venice: Franceschi, 1570.

Pallen, Thomas A. *Vasari on Theatre*. Carbondale and Edwardsville: Southern Illiniois University Press, 1999.

Panofsky, Erwin. *Perspective and Symbolic Form*. Trans. Christopher S. Wood. New York: Zone, 1997.

Pantin, Isabelle. "Poetic Fiction and Natural Philosophy in Humanist Italy: Fracastoro's Use of Myth in Syphilis." In *Fiction and the Frontiers of Knowledge in Europe, 1500–1800*, ed. Richard Scholar and Alexis Tadié, 17–30. Burlington, VT: Ashgate, 2010.

Parker, Holt. "The Observed of All Observers: Spectacle, Applause, and Cultural Poetics in the Roman Theatre Audience." In *The Art of Ancient Spectacle*, ed. B. Bergmann and C. Kondoleon, 163–79. New Haven and London: Yale University Press, 1999.

Parkinson, John. *Democracy and the Public Space: The Physical Sites of Democratic Performance*. Oxford: Oxford University Press, 2012.

Parronchi, Alessandro. "La prima rappresentazione della 'Mandragola.' Il modello dele' aparato. L'allegoria." *La Bibliofilia* 64 (1962): 37–86.

–. *La prima rappresentazione della Mandragola*. Florence: Edizioni Polistampa, 1995.

Patricius, Franciscus. *La città felice*. In *Utopisti e riformatori sociali del Cinquecento*, ed. Carlo Curcio, 119–212. Bologna: Zanichelli, 1941.

Payne, Alina A. *The Architectural Treatise in the Italian Renaissance: Architectual Invention, Ornament, and Literary Culture*. Cambridge: Cambridge University Press, 1999.

Peacock, John. *The Stage Designs of Inigo Jones: The European Context*. Cambridge: Cambridge University Press, 1995.

Pearson, Caspar. *Humanism and the Urban World: Leon Battista Alberti and the Renaissance City*. University Park: Pennsylvania State University Press, 2011.

Pedretti, Carlo. "Dessins d'une scéne, exécutés par Léonard de Vinci pour Charles d'Amboise (1506–1507)." In *Le lieu théâtral à la Renaissance*, ed. J. Jacquot, 25–34. Paris: Éditions du Centre National de la Recherche Scientifique, 1964.

–. *Leonardo Architetto*. Milan: Electra, 1981.

Pérez-Gómez, Alberto, and Louise Pelletier. *Achitectural Representation and the Perspective Hinge*. Cambridge, MA: MIT Press, 2000.

Pevsner, Nikolaus. *A History of Building Types*. Princeton, NJ: Princeton University Press, 1976.

Phillips-Court, Kristin. *The Perfect Genre: Drama and Painting in Renaissance Italy*. Burlington, VT: Ashgate, 2011.

Piccolomini, Alessandro. *Amor costante*. Ed. Nerida Newbigin. Bologna: Forni, 1990.

Pigafetta, Filippo. *Due lettere descrittive l'una dell'ingresso a Vicenza della Imperatrice Maria d'Austria nell'anno MDLXXXI l'altra della recita nel Teatro*

Olimpico dell'Edippo di Sofocle nel MDLXXXV. Padua: Valentino Crescini, 1830.

Pinelli, Antonio, and Orietta Rossi. *Genga Architetto.* Rome: Bulzoni, 1971.

Pirrotta, Nino. "Studies in the Music of Renaissance Theatre." In *Music and Theatre from Poliziano to Monteverdi*, 3–280. Cambridge: Cambridge University Press, 1975.

Pliny the Elder. *Natural History.* Cambridge, MA: Harvard University Press – Loeb Classical Library, 1962.

Plotinus, *Enneads.* Trans. A.H. Armstrong. Cambridge, MA: Harvard University Press, 1966.

Poggi, Paola. "Architectonica perspectiva: La prospettiva solida de *Le Bacchidi* e la voluta ionica di Baldassarre Peruzzi." In *Baldassarre Peruzzi* 1481–1536, ed. Christoph L. Frommel, Arnaldo Bruschi, Howard Burns, Francesco Paolo Fiore, and Pier Nicola Pagliara, 443–55. Venice: Marsilio, 2005.

Pon, Lisa. *Raphael, Dürer, and MarcAntonio Raimondi: Copying and the Italian Renaissance Print.* New Haven and London: Yale University Press, 2004.

–. *Learning to Look.* New York: Doubleday, 1991.

Pope-Hennessy, John. *Learning to Look.* New York: Doubleday, 1991.

–. "Some Aspects of the Cinquecento in Siena." *Art in America* no. XXXI (1943): 69–70.

Potolosky, Matthew. *Mimesis.* New York and London: Routledge, 2006.

Povoledo, Elena. "Origins and Aspects of Italian Scenography." In Nina Pirotta and Elena Povoledo, *Music and Theatre from Poliziano to Monteverdi*, trans Karen Eales, 281–2. Cambridge: Cambridge University Press, 1982.

–. "La sala teatrale a Ferrara: Da Pellegrino Prisciani a Ludovico Ariosto." *Bollettino del centro internazionale di studi Andrea Palladio* XVI (1974): 115–38.

Powell, John. *Music and Theatre in France 1600–1680.* Oxford: Oxford University Press, 2000.

Power, Cormac. *Presence in Play: A Critique of Theories of Presence in the Theatre.* Amsterdam and New York: Rodopi, 2008.

Preto, Paolo. *I servizi segreti di Venezia.* Milan: Il Saggiatore, 1994.

Prisciani, Pellegrino. *Spectacula.* Ed. Aguzzi Barbagli. Modena: Franco Cosimo Panini, 1992.

Quintilian, The Orator's Education. Trans. Donald Russell. Cambridge, MA: Harvard University Press – Loeb Classical Library, 2002.

Radford, Luis. "On the Epistemological Limits of Language: Mathematical Knowledge and Social Practice during the Renaissance." Educational Studies in Mathematics 52, no. 2 (2003): 123–50.

Rajchman, John. *Constructions.* Cambridge, MA: MIT Press, 1998.

Rancière, Jacques. *The Emancipated Spectator.* Trans. Gregory Elliott. London and New York: Verso, 2009.

–. "Painting in the Text." In *The Future of the Image,* trans. Gregory Elliott, 69–90. London and New York: Verso, 2007.

–. *The Politics of Aesthetics.* New York and London: Continuum, 2006.

Rasmussen, Steen Eiler. *Experiencing Architecture.* Cambridge, MA: MIT Press, 1962.

Rausch, Hannelore. *Theoria: Von ihrer sakralen zur philosophischen Bedeuntung.* Munich: W. Fink, 1982.

Rebhorn, Wayne A. *Courtly Performances: Masking and Festivity in Castiglione's Book of the Courtier.* Detroit, MI: Wayne State University Press, 1978.

Rewa, Natalie. "Introduction: Critical Perspectives on Design and Scenography in Canada." In *Design and Scenography,* ed. Natalia Rewa, xi–xxi. Toronto: Playwrights Canada Press, 2009.

Ricci, Corrado. "The Art of Scenography." *The Art Bulletin* 10, no. 3 (Mar. 1928): 231–57.

Rice, Eugene. *The Foundations of Early Modern Europe, 1460–1559.* New York: Norton, 1970.

Richards, David. *Masks of Difference: Cultural Representations in Literature, Anthropology, and Art.* Cambridge: Cambridge University Press, 1994.

Richter, Bodo. "Recent Studies in Renaissance Scenography." *Renaissance News* 19, no. 4 (1966): 344–58.

Riggs, David. "The Artificial Day and the Infinite Universe." *Journal of Medieval and Renaissance Studies,* no. 5 (1975): 155–85.

Riposio, Donatella. *Nova comedia v'appresento: il prologo nella commedia del Cinquecento.* Turin: Tirrenia, 1989.

Roberts, Helene. *Art History through the Camera's Lens (Documenting the Image).* Amsterdam BV: OPA, 1995.

Robinson, J.C. *Descriptive Catalogue of Drawings by the Old Masters, Forming the Collection of John Malcolm of Poltalloch.* London, 1876.

Romby, Giuseppina Carla. *Descrizioni e rappresentazioni della città di Firenze nel XV secolo: Con la trascrizione inedita dei manoscritti di Benedetto Dei è un indice ragionato dei manoscritti utili per la storia della città.* Florence: Libreria Editrice Fiorentina: 1976.

Rosand, David. "Theater and Structure in the Art of Paolo Veronese." *The Art Bulletin* 55, no. 2 (1973): 217–39.

Rosen, Mark. "Pietro Tacca's *Quattro Mori* and the Conditions of Slavery in Early Seicento Tuscany," *Art Bulletin* 97 no. 1 (2015): 34–57.

–. "Vasari and 'Vedute'," *Notes in the History of Art* 34, no. 4 (2015): 31–8.

Roskill, Mark. *Dolce's Aretino and Venetian Art Theory of the Cinquecento.* Toronto: University of Toronto Press, 2000.

Rowe, Colin, and Fred Koetter. *Collage City.* Cambridge, MA: MIT Press, 1983.

Rucellai, Bernardo. *De urbe Roma.* In *Rerum Italicarum Scriptores ad anno 1000 ad 1600.* Florence: Allegrini et Pisoni, 1770.

Rucellai, Giovanni. *Il Giubileo dell'anno 1450 secondo una relazione di Giovanni Rucellai.* Ed. Giuseppe Marcotti. Florence: Barbèra, 1885.

Ruffini, Franco. *Commedia e festa nel Rinascimento. "La Calandria" alla corte di Urbino.* Bologna: Il Mulino, 1986.

–. *Teatri prima del teatro: Visioni dell'edificio e della scena tra Umanismo e Rinascimento.* Rome: Bulzoni, 1983.

Ruzante. *L'Anconitana / The Woman from Ancona.* Ed. Nancy Dersofi. Berkeley and Los Angeles: University of California Press, 1994.

Rylands, Phillip. *The Timeless Eye: Master Drawings from the Jan and Marie-Anne Krugier-Poniatowski Collection.* Berlin: G+H Verlag, 1999.

Saalman, Howard. "The Baltimore and Urbino Panels: Cosimo Rosseli." *Burlington Magazine* 110, no. 784 (1968): 376–81+383.

Saint-Martin, Fernarde de. *Semiotics of Visual Language.* Bloomington: Indiana University Press, 1990.

Samaritini, Antonio, and Ranieri Varese, eds. *L'Aquila Bianca: Studi di storia Estense per Luciano Chiappini.* Ferrara: Corbo, 2000.

Sanesi, Irineo, ed. *Commedia del Cinquecento.* Rome: Laterza, 1912.

–. *Storia dei generi letterari italiani: La commedia.* Milan: Vallardi, 1954.

Sanminiatelli, Donato. *Domenico Beccafumi.* Milan: Bramante, 1967.

Sanpaolesi, Piero. "Le prospettive architettoniche di Urbino di Filadelfia e di Berlino." *Bollettino d'Arte* 1949: 322–37.

Santosuosso, Antonio. "A Society in Disarray: Satirical Poets and Mannerist Painters in the Age of the Italian Wars." In *The Renaissance in the Streets, Schools, and Studies,* ed. Konrad Eisenbichler and Nicholas Terpstra, 279–308. Toronto: University of Toronto Press, 2008.

Saslow, James. *The Medici Wedding of 1589: Florentine Festival as Teatrum Mundi.* New Haven and London: Yale University Press, 1996.

–. "La place du prince: Perspective et pouvoir dans le théâtre de cour des Médicis, Florence (review)." *Renaissance Quarterly* 59 no. 1 (2006): 147–9.

–. *The Poetry of Michelangelo.* New Haven, CT: Yale University Press, 1991.

Scaglia, Gustina. "A Vitruvianist's 'Thermae' Plan and the Vitruvianists in Rome and Siena." *Arte Lombarda* 84/85 (1988): 85–101.

Scamozzi, Vicenzo. *L'idea della architettura universale.* Venice: Valentino, 1615.

Schapiro, Meyer. *Words, Script, and Pictures: Semiotics of Visual Language.* New York: George Braziller, 1996.

Schechner, Richard. *Performance Theory*. London: Routledge, 2003.

Schich, Maximilian. "Complexity and Convention." In *Space between People: How the Virtual Changes Physical Architecture*, 32–9. Munich, London, and New York: Prestel, 2008.

Schironi, Francesca. "The Reception of Ancient Drama in Renaissance Italy." In *A Handbook to the Reception of Greek Drama*, ed. Beltine van Zyl Smit, 133–53. West Sussex: Wiley, 2016.

Scolari, Massimo. *Oblique Drawing: A History of Anti-Perspective*. Cambridge and London: MIT Press, 2012.

Seragnoli, Daniele. *Il teatro a Siena nel Cinquecento: "Progetto" e "modello" dramaturgico nell'academia degli Intronati*. Rome: Bulzoni, 1980.

Sergardi, Margherita. *Lingua scenica e terminologia teatrale nel Cinquecento*. Florence: Edizioni Internazionali La Nuova Europa, 1979.

Serlio, Sebastiano. *Libro primo [- quinto] d'architettura*. Venice: Melchiorre Sessa, 1551.

–. *Sebastiano Serlio on Architecture, Volume 1: Tutte l'opere d'architettura et prospetiva, Books 1–4*. Trans. Vaughan Hart and Peter Hicks. New Haven, CT: Yale University Press, 1996.

Servolini, Luigi. *Jacopo de'Barbari*. Padua: Le Tre Venezie, 1944.

Severino, Renato. *Meta-realism in Architecture: In Quest of the Ideal City*. Milan: Idea Books, 1995.

Shearman, John. *Mannerism*. London: Penguin Books, 1967.

–. *Only Connect ... Art and the Spectator in the Italian Renaissance*. Princeton, NJ: Princeton University Press, 1992.

–. *Raphael in Early Modern Sources*. 2 vols. New Haven, CT: Yale University Press, 2003.

Sherer, Daniel. "Error or Invention? Critical Receptions of Michelangelo's Architecture from Pirro Ligorio to Teofilo Gallaccini." *Perspecta*, 46 (2013): 76–121.

Stampino, Maria Galli. *Staging the Pastoral: Tasso's "Aminta" and the Emergence of Modern Western Theatre*. Tempe: Arizona Center for Medieval and Renaissance Studies, 2005.

Steinberg, Leo. *Other Criteria*. Chicago: University of Chicago Press, 1972.

Steinitz, Kate. "Le dessin de Léonard de Vinci pour la Représentation de la Danae de Baldassare Taccone." In *Le lieu théâtral à la Renaissance*, ed. J. Jacquot, 35–40. Paris: Éditions du Centre National de la Recherche Scientifique, 1964.

–. "Leonardo architetto teatrale e organizzatore di feste." *Lettura Vinciana 9* (Florence, 1970), 53–5.

–. "A Reconstruction of Leonardo da Vinci's Revolving Stage." *The Art Quarterly* XII, 4 (1949): 325–8.

Stinger, Charles L. *The Renaissance in Rome*. Bloomington: Indiana University Press, 1985.

Strong, Roy. *Art and Power: Renaissance Festivals, 1450–1650*. Berkeley and Los Angeles: University of California Press, 1984.

Sumberg, Theodore A. "*La Mandragola*: An Interpretation." *Journal of Politics* 23 (1961): 320–40.

Summers, David. *Real Spaces*. New York: Phaidon, 2003.

Szondi, Peter. *Theorie des Modernen Dramas*. Frankfurt am Main: Suhrkamp Verlag, 1963.

Tafuri, Manfredo. "Cesare Cesariano e gli studi vitruviani del Quattrocento." In *Scritti rinascimentali d'architettura*, ed. A. Bruschi, C. Maltese, M. Tafuri, and R. Bonelli, 387–467. Milan: Il Polifilo, 1978.

–. *Interpreting the Renaissance: Princes, Cities, Architects*. Trans. Daniel Sherer. New Haven, CT: Yale University Press in association with Harvard Graduate School of Design, 2006.

–. *Jacopo Sansovino e l'architettura del '500 a Venezia*. Padua: Marsilio, 1972.

–. "Il luogo teatrale dall'umanesimo a oggio." In *Teatri e scenografie*, 25–39. Milan: Touring Club Italiano, 1976.

–. *Venice and the Renaissance*. Cambridge, MA: The MIT Press, 1995.

Tasso, Torquato. *Discorsi dell'arte poetica* (c. 1569). Ed. Angelo Solerti. Turin: G.B. Paravia, 1901.

Tavernor, Robert. *On Alberti and the Art of Building*. New Haven and London: Yale University Press, 1998.

Testaverde, Anna Maria. "Spectacle, Theatre, and Propaganda at the Court of the Medici." In *The Medici, Michelangelo, and the Art of Late Renaissance Florence*, 123–31. New Haven and London: Yale University Press, 2002.

Todarello, Nazzareno Luigi. *Le arti della scena*. Novi Ligure: Latorre, 2006.

Tydeman, William. *The Theatre in the Middle Ages: Western European Stage Conditions, c. 800–1576*. Cambridge: Cambridge University Press, 1978.

Valentini, Roberto, and Giuseppe Zucchetti. *Codice topografico della città di Roma*. Rome, 1940.

van Eck, Caroline, and Stijn Bussels. "The Visual Arts and the Theatre in Early Modern Europe." In van Eck and Bussels, eds, *Theatricality in Early Modern Art and Architecture*, 8–23. London: AAH/Wiley-Blackwell, 2011.

Varey, John E. *Cosmovisión y escenografia: El teatro español en el Siglo de Oro*. Madrid: Castalia, 1987.

Vasari, Giorgio. *Le vite de piu eccellenti pittori, scultori ed architettori*. Ed. Gaetano Milanesi. 9 vols. Florence: Sansoni, 1906.

–. *Le vite de' piu eccellenti pittori, scultori e architettori: Nelle redazioni del 1550 e 1568*. Ed. Rosanne Bettarini and Paolo Barocchi. Vol. IV. Florence: Accademia del Crusca, 1994.

Vasari the Younger, Giorgio. *La cittá ideale: Piante di chiese (palazzi e ville) di Toscana e d'Italia*. Ed. Virginia Stefanelli. Rome: Officina, 1970.

Ventrone, Paola. "La feste del 1471 e i caratteri della cerimonialita religiosa." In *Le temps revient/'L tempo si rinuova: Feste e spettacoli nella Firenze di Lorenzo il Magnifico*, 21–54. Florence: Silvana, 1992.

Venturi, Robert. *Complexity and Contradiction in Architecture*. New York: Museum of Modern Art, 2002.

Vidler, Anthony. *The Scenes of the Street and Other Essays*. New York: Monacelli Press, 2011.

Vitruvius Pollio, Marcus. *De architectura: Translato commentato ed affigurato da Caesare Caesariano, 1521*. Ed. Arnaldo Bruschi, Adriana Carugo, and Francesco Paolo Fiore. Milan: Polifolio, 1981.

–. *Lucii Vitruvii Pollionis ad Caesarem Augustum de architectura liber primus -decimus*. Ed. Joannes Sulpitius (Sulpizio da Veroli). Rome: Eucharius Silber, 1486.

–. *On Architecture I–II*. Trans. F. Granger. Cambridge, MA: Harvard University Press – The Loeb Classical Library, 1955–6.

–. *Ten Books on Architecture: The Corsini Incunabulum with the Annotations and Autograph Drawings of Giovanni Battista da Sangallo*. Ed. Ingrid D. Rowland. Rome: Edizioni dell'Elefante, 2003.

Vives, Juan Luis. "A Fable about Man." In *The Renaissance Philosophy of Man: Petrarca, Valla, Ficino, Pico, Pomponazzi, Vives*, ed. Ernst Cassirer, Paul Oskar Kristeller, and John Herman Randall, Jr, 387–93. Chicago: University of Chicago Press, 1948.

Waddington, Raymond. *Aretino's Satyr: Sexuality, Satire, and Self-Projection in Sixteenth-Century Literature and Art*. Toronto: University of Toronto Press, 2004.

Walker, Joseph Cooper. *An Historical and Critical Essay on the Revival of the Drama in Italy*. Edinburgh: Mundell, 1805.

Waters, Michael. "A Renaissance without Order: Ornament, Single-sheet Engravings, and the Mutability of Architectural Prints." *Journal of the Society of Architectural Historians* 71, no. 4 (2012): 488–523.

Watt, Mary A. "*Veni, sponsa*. Love and Politics at the Wedding of Eleonora di Toledo." In *The Cultural World of Eleonora di Toledo*, ed. Konrad Eisenbichler. Aldershot: Ashgate, 2004.

Weinberg, Bernard. *A History of Literary Criticism in the Italian Renaissance*. Vol. I. Chicago: University of Chicago Press, 1961.

West, William. "The Idea of a Theater: Humanist Ideology and the Imaginary Stage in Early Modern Europe." In *Renaissance Drama XXVIII: The Space of the Stage*, 245–87. Evanston, IL: Northwestern University Press, 1999.

White, Hayden. "Interpretation in History." In *Tropics of Discourse: Essays in Cultural Criticism*, 51–80. Baltimore, MD: John Hopkins University Press, 1978.

White, John. *The Birth and Rebirth of Pictorial Space*. London: Faber and Faber, 1967.

Williams, Robert "Italian Renaissance Art and the Systematicity of Representation." In *Renaissance Theory*, ed. James Elkins and Robert Williams, 159–84. New York and London: Routledge, 2008.

Winton, Tracey Eve. "The Satyric Scene: Palldio's Villa Rotonda." In *Architecture as Performing Art*, eds, Marcia Feuerstein and Gray Read, 113–30. Burlington, VT: Ashgate, 2013.

Wittkower, Rudolph. *Architectural Principles in the Age of Humanism*. London: Norton, 1962.

Wohl, Hellmut. *The Aesthetics of Italian Renaissance Art*. Cambridge: Cambridge University Press, 1999.

Womack, Peter. "The Comical Scene: Perspective and Civility on the Renaissance Stage," *Representations* 101, no. 1 (2008): 32–56.

Wood, Christopher. "Countermagical Combinations by Dosso Dossi." *RES: Anthropology and Aesthetics*, no. 49/50 (2006): 151–70.

Woodruff, Paul. "Aristotle on Mimesis." In *Essays on Aritsotles Poetics*, ed. Amelie Oksenberg Rorty, 73–96. Princeton, NJ: Princeton University Press, 1992.

Worgul, Elmar. "Das Palastmodell Giuliano da Sangallos für Ferdinard I. König von Neapel. Versuch einer Rekontruktion," *Jarbuch der Berliner Museen* xxi (1979): 91–118.

Wright, Richard, ed. *Visual Attention*. Oxford: Oxford University Press, 1998.

Zaccarini, Donato. "Una scena cinquecentesca con la piazza di Ferrara," *Bollettino Statistico del Comune di Ferrara* II trimester 1925 (1926): iv–vii

Zambotti, Bernardino. "Diario ferrarese dall'anno 1476 sino al 1504"; and "*Diario ferrarese* (1409–1502)." In *Rerum Italicarum Scriptores*, ed. G. Pardi. Bologna: Zanichelli, 1925–37.

Zampelli, Michael. "'Lascivi Spettacoli': Jesuits and Theatre (from the Underside)." In *The Jesuits II: Culture, Sciences, and the Arts, 1540–1773*, ed. J.W. O'Malley, G.A. Bailey, S.J. Harris, and T.F. Kennedy, 550–71. Toronto: University of Toronto Press, 2006.

Zanre, Domenico. *Cultural Non-conformity in Early Modern Florence*. Aldershot and Burlington: Ashgate, 2004.

Zorach, Rebbeca. *The Passionate Triangle*. Chicago: University of Chicago Press, 2011.

Zorzi, Giangiorgio. "Le prospettive del Teatro Olimpico di Vicenza nei disegni degli 'Uffizi' di Firenze e nei documenti dell 'Ambrosiana' di Milano." *Arte Lombarda* 10 (1965): 70–97.

Zorzi, Ludovico. *Il teatro e la città: Saggi sulla scena italiana*. Turin: Giulio Einaudi, 1977.

Index

Page numbers in *italics* refer to illustrations.

www.ingramcontent.com/pod-product-compliance
Lightning Source LLC
LaVergne TN
LVHW090159080826
844660LV00013B/866/J

* 9 7 8 1 4 8 7 5 0 3 8 8 8 *